Walker Percy's
Sacramental Landscapes

Walker Percy's Sacramental Landscapes

The Search in the Desert

Allen Pridgen

SUP

Selinsgrove: Susquehanna University Press
London: Associated University Presses

Associated University Presses
440 Forsgate Drive
Cranbury, NJ 08512

Associated University Presses
16 Barter Street
London WC1A 2AH, England

Associated University Presses
P.O. Box 338, Port Credit
Mississauga, Ontario
Canada L5G 4L8

The paper used in this publication meets the requirements
of the American National Standard for Permanence of Paper
for Printed Library Materials Z39.48–1984.

Reprinted by permission of Farrar, Straus and Giroux, LLC:
Excerpts from *The Last Gentleman* by Walker Percy. Copyright 1966 by Walker Percy.
Excerpts from *Love in the Ruins* by Walker Percy. Copyright 1971 by Walker Percy.
Excerpts from *The Message in the Bottle* by Walker Percy. Copyright 1975 by Walker Percy.
Excerpts from *The Second Coming* by Walker Percy. Copyright 1980 by Walker Percy.
Excerpts from *Signposts in a Strange Land* by Walker Percy. Copyright 1991 by Mary Bernice Percy.
Excerpts from *The Thanatos Sydrome* by Walker Percy. Copyright 1987 by Walker Percy.
Reprinted by permission of McIntosh & Otis, Inc.
Excerpts from the Walker Percy Papers housed at the University of North Carolina at Chapel Hill. Copyright 1999 by Mary Bernice Townsend Percy, Ann Boyd Percy Moores, and Mary Pratt Lobdell.

Library of Congress Cataloging-in-Publication Data

Pridgen, Allen, 1943–
    Walker Percy's sacramental landscapes: the search in the desert / Allen Pridgen.
        p. cm.
    Includes bibliographical references (p.) and index.
    ISBN 1-57591-040-3 (alk. paper)
        1. Percy, Walker, 1916—Criticism and interpretation. 2. Religious fiction, American—History and criticism. 3. Quests (Expeditions) in literature. 4. Sacraments in literature. 5. Landscape in literature. 6. Symbolism in literature. 7. Deserts in literature. I. Title.

PS3566.E6912 Z8315 2000
813′.54—dc21   00-030120

. . . for the self that finds itself lost in the desert of theory and consumption, there is nothing to do but set out as a pilgrim in the desert in search of a sign.

—Walker Percy, "Why Are You a Catholic?"

Contents

Acknowledgments

Many organizations and individuals have contributed to the writing of this book. First of all, I am grateful to the Appalachian College Association for the generous Andrew W. Mellon Post-Doctoral Fellowships (1996–98). Alice Brown and Andrew Baskins at ACA were especially helpful and encouraging. Gary Poulton, president of Virginia Intermont College, and Rebecca Watson, former academic dean, were also supportive, graciously allowing me sabbaticals in fall 1996 and spring 1998 while I worked on this project at the University of North Carolina at Chapel Hill. Mark Harris unselfishly and good-naturedly assumed my duties as English Department chair while I was in North Carolina. At Chapel Hill, Joseph Flora was an invaluable advisor and reader, always able to tell me when I was succeeding in the chapters and when I was missing the mark. I also appreciate the assistance of the librarians in the Southern Historical Collection at Chapel Hill, where the Walker Percy Papers are housed. I am especially grateful to McIntosh and Otis, Inc., the literary agents for the estate of Walker Percy, who gave me permission to quote from the Papers.

In the last four years, I have published articles in *The Southern Quarterly*, *Renascence*, and *The Mississippi Quarterly* on the sacramental imagery in Percy's novels. I would like to thank Stephen Young, Ed Block, and Robert Phillips and the staffs at those fine journals for encouraging me in my work on Percy.

While I was in residence in North Carolina, friends and family were always ready to help with the challenges of finding suitable temporary housing. I'm sure Eileen Malan, Bill Thomason, Warren Person, and Mickey Barnes will not quickly forget the many times they helped me move in and out of rented apartments and houses.

My wife and son gave me what Percy calls the "greatest joy" at a time when I needed it most and could return it least. Linda, besides serving as a patient and perceptive reader of the various versions of the manuscripts, reminded me of the value of this research during the many times I became discouraged. Nathan was always understanding and amiable, never resentful about the added responsibilities he had to assume in my absence.

Most of all, I thank my mother Lois Pridgen-Barnes for showing me, and all who know her, the fullness of life Percy's pilgrims are so desperate to discover. This book is dedicated to her.

Abbreviations

Con	*Conversations with Walker Percy*, 1985
L	*Lancelot*, 1977
LC	*Lost in the Cosmos*, 1983
LG	*The Last Gentleman*, 1966
LR	*Love in the Ruins*, 1971
MB	*The Message in the Bottle*, 1975
MCon	*More Conversations with Walker Percy*, 1993
MG	*The Moviegoer*, 1961
SC	*The Second Coming*, 1980
SP	*Signposts in a Strange Land*, 1991
TS	*The Thanatos Syndrome*, 1987
WPP	Walker Percy Papers. Southern Historical Collection. Manuscripts Department. Wilson Library, University of North Carolina at Chapel Hill

A Way of Seeing

1
Introduction

In his fiction, Walker Percy picks through the deteriorating ruins of American suburbia and finds there wary residents trying to enjoy their culture's freedom and plenty while they desperately look around in the detritus for signs of life. He diagnoses in *The Moviegoer* (1961—National Book Award, 1962) and in the novels that followed—*The Last Gentleman* (1966), *Love in the Ruins* (1971), *Lancelot* (1977), *The Second Coming* (1980), and *The Thanatos Syndrome* (1987)— the existential malaise of these anxious middle-class Americans as they live out their days pursuing happiness in their comfortable suburban homes and efficient offices. He points out what has "gone wrong" (*SP*, 248) in their culture, a culture in which the best educated and wealthiest often unwittingly acquire in their search for life only a "death-in-life" (*SC*, 147, 155, 169, e.g.). Their search too often leads them to a paralyzing psychic "death" in which they are as alienated from themselves as they are from their pleasant neighbors and their intelligent colleagues.

Percy's essays and interviews also address the existential challenges of life in the ruins.[1] He explains in his nonfiction how the hapless suburban survivors of the American Dream often languish in an undetected ontological "death" that has its origins in the scientistic mind-set regnant in twentieth-century Western culture. This is a "mind-set" that values abstract "truth" and the achievement of self-satisfying interior psychological and emotional experience over the actualities of phenomenal reality. He believes that this kind of interiorized selfhood encourages a disregard for the world and for others who, of course, live outside the individual's private cognitive and emotional life. This disregard is, in effect, Percy asserts, a "devaluation of human life" (*SP*, 394) since it reduces the activities of the individual to a mere solipsistic pursuit of need satisfactions. But Percy also sees hope. His essays on language and religion are devoted to explaining some ways of knowing the world and the self that will defeat the living death he diagnoses in the novels.

Walker Percy's achievements in his fiction and nonfiction have not gone unnoticed. By the time of his death in 1990, Percy was recognized as one of the most important writers and thinkers of this century. In 1989, the National Endowment for the Humanities awarded him the prestigious Jefferson Award, an honor that the American government reserves for the country's most distinguished men of letters. His works have been translated into many languages and, even early in his career, academic critics began to explore the complexity of philosophical and theological ideas that he articulates in his essays and interviews and develops in his fiction. A scholarly conference solely devoted to Percy studies was held in 1989 at the University of Aarhus in Denmark. In the 1990s, two full-length biographies were published, as well as almost countless reviews, journal articles, critical studies, collections of essays, bibliographies, dissertations, and theses. In a 1995 bibliographical study, Henry Mills estimated that a complete bibliography of the commentary on Walker Percy's fiction and philosophy would include over nine hundred entries, both in English and in other languages.[2]

Most of this commentary has been in response to Percy's penetrating and unflinching examination of the death in the ruins, a death he saw at work in his own painful childhood. LeRoy Percy, his father, settled down in Birmingham, Alabama, after his Ivy League education and began trying to find a way to bear his daily existence in his law office, Presbyterian church, and country-club home.[3] He committed suicide in 1929 when his son was thirteen. In 1930, when Percy's mother moved with her three sons into the spacious home of William Alexander Percy in Greenville, Mississippi, the adolescent Walker saw in his "Uncle Will" (in fact, a cousin) another kind of searcher for life in a vanishing Old South culture. William Alexander Percy was a well-educated Southern gentleman who had found in Greenville a dignified and elegant way to live, but, as Percy would later point out in his novels and essays, his Uncle Will was also one of those romantics whose solitary devotion to their ideals often condemns them to a life of loneliness and disappointment. Evidently, Percy saw his mother as one more family member who fell victim to the despair he would later diagnose as epidemic among the wealthy and privileged. She died in an automobile accident in 1932, but Percy always believed that she committed suicide by intentionally driving her car off the narrow bridge outside Greenville.[4]

In 1942, Walker Percy faced his own demons at Trudeau Sanatorium at Saranac Lake, New York, where he was hospitalized after contracting tuberculosis from the cadavers he dissected while in medical school at Columbia. Percy was facing a life-threatening illness and an uncertain future, an existential predicament that led him to question the understanding of himself and the world that he had so far acquired. William Rodney

Allen maintains that Percy "reformulated himself psychically" during his three years at Trudeau.[5] It was this reformulation that provided him with the clues to a life and a self his study of chemistry at the University of North Carolina (1933–37) and his medical training at Columbia (1937–41) had so far failed to show him and his family had failed to model. He knew he was missing something, and he knew that his ignorance could lead him to suicide or to a future where he would simply play out roles as a physician, Southern gentleman, civic leader, and responsible father.

Prompted by this new philosophical doubt, at Trudeau Percy began reading existential philosophy and literature, modern language theory, and theology—initiating an intellectual and spiritual search that would continue for the rest of his life. Percy read in Heidegger, Jaspers, Marcel, Sartre, Camus, and Kierkegaard about the empty existence and self-alienation of the self who mistakes its abstractions for "truth" and its role-playing for authentic being. He could see in himself just this kind of disengaged, abstracted person—a cool, intellectual young scientist pursuing a medical career with absolute trust in the competency of his positivistic learning to show him the "truth" of human experience and himself. But Kierkegaard caused Percy to question his scientific certainties. Percy said later in a 1971 interview that he learned from Kierkegaard that science "cannot utter one single sentence about what a man is himself as an individual," cannot say anything "about what a man is or what he must do" (*Con*, 60). In 1974 Percy told the literature class he was teaching at Louisiana State University that Kierkegaard and the existentialists that he read at Trudeau were the sources for this ontological "discovery." Further, he said, they taught him about the "malaise," "bad faith," "Everydayness," "dread," and "anonymity" that afflict the modern searcher who yearns for some self-knowledge beyond scientific abstractions and "inauthentic" role-playing (WPP, series iv, box 40, folders 15-30).

Also at this time of reformulation at Trudeau, Percy began to read "philosophy of language," particularly Ernst Cassirer and Susanne Langer (*Con*, 106). It was this reading that first stimulated his interest in language symbolization as a source of knowledge and consciousness. A major feature of the worldview that Percy later developed in his fiction and in his philosophical essays is that human beings learn about themselves and their world by naming experience with language symbols. This language activity, of course, is a social activity whereby language users attach meaning to the experience they perceive. It is in this immaterial world of meaning that they create whatever knowledge they have of their existence; this shared semiotic world of meaning is their "reality." Such an epistemology and ontology obviously challenge the Cartesian, scientific assumption that an isolated thinking self discovers reality through its solitary, invisible cognitive processes and alone constructs an existence through its choice of roles.

But it was Percy's reading in Catholic theology at Trudeau that had the most influence on the novels and nonfiction he produced in the next four decades. Percy found in Aquinas and the Scholastics a "form of knowledge . . . different from scientific knowing," and different from the "ordinary epistemology" of modern "deterministic" science (*Con*, 204–5). It was this new knowledge that led to his conversion to Catholicism in 1947. Commenting on the importance of the Catholic faith to his writing career, Percy pointed out in a 1974 interview that he "didn't really begin to write until after . . . [he] became a Catholic" (*Con*, 88). Again, in a 1983 interview, Percy insisted that his faith was the single most important source for the ideas he developed in his writing: "I've been a Catholic ever since I've been writing, so the whole framework is, I suppose, Catholic" (*MCon*, 56).

After Percy returned to the South in 1946, married Mary Bernice ("Bunt") Townsend, and began to build his career and make his home in Covington, Louisiana, he knew that the knowledge his new faith had provided him would be necessary to show him what to do in order to have a life different from his father's and different from William Alexander Percy's. Particularly in his presentation of Will Barrett's wayfaring in *The Last Gentleman* and *The Second Coming*, Percy reflects on the self-deceptions inherent in lives like his father's. In these novels, Will's father defines himself in terms of personal codes of conduct and virtue that neither he nor the world can measure up to. Percy shows how such a self-definition can become a withdrawal from the phenomenal world, a retreat from a life defined as not honorable enough to live. Percy's father also depended on a Stoic, Southern sense of honorable conduct and Presbyterian rectitude for guidelines about what to do in constructing his unhappy life. And he, like Will Barrett's father, retired to the attic of his home one day and shot himself to death.

Percy could see a similar kind of inwardness and withdrawal in William Alexander Percy. Walker Percy greatly admired his Uncle Will— declaring that he was "the most extraordinary man I've ever known" (*Con*, 5). William Alexander Percy was the consummate genteel Southern gentleman: Harvard-educated attorney and community leader, paternalistic plantation master, highly cultured lover of fine music and poetry. While there was much to admire in this aristocratic figure, there was at the same time, Percy later saw, much to question. Percy's novels and essays warn again and again about the "dislocating" effects of the kind of aestheticism and noblesse oblige his Uncle Will represents. The self that habitually chooses the stimulations of aesthetic experience and the sense of worth granted by honorable conduct can easily develop into a self that is inclined to turn away from an actual life with others. This is a self that may be tempted to turn its back on a life that it perceives as less beautiful and less honorable than its idealized, interior version of existence. Percy could recognize the "extraordinary" in his Uncle Will, but he could also see in him how a lifetime of romantic self-indulgence in the pleasures of art and a lonely, Stoic devotion to honorable duties could degenerate into little more than a death-in-life.

Percy's forty-year career as novelist and philosopher began in the late 1940s, then, after a emotionally traumatic childhood, a brilliant academic career at the University of North Carolina and Columbia, a self-education at Trudeau in existential philosophy, literature, theology, and modern language theory, and his conversion to Catholicism. It is this complexity of psychological, intellectual, and religious experience that provided the sources for the worldview that Percy develops in his fiction and nonfiction, a worldview that is often presented in a highly allusive, ironic, nuanced style that challenges the reader's intellectual and aesthetic capacities.

The sheer volume of criticism in the twenty-five years after the publication of *The Moviegoer* (1962–87) attests to the complexities of Percy's intellectual, imaginative, and moral vision. J. Donald Crowley, in his "Introduction" to *Critical Essays on Walker Percy*, presents a thorough survey of this criticism.[6] Crowley points out Lewis Lawson's and Martin Luschei's pioneer work on Percy's philosophical and religious sources, his existential themes, the connections between his fiction and essays, and his interests in Old South Stoicism.[7] In the 1980s, Lawson continued to write groundbreaking essays and began to focus more on the relationships between Percy's language theories and his Christian and existentialist epistemology. A few critics in the 1980s, however, were beginning to become less enthusiastic about Percy's Catholic Christian worldview and complained of the didacticism and overt moralizing in the novels.[8] John Edward Hardy maintained in his 1987 study of the novels that he wanted to avoid as much as possible the religious and philosophical messages in Percy's fiction and emphasize instead "the art of Walker Percy's fiction."[9] Other critics in the 1980s tried other approaches. Anticipating the psychoanalytical studies of the 1990s, William Rodney Allen argued in *Walker Percy* (1986) that the sources for the themes in the novels could be found in Percy's childhood psychological experiences and in his Southern background. Ted Spivey, noting the Jungian influences in Percy in his *The Journey Beyond Tragedy* (1980) and *Revival: Southern Writers in the Modern City* (1986), was another critic interested in Percy's fiction as an expression of the author's psychological life.

Two full-length biographies, Jay Tolson's *Pilgrim in the Ruins* (1992)

and Patrick Samway's *Walker Percy: A Life* (1997), indicate the great interest in the 1990s in the relationships between Percy's fictional worlds and
his own life. Exploring the possible relationships, several critics have offered autobiographical and psychoanalytical readings of the novels. Bertram
Wyatt-Brown, in his chapter on Walker Percy in *The House of Percy* (1994),
reads the novels as therapeutic "outlet[s]" for Percy's "anger" and "bitter-
ness," an attempt by Percy to "distance" the "personal pain" caused by his
family.[10] Lewis Lawson's essays in *Still Following Percy* (1996) are a much
more informed and well-reasoned effort to explain Percy's fictional narratives through the writer's own experience. Lawson draws on his wide reading
in psychology and his impressive knowledge of Percy in developing his
argument that it was Percy's "maternal loss" that, more than anything else,
prompted him to create narratives about heroes in search of a woman's love,
a love that has the potential to reveal to the searcher "divine love."[11]

Other recent critics have continued to examine Percy's sources and vision. The essays in *Walker Percy: Novelist and Philosopher* (1991) are analyses
of the individual novels, commentaries on Percy's existentialism and Southern heritage, and discussions of Percy as a moralist.[12] Patrick Samway's
edition of the letters of Percy and Kenneth Laine Ketner, a scholar at Texas
Tech specializing in the semiotics of Charles Sanders Peirce, has been helpful
in re-emphasizing the importance of Peirce in Percy's thinking about symbolization, knowing, and the self.[13] Ann Futrell's book on Peirce and Percy
has also contributed to this important area of Percy source studies.[14] A
collection of essays edited by Lewis Lawson and Elzbieta Oleksy focuses
on the relatively unexplored subject of Percy's female characters and how
they function in developing the imaginative vision in the novels.[15] In his
Autobiography in Walker Percy (1996), Edward Dupuy uses current autobiographical theory to discuss Percy's Catholic Christian view of the self.

Many critics in the 1990s have emphasized that the single most important
feature of Percy's fiction and philosophy is his Catholic Christian "anthropology" (*MB*, 24); others find Percy's Christian messages tiresome and moralistic.
Gary Ciuba's study of the novels, *Walker Percy: Books of Revelation* (1991), and
John Desmond's collected essays in *At the Crossroads: Ethical and Religious Themes
in the Writings of Walker Percy* (1997) are two of the best critical works that
precisely and convincingly discuss the relationships between Percy's Catholicism, his cultural criticism, his concepts of the self, his epistemology, and his
understanding of language and symbolization. It is in these complex relationships that the reader can discover the richness of the worldview Percy created
in the body of his work. Ignoring these relationships, Kieran Quinlan offers a
simpler view of Percy's vision. Quinlan argues that the primary source of Percy's
philosophical and religious ideas can be found in the late 1940s orthodox Ca-

tholicism popular among intellectuals like Maritain, Merton, Flannery O'Connor, and Robert Lowell. This was the Catholic tradition embraced enthusiastically by Caroline Gordon Tate and Allen Tate, who served as Percy's early literary mentors. In his reductionist study, Quinlan asserts that the "vision" Percy acquired from this Catholicism is an "outdated Catholic Thomism" that is "no longer viable."[16]

Few serious critics besides Quinlan have been prepared to dismiss the profoundly informed philosophical and religious vision of Walker Percy as "an illusory spiritual pursuit,"[17] but instead it has been an assumption among almost all Percy scholars since Lewis Lawson and Martin Luschei that Percy's fiction and nonfiction demand the most rigorous and sustained research and analyses. And that is the assumption in the following chapters. The effort, primarily in the second chapter, is to define the most important features of the epistemology and ontology Percy develops in his novels, essays, and interviews and show how these have their roots in Catholic sacramentalism. The remaining chapters are devoted to explaining how Will Barrett in *The Last Gentleman* (1966) and *The Second Coming* (1980) and Dr. Thomas More in *Love in the Ruins* (1971) and *The Thanatos Syndrome* (1987) exemplify Percy's self-as-wayfarer in search of what to do in a sacramental world full of signs. These sacramental signs have the power to show them a life not available in the ruins of their culture, a life hidden from them as they desperately search for daily happiness in their professional achievements and family relationships.

In a 1974 interview, Percy said that this Catholic "sacramental view" provided him with "a way of seeing the world" that enriched his capacity to create his fictional wayfarers (*Con*, 88). It is a key element of his "Judeo-Christian anthropology" (*MB*, 24), a Catholic "anthropology" that asserts a "sacramental and historical-incarnational" (WPP, Series 2, D:27) understanding of individual and cultural experience.[18] Insisting on the influences of this "way of seeing" on his creation of his fictional worlds, Percy defined the imaginative landscapes in the novels as "a combination of the Catholic sacramental view and the South" (*Con*, 124). In the novels, Percy's vivid Southern settings become examples of the sacramental world where all make their journeys, and his heroes wayfarers making their pilgrimages with all others through a place where the signs in the created world around them have the capacity to reveal a world and a self beyond their knowing.

Will Barrett and Tom More are the two protagonists whose pilgrimages through the sacramental world are most thoroughly chronicled in Percy's novels. Percy's career as a successful novelist spans nearly thirty years, from 1958 when he began work on *The Moviegoer* to 1987 when *The Thanatos*

Syndrome was published. He spent about twenty of those thirty years developing the stories of Will and Tom in *The Last Gentleman*, *The Second Coming*, *Love in the Ruins*, and *The Thanatos Syndrome*. His other two novels are less detailed treatments of the sacramental search. In *The Moviegoer* (1961), Binx Bolling is an existential quester like Will and Tom, but this first novel, Percy says, is "more modest in its scope" than the later novels in its depiction of the search for sacramental signs of self and God (*MCon*, 4). *Lancelot* (1977) is a variation on the search motif developed in the other novels, Lancelot Lamar a gnostic quester who searches for evil and his own "salvation" from it (*MCon*, 79–80). Unlike wayfarers Will and Tom— who, after their discoveries about their predicaments, pledge themselves to a continuing search for signs—Lance thinks his search has ended. He is convinced that he has already found all the signs he needs to understand who he is and where he is and, at the end of the novel, intends to act on this knowledge to construct a new world in the Shenandoah Valley.

In their pilgrimages in the novels, Will Barrett, a lapsed Episcopalian, and Tom More, a "bad" Catholic, are wayfarers wandering through the sacramental postlapsarian landscapes of New York, Alabama, Mississippi, New Mexico, Appalachian North Carolina, and Feliciana Parish. They are trying to locate where they are, who they are, and what they should do in order to make a home for themselves in a world they find increasingly meaningless and purposeless. They are searching for some knowledge that will rescue them from the "death-in-life" that they repeatedly discover on the road, on the golf course, and in their suburban neighborhoods—a knowledge that will show them a life and a self they have so far been unable to locate.

These landscapes and the people in them are used symbolically in the novels to illustrate Will's and Tom's ways of seeing themselves and understanding their experience. Their ability to recognize the sacramental signs in the landscapes where they make their journeys and their ability to interpret the significances of these signs are indexes to their knowledge of themselves and their world. For the clear-eyed wayfarer, the desert he is traversing is, while filled with demons, also a sacred place, an incarnation of God. But Will and Tom only occasionally see with this clarity; most of the time they are oblivious both to the sacramental signs and their meaning. They do, however, finally achieve a "way of seeing" that defeats their suicidal despair and gives them the hope necessary to continue their searches. Will assents at the end of *The Second Coming* to a "possible" new life with Allie's love and, maybe, even with God's love (*SC*, 376). Similarly, Tom acquires some hope at the end of *The Thanatos Syndrome* when he agrees to follow Father Smith's advice to "wait" with a "good heart" for the new revelations about the world and himself that he will learn about "tomorrow" (*TS*, 363).

2

The Predicament: Where Are You?

The woman saw that the tree was good for food, pleasing to the eyes, and desirable for gaining wisdom. So she took some of the fruit and ate it; and she also gave some to her husband, who was with her, and he ate it. The eyes of both of them were opened, and they realized that they were naked. . . .

When they heard the sound of the Lord God moving about in the garden at the breezy time of the day, the man and his wife hid themselves from the Lord God among the trees of the garden. The Lord God then called to the man and asked him, "Where are you?" He answered, " I heard you in the garden; but I was afraid, because I was naked, so I hid myself."

—Genesis 3.6–10

The fearful, fallen Adam in the passage above has just been seduced into choosing what is "pleasing to the eyes" and has gained the "wisdom" that accompanies that choice. As a consequence, he faces a new and difficult existential question: "Where are you?" He is being asked to identify the nature of the unknown world that he is now required to enter, the world of suffering and death beyond the garden where, like Walker Percy's exiled heroes, he is about to "set out as a pilgrim" (*SP*, 314). Also like Percy's pilgrims, on his journey he will eventually be impelled by his "naked" alienation to ponder the effects of his recent choice and the knowledge it has brought him and led to wonder about what he has become and what he will do in the Fallen world of human history that will now be made in his image, not God's.

As a result of his fall, Adam has been banished from his home with God and sent out into a land where he will now have to search with his "opened" eyes for a way to make a life in the ruined landscape and for a way to discover what there is transcendent of the "seeing" that he has chosen in his ignorance and pride. Adam is the first to experience the "grave predica-ment" (*MB*, 144) Walker Percy's heroes face. In their predicaments, they are also alienated and alone as they search with the diminished vision that they have inherited from Adam for where they are, who they are, and what they should do (*MB*, 149) in the anxiety-filled world where they make their journeys. But their postlapsarian eyes, because they see dimly, can only show them illusions and lead them to erroneous or partial answers to these questions.

The predicaments of Percy's pilgrims are even more "grave" than Adam's because they live in a century and in a culture, Percy believes, that denies that there is any irrevocable gravity to the human condition. At least Adam is intensely aware that he is in a mysterious place that he does not under-stand and knows that there is no way for him to regain the paradise he has lost. But Percy's pilgrims journey in a society and in an historical era in which few believe that there is anything mysterious about where they are. Neither do they assume that there has been an aboriginal, irreversible Fall, an impoverishment of knowing that has exiled them forever from an Edenic existential condition. Instead, most assume the opposite: that human be-ings have the cognitive power to understand fully their predicament. They believe that they can observe and contemplate their environment, their so-ciety, and themselves and discover the "truth" about their world. Their investigations, they further assume, will uncover what is desirable and what is threatening in their existence. They then, logically, can pursue what their learning has shown them is satisfying and fulfilling and avoid or eliminate whatever causes discomfort. This is a scientistic worldview popular in this century that posits an ontology in which each individual is an autonomous self capable of discovering through his own thinking those experiences that will provide happiness. On the basis of its private discoveries, this self is entitled to the freedom to pursue its own version of happiness. Because, from this perspective, the individual's discoveries and the satisfactions they yield are potentially endless, a new Eden is always on the horizon.

Percy's pilgrims, under the influence of this worldview, often fail to rec-ognize that they are seeing with a clouded, Fallen vision and fail to understand how they are deceived by their culture's gnostic assumptions about the unlimited powers of the self to know and achieve. As a result, they frequently function in their lives with a misplaced confidence in their powers to know and act, habitually devoting themselves to futile quests for lives that their deficient eyes and limited minds tell them will be immea-surably more significant and satisfying than their current ones. They tend to pursue ego-satisfying occupational goals and achievements, cultivate emotionally satisfying relationships with their family and friends, and engage in the intellectual stimulations of science, art, philosophy, and theology in an effort to find the means for building fulfilling and happy lives. In a daily existence that sometimes seems to them purposeless and empty, even "farcical" and "demented" (*SC*, 4), they turn inward to their thoughts, feelings, and opinions, believing that within the recesses of their own minds they will discover the "truths" that will defeat the current despair and malaise that they see and reveal a new world.

Percy's fiction shows how these twentieth-century pilgrims are, in fact, seeing dimly while believing that they are seeing clearly. In their granting an absolute competency to their powers to envision and achieve a life made in the image of their desires and cognition, they are enclosing themselves within the narrow world of their individual perceptions and hiding from the voice that asks, "Where are you?" This voice is transcendent of their personal knowing and desire and demands that they recognize the "naked" reality of their being that is obscured by the limited vision they depend on to show them who they are, where they are, and what they should do.

From the perspective of Percy's Catholic Christian worldview, in order for them to escape their self-enclosure they need to turn their eyes to the sacramental signs in the incarnational universe. In Percy's sacramentalism, the doctrine of the incarnation affirms "a bond" between the physical world of the flesh and the anagogical world of the spirit,[1] and it is this bond that his wayfarers struggle to recognize. Percy says in "Physician as Novelist" that his heroes are in the process of recognizing that they are "wayfarer[s] in search of . . . [their] salvation." In order for them to have any success in their search, he goes on to emphasize, they also must realize that "the pilgrim's search [is] outside himself, rather than the guru's search within" (*SP*, 193). The sacramental signs of their salvation are immediately before their eyes in the phenomenal world, all creation a semiotic expression of a divine and infinite life. Although they do not always steadily improve in their ability to perceive this life,[2] they do become increasingly aware that they are living in a world that is formed by the facticity of "historical" "particularities," and, at the same time, they occasionally see signs in these "particularities" of a "God . . . [who] waits for us in things."[3] As Father Smith tells Tom in *The Thanatos Syndrome*, the knowledge that will defeat illusion and despair lies "out there" (*TS*, 121) in the mystery of the sacramental world of signs, not in the interior world of sensations, abstraction, and theory.

All of Percy's protagonists suffer from a blindness—sometimes partial, sometimes near-total—to the sacramental world and the messages available in its signs. This blindness is caused by their Cartesian, gnostic withdrawal into the closed interior reality of the self.[4] "Dislocated" and enclosed within their Cartesian subjectifications of time-space experience, Percy's self-absorbed heroes can rarely see beyond their abstractions and the emotional and psychological satisfactions they seek. But their encounters with the evil, suffering, and death in the world and the people in it often remind them of what is "out there" beyond their private feelings and ideas about life. They respond to these encounters by either retreating to their interior worlds or by taking tentative steps out into actual experience with others and the signs of their existence in a Fallen but grace-filled creation.

Will Barrett in *The Last Gentleman* and *The Second Coming* illustrates the difficulties Percy's heroes experience as they try to locate themselves in the actual created world. Will is symbolically enclosed in the basement of a New York department store at the beginning of *The Last Gentleman*, "dislocated" (*LG*, 20) from the world, others, and himself by his isolated "thinking" (*LG*, 3) about life. His journey to the openness of the New Mexico desert in the novel's final scenes suggests, perhaps, an incipient escape from the thinking and abstraction that have him so enclosed and so dislocated. It is in Santa Fe that he witnesses the excrutiating death of Jamie and helps Father Boomer in the baptism. Apparently, this death and sacramental rite awaken him to the possibility that there might be mysteries and "truths" utterly beyond the "objective" thinking he has always prized as a source of truth. When he leaves Jamie's bedside, he does not turn to his "magical" telescope and "scientific outlook" (*LG*, 29) in order to discover the significance of what has happened to him. Instead, he turns to another wayfarer whom he finds on the road with him. Will's new sense of engagement with the world outside his thinking is suggested when he "joyous[ly]" pursues Sutter in the streets of Santa Fe, pursues him with a "final question" (*LG*, 409) about the mysteries he has just witnessed at Jamie's bedside. He obviously believes he cannot through his solitary analyses arrive at an answer.

The middle-aged Will Barrett in *The Second Coming*, his youthful wandering in *The Last Gentleman* over, experiences a similar escape from his closed psychic world. Will's escape is implied by his leaving behind the frightening darkness of Lost Cove cave, his abandoning the Linwood golf course and country club, and his impending departure from St. Mark's nursing home. Throughout the novel, Will analyzes his painful memories of his father and the hunt in the Georgia swamp and examines the causes for the "death in life" (*SC*, 147, e.g.) that he is now living in the North Carolina mountains. He believes that through these interior explorations he will discover some "answers" (*SC*, 217) about his life that will relieve his suicidal despair. Near the end of the novel, Will begins to turn his eyes outward, and "things [take] on significance" (*SC*, 372) for him, "things" in the sacramental world he has been blind to for most of his life. Finally, in the hands of Allie and in the troubled face of Father Weatherbee, Will begins to see the possibilities for a life beyond his memories and beyond the perfect but sterile Linwood golf course.

Dr. Thomas More in *Love in the Ruins* is also lost in his interior world of emotion and thought. His desire for personal "happiness" (*LR*, 8, 18, 20, 138, 263, 311, e.g.) after the deaths of his daughter and faithless wife leads to his quest for "love" with Moira, Lola, and Ellen in the ruins of the local Howard Johnson's and to his messianic plans to use his medical knowledge to save mankind with his lapsometer. Tom More, like Will, spends much of his time alone with his thoughts in small, enclosed places. He plots military stategy while crouched in a dark "pine grove," tries to escape the chaos of the political upheavals in Paradise Estates by hiding in the "enclosed patio" (*LR*, 37) of his home, and dreams about his future "happiness" with Moira, Lola, and Ellen in the abandoned rooms of the ruined Howard Johnson's. In the final scenes, he begins, with the assistance of Father Smith and the sacraments of the Church, to turn his eyes outward to a "knowledge" (*LR*, 399) of himself as a participant in a sign-filled sacramental creation. Tom, after Christmas Eve Mass, barbecues a turkey at his "Slave Quarters" home and at this happy moment in his life senses that there is a divine presence that surrounds him, suspects that "the Lord is here" on this "holy night" (*LR*, 402).

In *The Thanatos Syndrome*, Percy presents an older and somewhat less exuberant Tom More who has not been able to maintain the hope and joy he briefly experienced at the end of *Love in the Ruins*. He is once more enclosed in an interiorized, scientifically defined self, whether alone in his prison cell, at his lonely office, or in front of Lucy's computer screen. Tom has resumed his career as a research-oriented psychiatrist isolated from the world and others by his pursuit of the abstract data and the scientific "truths" that he thinks will save himself and his neighbors from the "syndrome" he has discovered. As in *Love in the Ruins*, Tom again chooses his science and his own eyes in his efforts to discover "happiness" and "what to do" (*TS*, 88, 234, 354, 361, e.g.) and has difficulty sustaining his faith in the way of seeing that Father Smith and the Church show him. Father Smith's "Confession" finally causes Tom to reflect on the "horror" (*TS*, 254) in the actual Fallen world outside his data and to consider the possibilities "out there" in the incarnate creation where there are signs of the redemptive love that defeats the "horror" of suffering and death. An impending "epiphany" with Father Smith (*TS*, 370) and Mickey LaFaye at the end of the novel may open Tom to a new self and world.

Will and Tom, at the moments when they are most perceptive, become active, hope-filled seekers who take tentative steps—whether in the New Mexico desert, the mountains of North Carolina, Paradise Estates, or Feliciana Parish—toward a consciousness of those realities that transcend their cognition, the mystery Percy calls "the end of the quest" (*MCon*, 106). They do not, obviously, conclude the quest and transcend Fallen human experience with all its difficulties and frustrations. But they are at the ends of the novels on the verge of achieving an awareness larger than their past "happiness" or abstractions. They arrive at moments of clarity when they assent to the possibility that there may be signs that will tell them about a power that will redeem them from the painful predicament that imprisons them. They are willing to suspend their solitary search for solutions to all their problems and willing to join the other wayfarers who have decided that "the road is better than the inn" (*MB*, 89). By seeing their lives as an untraveled land that always stretches out before them, they begin to enjoy a new sense of hope and energy; they begin to see that their futures, while ambiguous and uncertain, are also open and volitional. Whatever success questers like Will and Tom enjoy emanates from the energy generated by the anticipation of the possibilities that lie just down the road. Will Barrett's "joyous ten-foot antelope bounds" at the end of *The Last Gentleman* (409) and his "heart leap[ing] with a secret joy" at the end of *The Second Coming* (411) are examples of the energizing effect of the wayfarer's achieving such a consciousness of himself in the world. Tom's exuberant dance around the barbecue grill on Christmas Eve night at the end of *Love in the Ruins* is motivated by a similar kind of awareness that there might well be a "true knowledge" (*LR*, 398) that can reveal to him a future that he heretofore has not been able to envision.

Lewis Lawson, commenting on Percy's heroes and their efforts to es-cape their closed consciousness and myopic vision, argues that they are striving desperately "to live in the present" of "space-time events,"[5] trying to perceive themselves in a present reality that they are closed off from by their subjective, Cartesian thinking. Lawson is emphasizing that the novels are about the heroes' ongoing struggles to escape what they presently are and about their efforts to develop a self they cannot yet perceive, not about how they are successful or unsuccessful in overcoming the problems in their lives. The novels are not stories about heroes defeating the challenges of their world and becoming "happy," but are instead tales about wayfarers who are, at best, trying to locate themselves accurately with others in that Fallen world Adam first identified as his place of exile. This is precisely what Tom is doing at the end of *Love in the Ruins* when he identifies him-self as a fellow exile with his neighbors in the "Slave Quarters" and what

Will is doing when he runs toward Sutter at the end of *The Last Gentleman*.

Patrick Samway, supporting Lawson's view of the Percyan wayfarer, says that Percy's pilgrim journeys toward a "horizon" where an infinite "source of reality" waits to transform his limited, closed consciousnesses into a new "plenitude of personal being."[6] Will, in his assenting at the end of his pilgrimage in *The Second Coming* to the possible significances of Allie's love and Father Weatherbee's "holy face" (*SC*, 411), is opening himself to this plenitude. Similarly, Tom at the end of *The Thanatos Syndrome* is also beginning to see anew and accept the possibilities of a life beyond his scientific knowing. In the closing scene, Tom sees the face of his patient Mickey LaFaye as a "mirror" of himself, sees both of them joined as they search together for a sign of the "terror"(*TS*, 371–72) within all postlapsarian selves that makes them look to the horizon for some salvation from their existential predicament. In moments like these, when they can see clearly, Will and Tom begin to conquer their self-absorption and alienation and begin to realize themselves as wayfarers "with you [all others] under God" (*LC*, 112) in a world filled with sacramental signs.

KNOWING AND LANGUAGE: WHAT'S OUT THERE?

In order for Will and Tom to begin to see the world and themselves in a more open and complete way, they must first locate themselves accurately, both in their physical environment and in the human social world of signs they inhabit. Heidegger calls these two existential "worlds" the *umwelt* and *welt*, respectively. In *Lost in the Cosmos* (110), particularly in the "intermezzo" entitled "A Semiotic Primer of the Self," Percy asserts that those who are desperate to "know . . . [their] self" must first define for themselves a mode of being in relation to these two worlds (*LC*, 87; *SP*, 290). Percy considered this "intermezzo" his most important philosophical statement (*Con*, 285), possibly because it makes explicit the importance of Heidegger's differentiation between the human, self-conscious world of sign creation and meaning and the physical environment that is the home for the rest of creation.

This semiotic placement of the self, according to Percy, has been a necessary ontological task since Adam's first self-conscious awareness of his nakedness; this is the way all "locate" (name), who they are and where they are in the world. "As soon as the self becomes self-conscious," he says, it "must be *placed* in a world. It cannot *not* be placed" (*LC*, 110). Self-placement is unavoidable because human beings use language and therefore live semiotically in a "world of signs" that they create with other humans. It is

in this immaterial world of meaning that they achieve whatever consciousness they have of the self and world (*LC*, 103). Their reality is not just the
physical environment they share with other beings, but also this shifting
and dynamic semiotic *welt*. Making a similar distinction between the world
of human cognition and the purely physical environment, Northrop Frye
points out that we live in a "mythological universe," not in "nature." According to Frye, imaginative literature speaks for this world of signs and
meaning and is an expression of our "body of assumptions and beliefs developed from . . . existential concerns."[7] For Percy, any discovery of a new
consciousness or any opening of the self to the mysteries in the sacramental
world can only be achieved in the context of this semiotic world of meaning, words offering "endless intelligible possibility"[8] as the self linguistically
interacts with others in naming reality. In Percyan epistemology and ontology, knowing is not accomplished by an isolated Cartesian, thinking
individual, but instead the self's knowledge of who it is and where it is is
socially constructed through language in the "*joint* act of designation and
affirmation by symbol" (*MB*, 282; emphasis added). Percy believes that "our
common existence is validated" (*MB*, 295) by this symbolization of language. Language transactions unite in a single world of meaning the
speakers, the listeners who understand the symbolization process, and the
signified universe being designated by their language signs.

Because language makes possible this intersubjective, shared world of
meaning, it can defeat alienation and estrangement. In the acknowledgement
of a shared semiotic experience with others, the individual can locate the
self as a participant in a world and cosmos that lie outside his private ideas
and feelings about his existence. For Percy, this is how one becomes "conscious": to be conscious is to know *about something* outside the perceiving
self, to know about it through language signs, to know *with another*, and
therefore to discover that one is in a sacramental and open world as Marcel's
"we are," not Descartes's "I-think" (*MB*, 283, 293, 295). At the conclusions
of *The Last Gentleman, The Second Coming, Love in the Ruins*, and *The Thanatos Syndrome*, Will and Tom are in the process of acquiring this kind of
open consciousness as they begin to recognize the facticity of their being
with others in the sacramental world of phenomena and as they begin to
question the authority of their own thinking as a source of "truth."

Percy's ideas about language, knowing, and being were derived, to some
extent, from his reading of modern philosophy and language theory, particularly the works of Charles Sanders Peirce, Susanne Langer, Ernst
Cassirer, Wittgenstein, and Heidegger. But in his earlier study of the medieval Scholastics he learned about a Catholic sacramental view of

symbolization and knowing that he believed anticipated in many ways these modern thinkers. This Catholic concept of a sacramental universe of signs continuously "speaking" to mankind of meanings that lie beyond immanent experience has its roots in the ancient Hebrew reverence for language as a divine gift and in a belief in a God ("the Word") who "became flesh and made his dwelling among us" (John 1.14). In the Judeo-Christian incarnational tradition, God speaks the world into existence, and Christ is the "Logos of God." Both God and Christ are transcendent sources of meaning and consciousness that lie beyond all human knowing, but they paradoxically exist and make themselves perceptible through signs in the sensible, incarnate universe. Words are also sensible, perceptible signs in physical experience that reveal immaterial meaning and consciousness. Language signs are absolutely, empirically existent in the actualities of time-space events, but at the same time are the sources of a human consciousness transcendent of physical phenomena.[9]

In "The Mystery of Language," Percy, exploring some of the parallels between the epistemologies of the Scholastics and modern linguists, asserts that in some ways the Scholastics' sacramentalism is "a far more adequate theory of symbolic meaning . . . than [the one] modern semioticists" (MB, 156) have developed. His reading of Aquinas convinced him that long before modern semiotics the Scholastics understood clearly the limitations of man's cognitive powers and knew that any access to more profound "essences" beyond those limitations can only be "indirect," "mediated by symbols" (MB, 156). Centuries before Charles Sanders Peirce, a modern philosopher very influential in Percy's thinking about semiotics, these medieval scholars pointed out that all knowledge emanates from man's symbolic activity.

In both Peirce and the Scholastics Percy saw an antidote to the modern scientistic subjectivity and romantic solipsism illustrated by Will Barrett and Tom More as they try to explore their inner lives for truth and happiness. In a 1989 letter to Patrick Samway, Percy maintained that he was attracted to Peirce because of the American philosopher's "attack on nominalism and his rehabilitation of Scholastic realism."[10] He was particularly attracted to the Scholastics' and Peirce's insistence that there is a real world of objects independent of individual perception and knowable only through language signs. Both Peircean semiotics and Scholastic theology assert that cognition is achieved through "reading" the signs in the actual, sensible world and by assuming that these signs can direct the "reader" of them to a knowledge beyond mere personal sensory data and the ideas based on that data. Peirce says, "the whole universe acts as a symbol . . . of God's very nature"; God reveals Himself "in living realities."[11] Obviously, this is a semiotic very similar to Catholic sacramentalism. Sacramental "seeing" is an analogical mode of perception exemplified explicitly in medieval biblical exegesis in which the Christian reader assumed that the scriptures speak metaphorically of a cosmos where God reveals Himself to human understanding through visible creation. The medieval reader's duty was to work his way up from his sensory perception of the world toward an understanding of how the particularities of the created world around him reveal analogically the mysteries of God.[12] When Tom More, at the end of *Love in the Ruins,* can see the "beast of a fish" he has just caught as a symbol of "Christ coming again" (*LR,* 387), he is exhibiting this analogical way of reading the sacramental signs in the world.

For modern semioticists like Peirce, and for the medieval Scholastics, the self has no knowledge of its being and no consciousness outside its transactions with the signs and symbols in the actual, sensible world—both the word signs of human language and the signs of the Word in the incarnate universe. From the perspective of this semiotic, the individual is not an isolated knowing self who observes a static world of phenomena separate from his being, but instead he is a symbol-mongering creature immersed in a dynamic universe and continuously wayfaring among these signs "in the neighborhood of being" (*MB,* 60). It is in this "neighborhood" that human language signs and the anagogical sacramental signs in the incarnational world continuously offer revelations as the pilgrim participates in the process of becoming that is forever occurring and forever being revealed in the universe. The source of all knowledge about the self and the cosmos is in this incarnational world of signs where mankind lives. Commenting on the universe as this kind of divine semiotic, Hugh of St. Victor declares, "this whole world is a book written by the finger of God."[13] Through the sensory signs in the actual time-space world of individual being, the Christian in search of a true knowledge of his predicament has the opportunity to ascend through sign reading from sense experience to spiritual truth.

Explaining further in "The Mystery of Language" how being continuously comes into existence through this sign-reading activity the Scholastics and Peirce recommend, Percy quotes Jacques Maritain, who speaks of the Scholastic notion of phenomenal things actually being present *"in alio esse"* in symbols (*MB,* 156). In *Ransoming the Time,* Maritain explains that for the Scholastics the signified thing is made present for knowing by its symbol, the signified object genuinely there *"in alio esse,* in another mode of existence."* In the Eucharistic wine and bread, for example, Christ is there *in alio esse* and therefore made knowable through those actual substances. The wine and bread "re-present" all the essential qualities of the Christ figure for the willing knower, and, as substitutes for what they stand for, they have "a certain presence—[a] presence of knowability." It is this "presence" in the symbol, not the actual signified thing, that is the source of the knowledge that makes up the interior life of human intellectual and spiritual activity.[14] In other words, the interior life that most equate with consciousness and the self is created out of the meaning that symbols make present and therefore knowable.

Aquinas, commenting on this relationship beween knowing and being that Maritain sees, asserts that human beings are able to know "something by becoming something" (MB, 297). From this perspective, there is no separate, autonomous knowing self detached from what it knows. Instead, individuals in the act of knowing are engaged in, and a part of, the flux of phenomena; they are continuously, through language symbolization, transforming actual things and their experience into meaning. This meaning, in turn, is what fills the interior life that each person defines as the self. Again, meaning is created through the presence of symbols, not things, and it is by the symbol's re-presenting phenomena (in alio esse) that the physical world and the immaterial self are joined in the process of knowing (MB, 296–97).

In his discussion of the role of Catholic sacramentalism and language theory in the development of Percy's ideas about language, knowing, and the self, Lewis Lawson says that for Percy language is a "sacrament," a "channel through which the human meets the divine," a way for the individual to enlarge his consciousness of the infinite world of meaning beyond his immanent environment.[15] Kathleen Scullin agrees that in Percy's essays and novels language is not only the means by which the individual connects with others, but it is also the way he transcends his current consciousness.[16] Percy, in "The Fateful Rift: The San Andreas Fault in the Modern Mind," discusses the possibilities of transcending one's current ego experience and achieving a fuller consciousness through the symbolization in language. In order to make his point about the potentially endless growth of the self made possible through language transactions with others, Percy quotes Gabriel Marcel, who asserts, "it may be of my essence to be able to be not what I am" (SP, 290; MB, 284). By its naming and knowing, Marcel is maintaining, the self has the capacity to transcend its current understanding of all that it perceives that it is.

In his fiction, Percy presents struggling selves who are working toward a recognition that they have not yet arrived at a full knowledge of "what" they are. Impeding their acquisition of such a consciousness is a modern language world made up of words that no longer signify adequately. Both Will and Tom search for a knowledge of their predicaments in a culture where, Percy believes, language has been "evacuated" (TS, 121) of meaning.

As Father Smith points out to Tom in *The Thanatos Syndrome*, there can be a deprivation of meaning in language that causes a subsequent deprivation of knowing and being among the language users. Words, Percy asserts, in "Naming and Being," can lose their ability to signify precisely and therefore "conceal" reality, closing opportunities for the individual "to discover being." Even an entire culture may suffer this "evacuation" of meaning, its inhabitants living by clichés and jargon that are empty of significance (*SP*, 135).

Percy believes that twentieth-century America is one of these linguistically deprived cultures. In a rationalistic, pragmatic culture like ours, Percy argues, actual time-space reality is obscured by a language that signifies a tree, for example, as "just a tree" (*SP*, 135). The actual tree itself, of course, is devalued by such designation and emptied of sacramental significance. Particularly in the case of religious language in this century, Percy maintains, the words are as worn out and empty as the language of television commercials. He says the Christian novelist shouting the "Good News" today might as well be shouting "Exxon! Exxon!" (*MB*, 116). Percy is identifying a modern cognitive orientation that Giles Gunn believes has functioned to "deprive" the language of literature and religion of its "reality" since the Middle Ages, and especially since the Romantic period. It is a kind of cognition that either sees a symbolic object as merely symbolic or sees the object itself as merely an object. In either case, there is a withdrawal from both the empirical and symbolic meanings of the object and a substituting for these meanings a purely personal significance (or absence of significance) that the individual, for whatever reason, happens to choose to attach to the object.[17]

Percy humorously satirizes this kind of "deprived" and "evacuated" language in *The Thanatos Syndrome* when he shows the Catholic Tom More's puzzled response to his wife Ellen's Pentecostal "personal encounter with Jesus Christ" and her finding "true happiness with her Lord and Saviour" (*TS*, 353). The glib religious language of television evangelists that Ellen mimics cuts her off from any further exploration of her spiritual life, and therefore from any new knowing and new being. The language makes her "happy" and satisfied, and therefore she has no impetus to search for Marcel's "not what I am." The language traps her in a complacent illusion of good feeling, a comfortable illusion that she has no reason to want to escape.

FINDING A PLACE IN THE DESERT: WHAT TO DO?

The self-knowledge Tom and Ellen need is particularly elusive in the twentieth-century primarily because of the scientistic assumptions about the self that Percy believes function to distort the individual's perception of who he is and where he is. In the America Tom and Ellen inhabit, most assume that human beings function as consumers and knowers of their physical environment, different only in degree from other organisms as they all pursue their need satisfactions. Most Americans are inclined to believe that personal happiness is the highest ontological goal and that the way to achieve happiness is to discover what is most satisfying to consume and pursue those satisfactions. Most also believe in the epistemological primacy of individual cognition, reluctant to admit that there is any "reality" beyond their current perceptions and knowing. These assumptions that the self is dependent on the stimulations that consumption in the physical and social world can provide and that there are no satisfactions available outside what the individual self can discover through his own cognition trap the modern self in the illusion that there is nothing to know and nothing to do outside his transactions with an indifferent environment.

Percy's best explanaton of the difficulties faced by his twentieth-century fictional wayfarers and their real-life counterparts as they try to discover a way of seeing and way of life larger than their private knowing and consumption is in his brilliant essay "The Message in the Bottle" (*MB*, 119–49). In this essay, Percy compares the existential predicament of the modern self to the situation of an amnesiac "castaway" on an island. This is a key metaphor in Percy's philosophy and theology, one he borrowed from Heidegger and Jaspers (*MB*, 146) and first used in his fiction in *The Moviegoer* (9).[18] Percy's self-conscious, amnesiac castaway in "The Message in the Bottle," Heidegger's *Geworfenheit* (*MB*, 146), anxiously roams about on the strange island among other equally alienated islanders, trying to discover "where he came from and who he is and what he must do" (*MB*, 149). His limited understanding of his predicament is symbolically implied by his isolation on the island from the vast unknown beyond the surrounding seas. His only access to knowledge is in this tiny place.

As he participates with the other castaways in his daily island activities, this modern exile may place himself in relation to his island world as either an organism that consumes the physical and cultural resources of his immediate environment or as a "knower" (a "scientist" in the original sense of the word) who wants to learn about the island and its activities through the language of its science and art. Or, more likely, he may choose both kinds of placement and play the roles of both consumer and knower. An alternative to these types of self-placements, and an existentially more authentic and productive one from Percy's perspective, involves the exile's recognition of his castaway condition and his turning his eyes to the open seas to "watch" and "wait" for messages that will bring "news from across the seas"

(*MB*, 140). In this waiting and watching posture, the castaway, first of all, is asserting that he believes there is something to know about himself and the world beyond his roles on the island; he is denying that his roles as consumer and knower of his environment are identical with his existential self. In addition, he is implying in his waiting and watching that he believes there is an immense and important realm of knowledge beyond the island that has the potential to open to him a radically new understanding of his predicament.

Twentieth-century castaways like Will and Tom, Percy maintains, have been encouraged to turn their eyes away from the open seas. They are victims of a pervasive scientific and social scientific epistemology and ontology that have "displaced" "man from the center of the universe" (*Con*, 223) and persuaded him to think of himself dualistically as either mere "bestial" organism or "angelic" transcendent knower.[19] Percy believes that it is the seventeenth-century mathematician Descartes who is responsible, more than any other single person, for this philosophical dualism in Western philosophy. It is a dualism that assumes a self that is alienated from phenomena and other selves, locked away in the invisible, isolated world of its own *cogito*. Descartes asserts that the *res cogitans*, the perceiving mind, is the disembodied agent that acquires knowledge by peering out at the *res extensa* (*SP*, 274), the objects of its perception. Inherent in this cognitive posture is a devaluation of human life, since the Cartesian observer unconsciously posits that his fellow humans are no more than objects to be observed and contemplated by his *cogito*. The actuality of individual people, organisms, events, and objects—all physical reality—disappear, transformed by the lonely *cogito* into abstract mental constructs.

Percy argues that this Cartesian dualism and the modern scientism that it has spawned are the principal features of an empirical worldview that relies primarily on the individual's visual data (as Adam chooses his opened eyes) for verification of the *cogito's* scientific "truths." Michel Foucault, in *The Order of Things*, discusses at length the features of physical reality that are hidden by such post-Cartesian, post-Enlightenment scientific methods of observing and studying the natural world. He points out how these methods of analyses inevitably result in a fragmented, incomplete understanding of experience.[20] Further, they nurture a sense of alienation and isolation from all that is not the scientistic observer's interior world of sensory perceptions, thoughts, opinions, and feelings. By such self-placement, the observer finds himself in a closed, self-made world of abstraction that has been generated and validated by sensory data, especially sight. He becomes a victim of what Percy believes is one of the essential dogmas of modern science—the belief that there are no realities "apart from the activity of the knower" (*MB*, 234). All reality outside the activity of the individual *cogito* is hidden from the Cartesian observer, and he therefore assumes that it is nonexistent.

The Cartesian objectification of the physical, phenomenal self as a being separate from the *cogito* encourages the individual to see himself as just another animal functioning in nature. This self-concept often leads to his locating himself as an "organism-in-an-environment," what Percy calls the "Self as Immanent." This "bestial" self sees itself as functioning much like other organisms—that is, it assumes that life is merely a matter of pursuing need satisfactions. In its pursuits, this kind of self may become either a passive "role player and consumer," or may set out to become an "autonomous self" who tries to create a satisfying life through its appropriation and mastery of the resources of the island (*LC*, 113). By such activities, the immanent self is likely to create a life devoted to an endless and self-defeating quest for happiness through need-satisfactions and role-playing. The primary danger in this kind of self-placement lies in the possibility of the castaway's identifying these "transaction[s]" (*LC*, 113) with the environment and other organisms with his existential self. He may, that is, have trouble distinguishing his authentic self from his activities. Consequently, in his constant role-playing he may become, Percy says, one of the many unauthentic, "frantic selves grop[ing] for any mask at hand to disguise their nakedness" (*SP*, 390).

A contrasting kind of semiotic placement that the modern, post-Cartesian castaway is tempted to choose is the "Self as Transcendent" (*LC*, 113). This is the "angelic" self that defines the world as *res extensa*, a place that it is somehow absent from except as a remote, transcendent knower of phenomena. In a secular age like the twentieth century, in which there is little faith in an actual transcendent metaphysical realm of "truth," science and art, Percy believes, are the only ways for this knower self to participate in a realm of knowledge higher than physical life. This transcendent self, therefore, searches for "truths" about his environment, the self, and his culture in the observations, analyses, principles, and abstractions of science and art, not in religion. The primary goal for this transcendent self is to acquire, through his study of the humanistic abstractions of science and art, a knowledge that the self can use to construct another reality within the confines of its own interior mental life that is "truer" and more significant than the mundane physical actuality of his daily life on the island. Because of this goal, this Cartesian knower castaway often exemplifies both Kierkegaard's aesthetic[21] and ethical stages of being: on the one hand, he defines himself primarily as an aesthetic, detached observer of physical phenomena, but he is also likely to see himself as a discover of the "truth" about life that his observations reveal. On the basis of these "truths," he is tempted to construct an ethical life that he believes mirrors the discoveries that he has autonomously achieved through his sensory data and his analyses of it. He decides what to do in life after his *cogito* discovers the truth about where he is. Will Barrett illustrates that he is just such an aesthete when he thinks he must "know everything before he . . . [can] do anything" (*LG*, 4).

The "angelic" castaway's Kierkegaardian, egoistic aestheticism inevitably leads to theorizing and abstraction, and therefore he often experiences an estrangement from actual phenomena and his authentic self instead of arriving at "truth." Paradoxically, his presumption of objectivity in his detachment results in an utter subjectification of experience because he must, because of his self-placement, look inward, Percy says, for self-satisfaction, self-development, and all knowledge about his island home (*SP*, 208). This interiorized self is closed off from experience, suffering from what Alfred North Whitehead calls a "misplacement of reality"; that is, this is a self that attaches greater significance to personal theories and abstractions than to the physical phenomena on which they are based (*SP*, 298). This is the "lost" self "in orbit" that Percy excoriates in *Lost in the Cosmos*, a self that mistakes its perceptions of reality for reality itself.

As Percy extends his castaway metaphor in "The Message in the Bottle," he explains that both the immanent and the transcendent castaways need to discover the possibility that there might be a dimension of being more significant than their knowing and need satisfactions on the island. The castaways need to be reminded that they are indeed castaways in exile from all knowledge that is beyond their island home and the abstractions of its science and art. Further, they need to know that their alienation from all that lies "across the seas" (*MB*, 140) accounts for their failures to achieve happiness, regardless of how well their needs are satisfied on the island or how much they know about island life through "island news" and island learning (*MB*, 130). They should not try to pretend that they are at home in their consuming and knowing on the island. Percy succinctly defines in his essay the castaways' urgent existential condition and their need to recognize where they are:

> To be a castaway is to be in a grave predicament and this is not a happy state of affairs. But it is very much happier than being a castaway and pretending one is not. This is despair. The worst of all despairs is to imagine one is at home when one is really homeless. (*MB*, 144)

Although Dr. Thomas More in *Love in the Ruins* obviously exemplifies the Percyan transcendent self who spends much of his time lost in his theorizing about saving the world with his miraculous lapsometer, he also has difficulty "break[ing] out of the iron grip of immanence" (*LC*, 122) that holds him fast in the assumption that the world is simply a Darwinian, menacing environment where he, and the other organisms, compete for survival and need satisfaction. But Tom is not a passive consumer, his aggressive posture toward his environment implied by his literally playing the role of soldier in the novel. His goal is to win his "happiness" (*LR*, 214) in his environment and defeat all the forces that prevent his attaining it. He is determined to become the autonomous consumer ridiculed in *Lost in the Cosmos*.

In the opening scene, Tom is fighting for his happiness, armed with a "carbine" and waiting to do combat with a hostile environment and culture. In a hellishly "hot," darkening "grove of. . . pines" (*LR*, 3–4), a buzzard circling ominously above him, Tom is prepared to fight for, and perhaps die for, the self-indulgent pleasures that he associates with a life of living happily with Lola, Moira, and Ellen. His life-or-death struggle is motivated by his desire for his future happiness in the ruined rooms of a long- abandoned Howard Johnson's motel—air-conditioned rooms furnished with three voluptuous women, "Campbell's chicken-and-rice" soup, "the World's Great Books," and "cases of Early Times" (*LR*, 8). While he waits alone in the grove, armed and combative, and plans for his future Eden of need-satisfactions, he is, paradoxically, quite comfortable (*LR*, 4) in the face of what he believes are the impending catastrophes and dangers. In his consciousness of his comfort in the midst of threat, Tom exemplifies Percy's immanent self (*LC*, 122) who seeks only personal ease. For this kind of self, comfort is prized over all other experience, so even catastrophe is welcomed because it prevents the psychic discomfort that accompanies stultifying boredom.

Will Barrett in *The Last Gentleman* exemplifies Percy's transcendent self, a self who, like the immanent self, does not know who or where it is. Unlike the often bestial Tom, however, the angelic Will habitually tries to place himself apart from the capricious pleasures and threats of the physical environment in order to search for the "truth" about his existence within the abstractions of his own mind. Throughout the novel, he intellectually detaches himself from the sacramental phenomenal world and his fellow castaways in a futile inner quest for a knowledge that will relieve his anxiety and malaise. Lost in his abstractions, Will is frequently oblivious to where he is in time and space, and therefore does not know what to do. In the opening scenes in Central Park, for example, Will is absorbed in his efforts to "engineer" (*LG*, 41) a new life for himself, and he is depending solely on his own thinking (*LG*, 29) and his scientific eyes to direct him in his search for "what to do"(*LG*, 4). He believes he can discover a new Eden of personal being solely by seeing anew with eyes augmented by the marvelous telescope that can "penetrate to the heart of things" (*LG*, 29). In his inner world of thought and desire, he is determined to "discover his identity" (*LG*, 79) through the "scientific principles and self knowledge" he feels he has acquired during his "five years of [psycho]analysis" (*LG*, 41). He is completely absorbed in his dreams of the Edenic life he believes he can create and therefore incapable of perceiving the actualities of his immediate environment. Central Park, in contrast to the life Will contemplates and desires, is a dark, conspicuously postlapsarian garden, a "worn," "tough" place that has been "put to hard use by millions of people" (*LG*, 4). Humorously emphasizing Will's detachment from phenomenal reality, Percy implies that the ominous gunshots and fires of nearby rioting Harlem are obvious signs in the landscape that should jolt the dazed Will out of his reveries and remind him where he is.

The Sacramental Landscape

Percy speaks explicitly in his interviews and essays about the importance of the symbolic sacramental landscapes where his protagonists make their quests for signs that will tell them about their predicament. In a 1974 interview in which he acknowledged the influences of Gerard Manley Hopkins's sacramentalism on his fiction, Percy maintained that his novels express a "Catholic attitude toward nature . . . as a sacramental kind of existence" (*Con*, 124). In "Notes for a Novel about the End of the World," he says that a Catholic "incarnational" worldview is an essential philosophical assumption in his fiction (*MB*, 111). Again, in "Another Message in the Bottle," he echoes Flannery O'Connor when he declares, "it is my conviction that the incarnational and sacramental dimensions of Catholic Christianity are the greatest natural assets of a novelist" (*SP*, 366). Percy believed, along with O'Connor, that the Catholic faith opens up for the writer of fiction a sacred "added dimension" of reality.[22] In a 1986 interview with Patrick Samway, Percy expressed his sacramental worldview in a particularly direct way: "things in the world . . . mirror in themselves, however dimly, something beyond themselves" (*MCon*, 129).

In a 1952 letter to the then-recent Catholic convert and struggling young novelist, Caroline Gordon suggested to Percy some techniques that would enable him to dramatize this Catholic sacramentalism in his fiction. Gordon served as a literary mentor for both Percy and Flannery O'Connor early in their careers. Besides stressing in the letter the importance of the thematic complexity and profundity that the Catholic faith makes available to the Catholic novelist, Gordon strongly advised Percy to avoid abstraction in his fiction and strive for concrete settings and events. She emphasized the importance of vivid and sensuous imagery, particularly for the novelist with a sacramental view of nature for whom "each image and symbol . . . reveals something of infinite reality."[23]

Percy's vivid landscape imagery in *The Last Gentleman*, *The Second Coming*, *Love in the Ruins*, and *The Thanatos Syndrome* shows that he eventually learned how to create the kind of fiction Gordon describes in her letter. The imagery in Percy's novels emphasizes that the world through which his wayfarers make their pilgrimages is a sacramental, mysterious place full of signs and, anagogically, an expression of the Word that discloses whatever truth there is. One critic has precisely named these landscape images in Percy's fiction "Christological hierophanies" because they serve as reminders of O'Connor's "added dimension" of experience.[24] In these symbolic sacramental landscapes, the protagonists are engaged in the difficult process of shedding their abstractions and illusions about where they are and acquiring a new, if incomplete, consciousness of themselves as "fully incarnate beings" (*MCon*, 148).

Percy places Will Barrett in such a symbolic landscape in the opening scene of *The Second Coming*. Will is alienated from others and unconscious of his existence in sacramental nature, his condition caused by his locating himself in the interior world of his memories, feelings, and ideas. While he is playing a pleasant round of golf with his wealthy friends, he observes closely the natural world around him, but he is incapable of reading accurately the sacramental signs in it. He is, therefore, from a Christian sacramental view of experience, not entirely conscious of where he is. Before him on the seventeenth green he sees a "low ridge of red maples . . . in the brilliant sunlight" that looks like a Pentecostal "tongue of fire" (*SC*, 6), but he attaches little significance to his observation. He vaguely senses that he is experiencing a "sign" (*SC*, 3) of some sort, but it does not prompt him to locate himself in the immediacy of time and space where the sign, of course, exists. This sign instead lures him away from the present moment and events and transports him into his inner world of depression and into his thoughts about the "farcical" and "demented" (*SC*, 4) state of the world. Again, when he sees the "scarlet and gold hillsides of the Appalachians" (*SC*, 7), he responds by retreating into his own mind, this time into his memories of Ethel Rosenblum and lost love, and eventually into his theories about the Jews leaving North Carolina.

In the final scenes of *The Thanatos Syndrome*, Percy uses the same kind of sacramental landscape imagery to suggest that Dr. Thomas More may be descending from the transcendent orbit of abstractions in which his science has trapped him and gaining a fresh awareness of the flesh-and-blood, incarnational world. Earlier in the novel, the insolent Chandra curtly diagnoses Tom's habitual abstraction by proclaiming that he is simply "too much up in [his] head" (*TS*, 40). He reveals this detachment from the world and others when he and his cousin Lucy are studying the "syndrome." He is devoted to gathering data about the strange plague that has assaulted south Louisiana, his victimized patients mere case studies that can help him find the answer to this medical problem. He considers the victims of the syndrome just blips on Lucy's computer screen—bits of data to verify or disprove his theories about the interesting disease that he is studying. But at the end of the novel, when he is working in his office face to face with Mickey LaFaye, Tom appears to have begun a re-entry from his orbit. As he tries to use his psychiatric medical knowledge to help Mickey, he is engaged with her in an intimate intersubjective act of language and therefore turning his attention to the signs outside his interior abstractions. At least at this moment, he is escaping the self-absorption Chandra earlier diagnosed. In the closing scene, Tom's incipient new consciousness of where he is is implied by Percy's symbolic description of the world that surrounds his office, the world that he will inevitably enter when his work day is finished: "the morning sun [is] booming in over the live oak, the air yellow and clear as light" (*TS*, 366). When Tom leaves his office, he will walk out into a sacramental world that bristles with energy and hope.

The images of earth, sky, trees, and fire in these scenes from *The Second Coming* and *The Thanatos Syndrome* are the kinds of images Northrop Frye in *The Great Code* and in his earlier *Anatomy of Criticism* calls "apocalyptic," Frye arguing that such imagery is particularly characteristic of mythic literature that imaginatively presents "reality in the forms of human desire."[25] For example, in the biblical story of Christ, Jesus is the metaphorical wanderer who, like all humankind, is wayfaring toward a redeemed, spacious, free, paradisiacal world.[26] This mythic new Eden toward which Christ is journeying represents a return to all that human desire embraces, that original unity and harmony that was lost by man's choosing his own eyes in fallen Eden. It is a return to all that is life-affirming, a return to the tree of life and the water of life. Christ is the central metaphor in this apocalyptic vision, for he symbolically embodies all the cosmos in a dynamic, living world of plenitude in which fire, water, air, and earth are harmoniously joined as described in the Old Testament Book of Wisdom (19.18–21). Metaphorically, the Body of Christ holds all elements of existence together in identity. He is the body and blood of the animal world, the wine and bread of the vegetable world, the life-giving waters of the earth, and the air, wind, and fires of the heavens that are the sources and sustainers of nature.

Percy's use of this kind of apocalyptic imagery gives his fictional land-scapes an "added dimension," and therefore the events and characters in the fictional worlds of his novels also take on an additional thematic dimension. Will and Tom and their struggles to locate themselves in their *umwelt* and *welt* become parabolic illustrations of a universal human quest in cosmic, sacred history, a history that promises that all wayfarers in the Fallen world are returning to a true knowledge of where they are and who they are beyond ego experience. But they, like Will and Tom, have not yet returned, and, therefore, they should understand that the place they currently inhabit is an exile from their final home. They must learn *where they are*, learn that they are in exile in an imperfect place where, O'Connor says, "the good is under construction" among the "grotesque,"[27] lonely, and anxiety-filled lives that surround them. Will and Tom, living their lives in suburbs and on golf courses that sometimes seem to them to offer little more than "death in life" (*SC*, 147), must, like all other wayfarers, try to read the signs of the "good" that O'Connor and Percy believe is continuously coming into being through the Incarnate Word. When Will and Tom can successfully define themselves as active "seeker[s] and wayfarer[s]," Marcel's "Homo viator" (*SP*, 290), they become hope-filled searchers for these signs—on the road, "on the move" (*SP*, 369). As they make their search for their home "across the seas," look toward an open horizon of being, in the air and earth around them are the sacramental signs that can tell them where they are, who they are, and what they must do.

Will Barrett:
In the Desert and on the Links

3

The Last Gentleman: Waiting in the Desert

Love will disappear from the face of the public world, but the more precious will be that love which flows from one lonely person to another . . . the world to come will be filled with animosity and danger, but it will be a world open and clean.
　　　　　　—Romano Guardini, *The End of the Modern World*

Will Barrett in *The Last Gentleman* (1966) has known since childhood that there is "something . . . missing" (*LG*, 9) in his life, a cognitive "gap" (*LG*, 12) that prevents his knowing who he is and "what to do" in order to "live his life." Since adolescence, he has been devoted to a search for "the great secret of life" that will teach him how to live and show him how to conquer the alienation and self-estrangement this "gap" causes. Will knows that the absence in himself that he cannot name has something to do with a legacy that he has inherited from his honorable but self-destructive Southern family. It is the same legacy responsible for his father's romantic demand for a life of "honor" and for his subsequent refusal to endure a life that was simply not noble enough to meet the standards of his abstract moral and social codes. But he also knows that the secret is rooted specifically and uniquely within him, in the "nervous condition" that he has suffered since childhood. As a result of his understanding of his past and his definition of his psychological life, Will has lived his brief life resigned to an unfocused and existentially paralytic interior search for a self and a life that he believes has been hidden from him. He spends his days "watch[ing]" for "something . . . to happen" (*LG*, 10–11) that will reveal the secret to him.

　　Will's interiorized search is a function of an habitual "angelic," transcendent self-placement that encourages him to withdraw from his immediate time-space experience. This inclination to withdraw into his cognitive experience is illustrated in the opening scene of the novel when he lies "thinking" in Central Park (*LG*, 3). Because he believes that the secret lies utterly within his personal past and his private consciousness, Will has always believed that living his life is, first of all, a matter of discovering "what to think" (*LG*, 9). He has assumed that this interior quest for knowledge will finally show him how to live an Edenic emotional and psychological life in the "bestial" immanent world of need satisfactions—a life radically different from his father's and different from the alienated and troubled existence he has endured in his seven years of "wandering" (*LG*, 12) that have led him from his Mississippi home to New York City.

But Will's search has been unsuccessful and left him abstracted and self-enclosed in his memories, thoughts, and analyses, cut off from the daily, ordinary events of his life by his continuous contemplations of the self that he might become or could have been. His search has left him more isolated than ever before from a consciousness that will defeat the suicidal despair that made his father's life, with all of its ideals, an illusion, a failure, and a waste. It is a search that by its very interiorized nature precludes his finding himself as an incarnate human being participating with others in a creation that exists outside his cognitive activities. From a Christian perspective, Will has forgotten who and where he is, forgotten that he is "a pilgrim and participant" in a Fallen world. As a result, he has become a homeless "angelic" seeker of self-knowledge who at the same time futilely seeks ways to make himself happy by satisfying his daily physical, social, emotional, and psychological needs.[1]

In a 1971 interview with John Carr in which Percy discussed some of the differences between the protagonists of his first two novels, he maintained that Will Barrett in *The Last Gentleman*, unlike Binx Bolling in *The Moviegoer* (1961), "was really sick. He didn't know where he was." In a medical sense, Percy maintained, Will "was . . . a great deal worse off than Binx" (*Con*, 66), his mental illness causing his frequent confusions about "where" he is. Besides these "dislocations" in space, Will, Percy explained in an earlier interview, also suffered from frequent "disoriention[s] in time," his "fugue[s] of amnesia" repeatedly resulting in his "wak[ing] up somewhere, not knowing where he was" (*Con*, 13). Because of this condition, Will is continuously assaulted by déjà vu that transports him into his painful family past and isolates him from present time-space experience. Will's dislocations obviously interfere with his ability to make discoveries about the missing features of his self and frustrate his efforts to fashion satisfying social and emotional relationships with his family, friends, and acquaintances. And, since it is in the existential immediacy of phenomenal creation that the sacramental signs of the infinite, atemporal dimensions of human experience can be found, Will's limited powers of perception close him off from a consciousness that could reveal to him the fullness of being promised by a Christian view of human history.

Will's medical condition is used in *The Last Gentleman* as a metaphor for the general psychic "dislocation of man in the modern age" (*Con*, 11) that Percy believes afflicts the post-Christian, scientistic Western world. Will is a modern Everyman whose angelic-bestial self-placement causes him to become a victim of this "dislocation" (*LG*, 13,19,20, 98, e.g.). Edward Dupuy explains that Percyan heroes like Will "negate the present," and become "lost in recollection" as they reconstruct their pasts and imagine their futures.[2] Will exemplifies this kind of self-placement in time. Enclosed in the ghostly Cartesian recesses of his mind, Will spends much of his time lost in the past or lost in the bewildering variety of possibilities for action in the future. *The Last Gentleman* is essentially about Will's efforts to place himself in actual time and space and thereby discover where he is.[3]

Will's confidence in his cognitive capacities as he attempts to construct a meaningful past and a "happy, useful" (*LG*, 385) future leads him to feel that it is necessary "to know everything before . . . do[ing] anything" (*LG*, 4). This epistemological and ontological posture causes him to live "in a state of pure possibility" (*LG*, 4) and creates an anxious self-consciousness that interferes with his daily attempts to "live his life" in the immediately present immanent world of work, family, and social relationships. Like Prufrock, he is hopelessly enervated by the infinite choices for action that such thinking generates, "lost in his own potentiality" (*LG*, 214) and unconscious of present time. Kierkegaard, in *Fear and Trembling*, warns that such a belief in "everything being possible" is the mark of "fools and young men"; it is "a great error," he says, because obviously "much is impossible in the finite world."[4]

Will, like Percy's other wayfarers, is closed off from a knowledge of himself and the world primarily because he has been seduced by a modern scientism that encourages him to believe that he is an autonomous self who can discover his "identity" and create an immanent life of his choosing through his "objective," "scientific" (*LG*, 18, 28, 29, e.g.) thinking and knowing. One night while traveling south with his newly adopted Vaught family, Will reveals in his casual ruminations about himself how this absolute trust in the competency of his intellect to discover "truth" inevitably leads to self-deception and isolation. As he sits on the porch of a motel in the hills of Georgia, Will reflects on his transcendent urge to know, the "old itch for omniscience" (*LG*, 170, 214) that has become for him a recurring and habitual cognitive condition. He explains this itch as the yearning for the acquisition of both "bestial" "carnal knowledge" and "perfect angelic knowledge" (*LG*, 170), an epistemological goal that implies that Will unwittingly wants the ability to know existence both as a beast knows it (consumption) and as a spirit knows it (transcendent cognition). From Percy's Christian perspective, Will's Faustian desire for such angelic-bestial knowledge represents an ontological misplacement, since to know oneself is to know that all human beings are neither beasts nor angels, but incarnate "wayfaring creature[s] somewhere between" (*MB*, 113) in a physical creation that, like its inhabitants, is a mysterious union of matter and spirit. The Christian self locates itself in the present moment, between the finite and the infinite, neither entirely a beast who merely consumes nor a ghostly "angel" who merely thinks.[5]

What is most attractive to Will about omniscience is that it allows him to imagine that he has disappeared from the actual world, become a disembodied Cartesian intelligence as invisible as his thinking and the knowledge it yields. He muses on the motel porch about his desire "to know without being known" (*LG*, 170). Percy explains repeatedly throughout his work that such isolated knowing by an unseen *cogito* is impossible since all individual consciousness is achieved through language transactions with others in the semiotic world of meaning that all share (*MB*, 283, 293, 295). Will's feeling that he must ("had to") be separate from this semiotic source of meaning and consciousness suggests, then, that he is being compelled by his self-placement toward a psychic nonexistence, a psychic death that he mistakes for life. Sutter, in his "casebook," precisely diagnoses Will's dislocation and alienation from reality when he points out that Will wants to "cling to his transcendence" while simultaneously learning "how to traffic with immanence . . . in such a way that he will be happy." Sutter concludes that such a goal is "self-defeating," the misguided quest of the bifurcated Cartesian self that radically separates spirit and flesh (*LG*, 353). He is arguing that the angelic self, when it descends into the immanent world in order to pursue the happiness that bestial need satisfactions grant, must necessarily relinquish the detachment it enjoys and therefore surrender the possibilities for knowing that were available in its transcendent orbit.

Will is in a grave predicament. He has become an alienated, homeless "watcher . . . listener and . . . wanderer" (*LG*, 10–11) among the strangers of New York City, utterly isolated from any sort of intersubjective communication with others and living a death in life he cannot, because of his estrangement from reality, identify. At age twenty-five, he works the night shift as a janitor at Macy's, symbolically self-enclosed and buried in "a tiny room three floors below street level." When he joins the New Yorkers on the crowded city sidewalks each morning after work, he makes his way to his solitary bed in his "cell in the Y.M.C.A." (*LG*, 18–19), so "dislocated" that he "hardly knew who he was from one day to the next" (*LG*, 20). He is Romano Guardini's modern "abstracted" "mass man" who is so lost to himself that his life becomes mere meaningless role-playing.[6] And there is little hope for Will's acquiring the ability to ameliorate his often alarming sense of dislocation from himself and the world. Deaf in one ear and mildly aphasic (*LG*, 8), Will is semiotically challenged, his ability to receive and send signs impaired. He is therefore limited in his capacities to develop his consciousness through the language transactions with others that Percy posits as the source of all knowing about the self and its place in the world with others.

Will, at this point in his life, has been a pilgrim on the road and on a search for seven years, but he has not been wayfaring toward any new, open consciousness of a self and life in the incarnate physical world beyond his mental constructs of experience. Instead, he has been only wandering aimlessly within his psyche for endless choices for being and action. This impaired and failed wayfarer now limps around New York on a bad knee trying to discover "what to do" in the narrow confinement of an interior life where he thinks all "possibilities" (*LG*, 4, 10, 81, 160, 162, 175, 214, 356, 385) lie. Usually "as objective-minded and cool-headed as a scientist" in his doomed search, Will has explored the resources available on every transcendent avenue of his *cogito*. He has read "well-known books on mental hygiene" and aspired to the "mature" "emotional gratifications" offered by the arts and "rewarding interpersonal relationships." Will has even tried "to learn from the psychological insights of the World's Great Religions" (*LG*, 11-12), although he claims no religious convictions.

There is some hope for Will, however. While his transcendent psychic posture causes him serious dislocations, he is intensely conscious that there is something wrong with him and that this affliction is hiding "the great secret" from him. This consciousness motivates him in his continuous, unrelenting search. Will is, Percy told John Carr in a 1971 interview, "a real searcher," a serious and anguished wayfarer in Kierkegaard's "religious mode" who is "passionate[ly]" "after something." Contrasting Will with Binx Bolling, his first fictional wayfarer, Percy explained that Will's pilgrimage is much more difficult than Binx's search in *The Moviegoer*. Binx, Percy explained, "lived almost entirely in . . . the esthetic mode . . . cultivating . . . feeling . . . and having sensations" in the "desert" of American suburbia; at the end of the novel he finally "jumps" to the "religious" sphere and becomes a "believer." Will too "goes to the desert to seek something," but he, Percy went on to say, is the anguished Kierkegaardian "religious" searcher who knows he is homeless—a "drowning man . . . on the ragged edge" (*Con*, 66–68). Will's journey in *The Last Gentleman* from New York to New Mexico concludes not with an easy revelation but with a mysterious encounter with death and salvation in a hospital in Santa Fe, an encounter that he knows he does not fully understand.

The Last Gentleman is about Will's initiating at the beginning of the novel a vigorous new search after the seven years of failure that have led him to his current predicament in the lonely rooms at Macy's and the Y.M.C.A. Will believes that this time he will discover in his search the secret about himself and all human life that he has since childhood sought and thereby radically transform his life, engineer a future marked by self-knowledge and happiness. Unfortunately, this new search seems doomed from the beginning. The fact that Will makes his dramatic decision to "set forth into the wide world" while he is alone and enclosed in the claustrophobic Otis cab (*LG*, 41) of the Y.M.C.A. elevator symbolically suggests that he continues to be isolated and self-enclosed in his angelic thinking as he plans his exciting new future life in the openness of the world.

Will's purchase of a sophisticated telescope to assist him in his search suggests that he continues to depend on the same transcendent eyes that he has relied on in the past. Until he decides in New Mexico that he is "through with telescopes" (*LG*, 358), Will believes that the telescope will serve as an invaluable complement to his naked scientific (*LG*, 41) eyes. The telescope, of course, is a tool that has been essential for scientific "seeing" since pre-Cartesian empiricism, the philosophical source of the modern scientistic way of seeing that Will believes will show him the truth about life. What this instrument does, however, is merely assist the seer in his efforts to accumulate visual data, data that reveals a world no larger than the fragments of phenomena that appear in the lens of the telescope. Will has faith, however, that the telescope has other powers, that it can expose "the heart of things" and therefore help him change "his very life" (*LG*, 29).

And it does change his life—in ways that his objective observations and his scientific thinking could never reveal. Ironically, it is this scientific instrument that is responsible for Will's search for self-knowledge being transformed into a quite unscientific pursuit of the emotional and sexual pleasures of romantic love after he sees Kitty Vaught accidentally appear in the lens one summer day in Central Park (*LG*, 7). This first encounter with the enticements of love initiates Will's search for love and happiness with Kitty and the Vaught family at their Alabama "castle" (*LG*, 189) on the golf course. The image of Kitty in the telescope urges Will to seek an emotional Eden with his Southern Eve in her family's upper-middle-class version of paradise in suburban America.[7]

The first four chapters of the novel are primarily devoted to chronicling Will's adventures in New York, on the road South with the Vaughts, and at their home as he tries to analyze and understand his emotional and psychological entanglements with the new family he has joined. Their intimacy demands that he adopt some new roles and step out of the isolated self-enclosure that his detachment and objectivity have created. Most important, his love for Kitty requires that he define the experience with another that the word *love* signifies and that he decide what to do in order to achieve the happiness that love seems to promise. Will is not at all confident about such intersubjective experience: "Love, he thought, and all at once the word itself went opaque and curious. . . . Do I love her [Kitty]? I something her" (*LG*, 104).

Besides struggling with questions about what he feels and how he should act in response to his love, Will spends much of his time envisioning and planning a future with Kitty that will be filled with a love and happiness he has never known and trying to create and adopt a self that will be able to function effectively in that future. He is certain that his "scientific principles" and "self-knowledge" (*LG*, 41) will enable him to construct a perfectly tranquil life: Kitty in the kitchen of a spanking new "G.E. Gold Medallion Home" (*LG*, 283) and he down at Chandler Vaught's Confederate Chevrolet dealership selling Chevys to his amiable neighbors. Unfortunately, his memories of his father and his family's past continue to haunt him while he tries to construct a present and future life with Kitty and her family, and his recurring "dislocations" prevent Will from sustaining the roles he is attempting to play out with the Vaughts. He knows there is still a gap, "something missing" about himself that his thinking has not yet located and that he may not be able to find in the happiness that his role-playing with the Vaughts provides.

In the final chapter of *The Last Gentleman* Tom temporarily "forgets" (*LG*, 294) his dreams of a future with the Kitty and her family and, eventually, gives up trying to see with his telescope. Will's search takes another direction, and he begins to direct his eyes outward to existential possibilities beyond his personal happiness and scientific seeing. Guided by Sutter's Esso map he found in the doctor's vacant apartment, Will awakes the morning after being knocked unconscious on the rioting university campus in Alabama and, leaving Kitty and her home on the golf links behind, heads toward Santa Fe to find Sutter and Jamie. On this drive from the Vaughts' "paradise" in Alabama to New Mexico, Will discovers some other gardens and some other kinds of love perhaps more important than his emotional satisfactions with Kitty in his self-constructed American Dream future. And he encounters in these gardens some ways of seeing that make him

wonder about the efficacy of the omniscience that he desires. Will's journey into the open desert of the American West is a journey out of his
self-enclosed knowing and need satisfaction and toward an incipient new
capacity for seeing where he lives in the Fallen, sacramental world with
others. With Father Boomer in the Santa Fe hospital, he begins to recognize the possibilities of a self that is living in a creation infinitely richer and
more mysterious than the fragments of reality exhibited in the tiny world
(*LG*, 5) of the telescope's lens.[8]

FORGETTING AND REMEMBERING

Primarily because he is so often either lost in his contemplations of his
childhood past with his father or self-absorbed in dreams of his future
marriage with Kitty Vaught, Will throughout the first four chapters of *The
Last Gentleman* is incapable of locating where he is as an incarnate being in
the sacramental landscapes through which Percy shows him wayfaring. He,
therefore, often misinterprets the signs around him or simply ignores the
sacred "added dimension" of his environment.[9] Sometimes, he literally does
not know where he is (*LG*, 240, 269, 292, 293). For example, when Will
and Forney Aiken, the "pseudo-Negro," arrive in Levittown, Pennsylvania,
on their way south, Will wonders, "Where is this place?" (*LG*, 138-39).
Later, finding himself beside a strange highway at sunrise, he wonders how
he got there and "stud[ies] his map" in order to try to calculate mathemati-
cally where he is (*LG*, 151).

Will tends to look out at the world and his fellow exiles in it with the
solipsistic eyes of the Kierkegaardian romantic aesthete who locates where
he is within the thoughts, feelings, and memories of his own consciousness. As a result of his aestheticism, Will frequently forgets that he is living
in the present, actual world and experiences the alienation and psychic lifelessness that accompany this detachment from the finite particularities of
existence and their significances. "Cheerful" and feeling "good" as he strides
up Broadway after a night's work at Macy's, Will thinks how "pleasant" it is
that he has a "mind wiped clean as a blackboard" and is able to forget
"everything" (*LG*, 46). Will, like Kierkegaard's aesthete, tries to forget—
tries to erase from his consciousness an awareness of all unpleasant experience
in order to remember only what is pleasure-producing. Kierkegaard says
the aesthete, because of this habit of mind, "live[s] as one dead" in the
emptiness of his interior castle, a self-constructed palace decorated with
the pretty but lifeless pictures of reality that he has collected.[10]

One of Percy's epigraphs to *The Last Gentleman* is a quotation from *Ei*-

ther/Or in which Kierkegaard says, "if a man cannot forget, he will never amount to much." But the Danish philosopher is not in this passage applauding the kind of "aesthetic" forgetting that Will demonstrates. Instead, he is talking about the Christian "Knight of infinite resignation" who has mastered the art of forgetting and has thereby "cut away what . . . [he] cannot use" in achieving his salvation. The "Knight" has forgotten the trivialities of worldly concerns, Kierkegaard says in *Training in Christianity*, in order to remember who he is in "the Lord Jesus Christ."[11] This is the kind of forgetting that Will reads about in Sutter Vaught's nihilistic casebook as he lies in the bunk of his snug Trav-L-Aire in Texas. Sutter, in the rambling philosophizing about transcendence and immanence that fills the book, expresses his philosophical reservations about his sister Val Vaught's Catholic Christian belief that people need "to forget everything which does not pertain to . . . [their] salvation" (*LG*, 354). Val is echoing Kierkegaard's description of the Knight, a man who forgets what the world encourages him to desire and pursue in order to remember the fullness of life that can be gained through the redemptive power of the Incarnation.

Will may be, as Percy asserts, a "religious" Kierkegaardian searcher, but he is also the Kierkegaardian aesthete who has not developed the power to remember what guides the "Knight of infinite resignation" in his search. Because Will is only nominally Christian, he is not inclined to think very deeply about any redemptive "added dimensions" of his experience. His epistemological limitations are illustrated when Sutter, in a conversation with Will at the Vaughts' house in Alabama, asks Will if he "believe[s] that God entered history"—if he believes, in other words, in the Incarnation. Will perfunctorily replies that he has never "really thought about it" (*LG*, 221). Early in the novel, when Chandler Vaught is talking with Will in the New York hospital where Jamie is being treated, he asks Will about his "religion." Will answers that he is an Episcopalian, but he silently registers the fact that "he had never given the matter a single *thought* [emphasis added] in his life" (*LG*, 78). In the final scene in the hospital in Santa Fe, as Father Boomer questions Will about Jamie's baptism, Will again thinks that "in his entire lifetime" he had not "given such matters a single *thought*" (*LG*, 397; emphasis added). At the Vaught "castle" (*LG*, 189) in Alabama, Will tells the Catholic Val Vaught that he doesn't "know what the word 'salvation' *means*" (*LG*, 212; emphasis added).

Will's responses in these scenes indicate that the objective (*LG*, 11, 18, 28, 29) consciousness he has depended on to reveal life to him has made him forget that there may be experiences outside his thoughts and the meanings he constructs. From such a perspective, the only possibility for any salvation from the existential diminishments that he has clearly identified in his wandering lies in the relief that he himself can "engineer" from day to day through his thinking, role-playing, and pursuit of happiness. Will is inclined to forget the physical reality beyond his thinking and enclose himself in an aesthetic psychic death where the sacramental signs that can show him a life of love with others under God (*LC*, 112) remain obscured from his sight and therefore impotent.

What Will does remember, and frequently, is his adolescent life in Ithaca with his father, or, more precisely, bits and pieces of that past that he tries to analyze in order to find the "great secret" of himself that he thinks is hidden somewhere in his memory.[12] Ironically, it is this fragmentary and incomplete remembering of his past and his attempts to explore these memories in order to arrive at some dramatic new self-discovery that encourage Will to forget his immediate, actual life. For example, in the opening pages of the novel, when Will recalls the summer after he left Princeton, he reveals the interiorized self that has functioned to hide reality from him. He remembers vividly "the dreadful hay fever" he suffered while he labored miserably in the dusty library conference room of his father's law firm. Symbolically sick and enclosed in his family's past as he pored over the aging law books and tedious legal documents, Will's affliction and abstraction prevented him from seeing much significance to the wondrous and dynamic life beyond the window sill in the fecund fragrant summer air of his Mississippi Delta hometown. Percy's imagery emphasizes the sacramental energy and beauty that radiates from the dense reality that Will casually ignored while he tended to his swollen and irritated nose. The "dark lustrous green" oaks turned "yellow with pollen" in the "glittering" streets where his neighbors and friends went about their daily lives, and the "quarrels of the sparrows" and the "towering sound of the cicadas . . . filled the white sky." Meanwhile, Will looked away from these signs, preferring to concentrate his attention on the damaged "violet" membranes of his hay fever-ravaged nostrils (*LG*, 16)—a literal turning inward to the fleshy symptoms of his sickness and away from a beauty that has the potential to make him wonder about its significances.

Now, when Will recalls these events, he continues to direct his gaze inward, finding this memory of a summer in Ithaca significant not because it reveals his failures to see beyond the window sill, but because that summer was the summer his father died. He believes that this death is somehow crucially connected with the "nervous condition" (*LG*, 13) that presently afflicts him and that by analysis of the memory he can discover that connection. He is not interested in the actualities of the past events but only in his explorations of their effects on his current mental and emotional state.

Will is interested exclusively in his own psychological and emotional experience and his intellectual analyses of it, these particular events from his past significant only because they provide some data that he may be able to use in his search for some secret of his interior life that he cannot yet define. Just as his hay fever once diverted his attention away from the phenomenal life in the streets of his Southern home and its significance, so now his exclusive interest in his possible psychological illness prevents him from turning his eyes outward to locate himself in the immediacy of his present time-space experience in New York and the sacramental signs there.

Will's memories and self-analyses also interfere with his efforts to find himself in intersubjective social experience. He is able to recognize the "trouble" he has always had with "groups" (*LG*, 19), but, humorously, does not consider that "groups" of people have indeed been a conspicuously troublesome problem for all human beings since the creation of Eve and the subsequent population of the planet—particularly in New York City. Will does not identify his social anxiety as a symptom of a universal homelessness and exile that all share, but instead sees it as a symptom of his unique nervous condition (*LG*, 19). Percy explains in "The Message in the Bottle" that the anxiety and sense of alienation that Will feels in groups are universal human responses to existence, the inevitable consequence of all people being castaways in exile since the Fall from a home that they cannot remember.

Unable to locate himself in this common predicament, Will defines his social trouble as a personal psychological problem and again searches his past for an explanation for the causes of this feature of himself. Analyzing the difficulties he has with groups, Will recalls a childhood summer when his father and stepmother sent him off to camp while they vacationed in Europe. He ran away from the Christian summer camp one night after being encouraged by the "tribe" of other campers to commit himself to a life with Christ. He returned to his home and spent the rest of the summer reading comics in a tree house, his eyes focused on the garish pages while a Hopkinsian sacramental "sea of dappled leaves"[13] tossed his raft-like home in the "tall sycamore" (*LG*, 13). Will's preference for his elevated summer home and the solitary diversion provided by his reading suggests the psychic comfort he achieved by isolating himself from the other children and the sacramental signs right outside the tree house—by ascending to the lonely orbit of his transcendent and detached self. This escape was Will's self-deceiving alternative to assenting to the intersubjective engagement with the tribe around the campfire and to the news they might bring about who he is and where he is in a creation redeemed by the Incarnation of Christ.

Will's trouble with groups persists into adulthood because he continues to adopt a transcendent posture in his negotiations with the world and others and continues to look exclusively inward for any redemption from the discomfort that the existence of other people causes him. Now, however, he does not simply run away, but instead attempts to ameliorate his anxiety by "improv[ing] his group skills" through the "role-playing" recommended by "the social scientists" he depends on for information about who he is and what he should do. Will is particularly successful at this role-playing, but, ironically, these efforts to make himself happy further dislocate him as he tries to construct in his mind the kinds of selves he thinks could perform well with others and imagines the lives that these selves might enjoy. He says that "there were times when he took on roles so successfully that he left off being who he was and became someone else" (LG, 19–20). In other words, he ceased to exist and experienced a kind of existential death. He recalls, for example, "a few winters ago" when "he became an Ohioan" after a week or so of socializing with several of his coworkers at Macy's, all natives of the Buckeye state. After a few outings with these carefree Midwesterners, Will says the consonants began to "snap . . . around in his [Southern] throat like a guitar string," and he began to call "Carol" "Kerrell." He drank beer and "had not a thought in his head nor a care in the world" (LG, 20).

Will's estrangement from the phenomenal world and from other people may have its roots in his father's similar aesthetic detachment. In Will's memory of the night his father killed himself in the attic of their family's home (LG, 99–101), Will recalls a proud man who also preferred the aesthetic pleasures of his inner life over the groups that he felt doomed to endure—in his case, the "fornicator[s] and hypocrite[s]" (LG, 101) of his hometown.[14] As he paced the street in front of their home, his father listened to the Brahms from their Philco, quoted Montaigne's skeptical aphorism about mankind's madness and his "mak[ing] gods by the dozens," and bitterly lamented the absence of honor and character among the citizenry of Ithaca. Unconscious of the sacramental "dapple of light and leaves" (LG, 99) above him in the night, his father was literally and symbolically in the dark, in aesthetic orbit and therefore alienated from those in his hometown who did not make their lives in the interior world that he constructed. Ed Barrett's choice that night was the logical choice for the self-transcendent aesthete who wishes not to exist in the imperfect world that he perceives.

While absorbed in this memory as he saunters through Central Park on a summer night, Will illustrates that he is as much in orbit now as his transcendent father was that night in front of the family home. Will strolls through the park just as he journeys through his life, "lost in thought" and "somewhat dislocated." In this semiconscious state, Will withdraws into his memories of himself as a thirteen-year-old sitting on the porch steps of his home and watching his father pace up and down the sidewalk. As Will makes his way through the park, he is absorbed in the memory and pays little attention either to the threatening gunshots he hears from nearby Harlem or to the beautiful "gold green spaces in the rustling leaves" that are created by the dim lamps in the park (*LG*, 98). He is oblivious in his reverie to both the beauties and dangers of this postlapsarian garden, estranged from this imperfect but beautiful creation and its inhabitants as he makes his dazed journey through it.

There are moments in New York and on the road south that Will escapes his memories and looks out at creation, but when he does he sees darkly, usually unable to identify where he is. Abstracted, he does not locate himself as a participant with others in a Fallen world that in its ruins still contains the sacramental signs of redemption and new life. In the very first scene in *The Last Gentleman*, for example, Will looks around in the "Great Meadow" of Central Park, a pastoral refuge from the bustling and violent anonymity of the city that is at once the "smudged," sullied garden of Hopkins's "God's Grandeur" and a garden charged with the divine presence that revealed itself to humankind in the breezes in Eden (Genesis 3.8). The park, although green with the new life of early summer, smells like a "zoo," and the grass is "coarse and yellow as lion's hair and worn bare in spots, exposing the tough old hide of the earth." Will thinks of it as a "bear garden" (*LG*, 4). This is a postlapsarian garden created by violent and foul-smelling exiles from Eden, who, even in their well-intentioned attempts to create a place of beauty and safety, create an oppressive, zoo-like enclosure.[15] This zoo is an appropriate symbol of the closed, postlapsarian human consciousness that built it.

But Will fails to see the metaphorical implications of the garden; he is too objective and scientific, too literal-minded, to extend the zoo metaphor and see himself as one of the trapped, helpless creatures in the zoo. Instead, he thinks to himself as he idly surveys the grounds, "it is a good thing to see a park put to good hard use by millions of people" (*LG*, 4). He fails to recognize that the zoo clearly is not a good place but a damaged garden created by a humanity seriously and universally diminished by the estrangement from the fullness of its original self and life described in Genesis. He cannot see that New York's city planners have built the only garden that Fallen mankind is capable of constructing, a blasted and oppressive garden where individuals are as lonely, displaced, and alienated from each other as animals in the cages of a city zoo.

Will is unable to explore these symbolic implications of where he is and thereby unable to locate himself in communion with others in an aboriginal Fall, and he is also blind to the sacramental signs in the Great Meadow that point to the ongoing process of redemption that the Catholic Christian faith posits as the most important feature of human history since the Creation and the Fall. When he looks up to the beautiful sky, "mild and blue" and "whitened" by a light haze, he does not locate himself in the open serenity and vastness of the cosmos that is suggested by these images. And his secular consciousness certainly will not allow him to associate the white and blue radiance in the life-giving heavens above him analogically with Christ and the Virgin Mother, the sources of the life and love that hold the ruined garden in their embrace.

The peregrine falcon Will is waiting in the park to spot with his telescope was intended by Percy as another sacramental symbol of the awesome power and majesty of Christ, his choice of this image, he says, inspired by reading Gerard Manley Hopkins's "The Windhover."[16] But Will cannot read this Christian sign because of his scientific and romantic way of seeing.[17] The beautiful and elusive bird has significance for Will only because it provides him with a subject for a spectacular photograph. Will's desire to photograph the falcon after he captures it in the "brilliant *theater* of the lenses" (*LG*, 5; emphasis added) of his telescope shows that he has the same kind of detachment and abstraction from the world that marks Kierkegaard's aesthete. William Barrett, in his discussion of Kierkegaardian aestheticism in *Irrational Man*, notes that the words *theatre, theory,* and *aesthetic* have the same Greek roots.[18] The theater metaphor suggests that Will chooses to locate himself as an invisible spectator who sits in the darkened audience and watches the spectacle of life, his goal the private sensory, intellectual, emotional, and imaginative stimulations the performance can produce within him. He, like Kierkegaard's romantic aesthete, prefers to live in the isolated "palace" of his consciousness, only descending occasionaly into finite reality to bring back pictures of phenomena.

Will's abstraction from creation and his blindness to the sacramental signs in it are vividly and humorously demonstrated when he finds himself one "white misty morning" "moderately disoriented" beside a highway somewhere in Virginia. He has left New York and has been hitchhiking toward Williamsburg, Virginia, planning to rendezvous there with the Vaughts and join them on their meandering trip home to Alabama. Experiencing again one of his "interior dislocations," Will tries to remember "where . . . he . . . spent the night" and where he is now. Comically, instead of looking out at the physical actualities of this strange place, Will begins to study his Esso map of Virginia, a mathematical, abstract picture of where he is. This spatial dislocation precipitates in turn an ontological uncertainty that prompts him to try to verify who he is. Will examines his face in the "steel mirror" he keeps in his backpack and "consult[s] . . . his wallet" to make sure he is in fact Williston Bibb Barrett (*LG*, 149–51).

While his eyes are turned to the image in the mirror, the data in his wallet, and the lines on the Esso map, Will remains oblivious to the wonders of the living creation that surround him and therefore oblivious to the divine presence intimated there. The sun rises on the "white-oak swamp" and "warm[s] his back," "Sapsuckers [are] yammering," "green confettilike plant[s] . . . float . . . on the black water," "the fluted trunks and bald red knees of the cypress" stand silently by the water, and "the first fall specklings of the tupelo gums" (*LG*, 151) dot the dense fecundity of the tropical forest. The swamp is spectacularly alive, awaking in the life-sustaining sun and water and breaking into a parade of color and sound while the self-absorbed Will ignores it all and searches the recesses of his pack for documents that will give him verification of where he is and who he is. Distracted by this search in his pack, Will misses the significance of the fact that he is included in the miraculous complexity of life around him, a life that pulses with energy, beauty, and mystery. He has forgotten that the sun warming his back is the same sun that sustains all finite life, and he therefore remains unconscious of the significances it may have as a sacramental symbol of an infinite life that is the source of incarnate creation.

WHERE DOES LOVE PITCH ITS TENT?

What Will tries to remember from the moment in Central Park that he "falls in love" with the image of Kitty in the telescope's "theater" until he is separated from her on the rioting university campus in Alabama (*LG*, 291) is the exhilarating new emotions she provokes in him now and the Edenic happiness he believes she can provide for him in the future.[19] In New York, on his trip south with the Vaughts, and at their home in Alabama, Will is repeatedly dislocated from his immediate environment and from Kitty, psychically enclosed in his contemplations of his feelings and thoughts about his new love. When he is not overwhelmed by his sexual desire for her, he indulges in romantic dreams of an easy, Kierkegaardian ethical life that he could construct by loving Kitty and going "back to the South, finish[ing] his education, . . . be[ing] a business or professional man, marry[ing] him a wife and liv[ing] him a life." He envisions himself in a "good little house in a pretty green suburb" with "a pretty little wife in a brand-new kitchen with a red dress on" (LG, 88). Unconsciously, Will wants a life, like this romanticized one, that would replace his life of desperate wandering in search for the "great secret." He could then have a home where he would not have to agonize about who he is, where he is, and what to do. His physical, psychological, emotional, and social needs satisfied by such a stereotypical middle-class ethical existence, he would be released from the incessant existential demands of his past and his present predicament. In the suburbs, he could discontinue his life as religious, wayfaring searcher and disappear into the anonymity of upper-middle class American role-playing.

His having this life and becoming this self, Will knows, depend on his being sure that the relationship he has with Kitty amounts to love and not just lustful physical desire. He is troubled by the "bestial" sexual needs she stimulates in him and knows that he must locate and define some dimensions to his feelings that transcend these base needs if he is ever going to experience love and not mere selfish need gratification. This new love experience with Kitty demands that Will make the connection between the immanent needs of the body and the transcendent emotional, spiritual, and psychological experiences of the self, and he is ill-prepared for the task. Will's angelic-bestial consciousness has always made it difficult for him to connect body and spirit.

When Will tries to reflect on the immanent and transcendent facets of his love for Kitty, he remembers his genteel father telling him never to "treat a lady like a whore or a whore like a lady" (LG, 100). This bit of advice reinforces the flesh/spirit bifurcation that dominates Will's objective consciousness and makes the intersubjective intimacy that he desires with Kitty difficult. His father's advice suggests that "ladies," embodiments of angelic moral qualities and noble character, require gentlemanly role-playing, whereas the bestial physicality of "whores" permits the gentleman to descend into immanent reality and sexual pleasure. This concept of love is based on a romantic, Cartesian division of flesh and spirit that not only dehumanizes women by its abstract categorizations, but also encourages the "gentleman" to define his romantic relationships as being merely two different kinds of need satisfaction. It is an ontology that suggests that a man should seek the satisfying of his sexual needs in his relationships with some women and that with "ladies" he should attend to his other needs by seeking the ego gratifications that come from playing out the role of aristocratic Southern gentleman and the moral and social codes inherent in that role.

Will's attempts to love Kitty are thwarted by his inclination to position himself in relation to the world as just such an aesthetic, self-enclosed satisfier of needs. The encounters that Will has with Kitty often take place in symbolic settings that emphasize that Will suffers from this kind of self-enclosure and dislocation. Their first intimate meeting, for example, takes place in a dark, heavily wooded section of Central Park, beneath "a shallow overhang of smooth rock" where "no sound . . . or sight" from the city can be detected. The fires from Harlem are only a distant red glow in the night sky, and the gunfire being exchanged between "the cops and the Negroes" is no more than "a faint crepitant sound like crumpled newspaper" (*LG*, 107–8). Will, in this remote, hidden place with Kitty, becomes "like a blind man" (*LG*, 111) in his pursuit of the pleasures of eros. Like Cupid, a god who comes to the mortal Psyche only at night, so Will is attempting to descend from his transcendent orbit to seek a union with Kitty. He literally cannot see where he is nor see immediately in front of him the naked woman that he is trying to love. Symbolically, Will is blind about what constitutes love, uncertain whether he should merely respond sexually to Kitty's "astounding and terrific melon immediacy of nakedness" or rhapsodize about how "love is everything" (*LG*, 109–10). Is love some mystical, transcendent human experience that requires him to see that there is something glorious and special about Kitty? Is she whore or lady? Flesh or spirit? Beast or angel? Is this eros or agape? "Where," Will wonders, "does love pitch its tent?" (*LG*, 107).

After Will leaves New York and joins the Vaughts' entourage at the Coach-and-Four Motel in Williamsburg, he begins his brief sojourn south with Kitty's family and his pursuit of love and happiness with them. The G.M.C. "Trav-L-Aire" he and Jamie use for the journey is a vehicle appropriate for an abstracted, detached, self-enclosed aesthete like Will who spends much of his life traveling in the rarefied air of his transcendent orbit. Will, when he sees the camper truck in the parking lot of the motel, thinks that it offers "a good way to live nowadays" because it allows its owners to be "in the world yet not of the world, sampling the particularities of place yet cabined off from the sadness of place" (*LG*, 153). The living arrangement that the Trav-L-Aire furnishes is ideal for the "cabined off" aesthete whose goal is to avoid the "sadness" of the real world and from time to time dip down into the Fallen, finite world to sample its particularities and savor the sensations that they stimulate.

And this is exactly what Will does on the journey south in his new mobile home. By the time he and Jamie reach the Carolinas, Will has decided that "the camper was everything he had hoped for and more." At nights (for Will, as for Cupid, the "best" times [*LG*, 161]), they set up the telescope and become godlike, invisible spectators in "the lonesome savanna" and watch in the scientific lenses the "jewel-like warblers" that "swarm . . . about the misty oaks." Occasionally, they "stroll to a service station or fishing camp" for groceries or supplies, Will experiencing at these times "the pleasantest sense of stepping down from the zone of the possible to the zone of the realized." Then back to the cabin and the "unrealized" possibilities of his private interior world. When they retire for the evening from their observations and casual encounters with the phenomenal world, Jamie reads books on mathematics while Will escapes into English detective stories. He likes the "disguised" English heroes in these novels who are adept at "hiding" in their "burrow[s]" and "notic[ing] things" —- "observing" the people and events that interest them "without being seen" (LG, 161–62). Will repeatedly alludes to these detectives (LG, 170, 174, 190, 194, 205, 214, 337), obviously imagining them as models of the kind of detached, invisible observer he would like to be.

In order to enjoy the pleasures of the love he is seeking with Kitty, however, Will has to step down from the camper into the only place where love's tent is pitched, into the physical world where exquisite warblers as well as sadness dwell—where no one has the luxury of remaining a disembodied observer. Will is not comfortable on the trip when he descends from the cozy confines of the Trav-L-Aire, leaves his telescope in its case, and takes a look at a world larger and more diverse than the fragments of creation he selects for his distant observations in the telescope. When, for example, he and Jamie join Kitty and the Vaughts in Charlestown [Charleston], Will is disappointed, even disgusted, by "the gardens" of the city. He notices only the "evil-tempered mockingbirds," "oily camelias," and the "bitter"-smelling water on the "hairy leaves of the azaleas." As he stands with his love and her family among the luxuriant color and splendor of Charleston's famous gardens, Will "close[s] his eyes" and turns inward to focus on his evaluations of his sensory responses to the creation before him—the smells, sounds, and sights in the gardens that cause him unpleasant feelings. Thinking of the future and of "death," Will is lost in his private inner world of thought and feeling, conscious only of an oppressive "hot sun" that causes him to feel physically "sick" in this repulsive, but actual, garden (LG, 163–64).

The flesh-and-blood reality of Kitty also continues to cause him discomfort as he persists in his efforts to discover how he can adequately love her in the here-and-now actuality of a hirsute and greasy Fallen Eden. Will is having trouble acquiring at all times the good feelings he believes his love should provide and is continuing to fail in reconciling his romantic, idealized illusions about his relationship with Kitty with his (and her) sexual passion. Spirit or flesh? One night while they are in South Carolina, he and

Kitty meet at the ice machine of the Quality Court at Folly Beach where the family is staying for a few days. They walk out onto the tranquil beach, "the moonlight curl[ing] along the wavelets." In this stereotypically romantic setting, Will holds his "charms in his arms" and promises himself that he will no longer love Kitty as he did in Central Park, subjecting her to "grubby epithelial embraces" and thereby transforming himself into an ignoble, bestial fornicator. He will restrain his sexual appetites, he vows silently, until they are in their perfect "honeymoon cottage . . . small by a waterfall" (*LG*, 166). And he can only hope that Kitty will remain equally chaste.

But as they kiss, Kitty "work[s] her mouth against his," and Will's idealized, angelic vision of her as a sweet, innocent young lady vanishes before the undeniable physicality of her behavior. Not only does her seductive kiss shatter his dream of Kitty in the cottage, but it also interferes with his efforts to retain his identity as the fictional honorable "gentlemanly engineer" who is "court[ing] [her] . . . in the old style" of Old South ladies and gentleman. Her "whorish" kiss makes him realize that love for her, as for him, may be just "a naked garden of stamens and pistils," a purely sexual, biological reality no more mysterious or complicated than the sexual activity of flowers described in a high-school biology text. In this moment with Kitty on Folly Beach, Will becomes aware of the folly of his believing that he can be the gentlemanly self he has just constructed in his mind's eye. He knows there may be no storybook "cottage by the waterfall" where his sweet Kitty awaits him.

This realization compels him to drop his gentlemanly role and respond to Kitty the "Whore" with a similar bestial self of his own. The "old motel lewd-longing" possessing him as they return from the beach and make their way to their rooms down the darkened Quality Court passageway, Will tries to lure Kitty into the motel's service room. In this aggressive effort to satisfy his momentary lust in this tiny room, Will is symbolically choosing the dark, self-enclosed world of his desires and their satisfactions over the vast and beautiful openness of the moonlit beach and ocean he has just abandoned. Again here, as earlier in his awkward and aborted tryst with Kitty in Central Park, Will becomes a blind man, unable to locate where he is and who he is with another incarnate, flesh-spirit self. He cannot see that he is in a Fallen Eden where both moonlit beaches and shadowy motels filled with strangers make their home. In the darkness of the motel, Will feels that the "lewd-longing" that afflicts him and his love at this moment is "the mortal illness of youth" that prevents their achieving any kind of union more spiritual or more joyous than the mechanical reproductive experiences of soulless "stamens and pistils." Will is "bereft" by his realization that he and Kitty cannot be the gentleman and lady on the beautiful beach, that they and all others have longings that can only be satisfied in secret, dark places. A "piercing sorrow" sends him "careening down" the darkened Quality corridor toward his lonely room (*LG*, 167-68).

A few days later and a few miles south of Folly Beach on the Georgia coast, Will finds himself once more trying to identify who he is and what to do in his courting of his whore/lady, and again he seeks out a small, enclosed place, a symbolic refuge from the larger world beyond his thoughts and feelings about his love. A tropical storm beating in from the south, Will and Kitty leave the resort hotel where the Vaughts are staying and retreat to the Trav-L-Aire that is tied down safely "in a hollow of the dunes." In this womblike place, Will is exhilarated by the storm and by his and his love's isolation from the dangerous winds and rains just outside "the alumi-num skin" of the camper. He feels that they are as safe and "snug as children" and that "it might be possible for them to enter here and now into a new life" (*LG*, 174–75). In the course of Will's dreams of this new life, the storm outside passes, and he and Kitty sit at the Formica table inside the Trav-L-Aire and gaze out at the facticity of the living world beyond the aluminum "skin" that Will feels contains them—peer out at "round leaves of the sea grapes" and the fiddler crabs that are "scoot[ing]" across the sands to their actual "burrows" (*LG*, 180).

But no rebirth into a new life takes place. As Will lies with Kitty in the camper and they talk of their love and future, Will is again assaulted by the ontological confusion his father's advice about how to treat ladies and whores has precipitated: "what am I, he wondered: neither Christian nor pagan nor proper lusty gentleman, for I've never really got the straight of this lady-and-whore business." Trying to be proper as they lie together, Will whispers "sweet love-murmurings into her ear" and fantasizes about their future to-gether in their romantic cottage; Kitty becomes once again in this fantasy future a sweet bride in a "brand-new kitchen" bright with "the morning sun streaming in the window." He tells her twice, "I dream of loving you in the morning" (*LG*, 180). His dream of loving, however, is disturbed by a not very ladylike Kitty in the bunk with him. Will feels her come "on at him like a diesel locomotive" (*LG*, 173), the immediacy of her "whorish" gazes and kisses threatening his visions of her as sweet wife and him as dutiful and gentlemanly husband. She is not the lady he has seen in his dream, and therefore he cannot be her imaginary future husband. Will is confused about who he should be and what he should do now in this actual moment and place in response to his love for Kitty, what to do in order to love this actual person in his arms while he waits for some indefinite future morning that has no more reality than a dream.

LOVE IN THE GARDEN

When Will returns home to the South and moves in with the Vaughts (*LG*, 185–289), he enrolls at the local university in order to pursue the normal career and life he plans to have with Kitty. He is more determined than ever to love Kitty in a proper way and to "engineer" a future in which he will "be happy and at home too." But Will's predicament becomes worse. He unexpectedly feels more homeless and less happy than he did in New York. "His homelessness," Will reasons, "was much worse in the South because he had expected to find himself at home there." It seems to Will that "everyone . . . [is] happy" in the South, his feeling of alienation, there-fore, a truly aberrant adjustment to this environment. At the "intersubjective paradise" of the university—a youthful microcosm of this New South cul-ture—he is aware of his radical estrangement from others. He cannot figure out how to speak with his fellow students, and his anxiety causes his "knee . . . [to leap] so badly that he had to walk like a spastic" (*LG*, 204). Main-taining certainty about time-space reality becomes difficult as his "memory deteriorate[s]." Will more frequently wakes "not knowing where he [is]" (*LG*, 186). His crippling dislocations are exacerbated as he returns to his old habit of "forgetting everything" (*LG*, 46) about his present reality in order to construct an interior life, this time one with Kitty Vaught and her family.

But, ironically, Will thinks that the Vaughts' home is "a good place to live," primarily because it provides him with a situation in which he has "no duties" and has plenty of time to "collect . . . his thoughts" (*LG*, 191). Will is free from daily obligations to others, and this detachment allows him to reduce his life to the collecting of bits of cognitive experience that for what-ever reasons interest or amuse him. What Will is enjoying at the Vaughts' home is the freedom to be the aesthetic child that Kierkegaard describes in *Either/Or* as one who both remembers and forgets easily in order to "enjoy" a content life without the disturbances that daily imperfections cause.[20] At the Vaughts, Will literally regresses to a childlike role as a wealthy student who depends on his family for the practical, psychological, or emotional needs he might have while he pursues whatever knowledge interests him at the university and whatever pleasures his love for Kitty might yield.

In the walled "ruined garden" (*LG*, 200) at the Vaughts' "castle" and on the paradisiacal, artificially Edenic golf course that surrounds it, Will, how-ever, begins to awaken out of this aesthetic unconsciousness. Here, in this attractive but Fallen Eden in Alabama, Will meets others who have, like him, searched for love and happiness, but have discovered in their searches some dimensions of "love" and the self that he has not adequately considered. From Sutter, Will sees how the marital "love" he depends on for his future happiness with Kitty can degenerate into malice and loneliness. Sutter also shows him the dangers of an "angelic," transcendent consciousness like his own, one that looks inward and nowhere else for the "great secret" of human existence. In Sutter, Will can see an example of a man who has "exhausted the aesthetic sphere" Will has been exploring for a lifetime and a quester who has subsequently arrived at "despair" (*Con*, 204). Rita, Sutter's estranged wife who believes in pursuing a life of "beauty and joy" (*LG*, 244) through the arts and humanistic learning, shows Will an example of the self-delusions and self-aggrandizement inherent in a romantic conscious-ness that isolates itself in its private dreams of the good and the beautiful. Finally, from the Catholic Val Vaught, Will hears about "the love of Christ" (*LG*, 211), a love utterly different from the "happiness" provided by per-sonal need-satisfactions—in fact, a love that paradoxically pitches its tent in the suffering and death that Jamie exemplifies and in the sorrow he causes.

When Will first arrives at the Vaughts' ruined garden, he is content to remain the detached aesthete and to enjoy the freedom he has to collect thoughts that interest him. For Will, the garden is an ideal place to escape into his interior world of abstractions and self-constructions; from his per-spective, it is ruined only in the sense that its abundant summer growth is now diminished by the encroachment of fall. The first time we see Will in the garden he, Jamie, and Kitty have just returned from the university. They are relaxing together in the October sunlight while they casually inspect their new textbooks. Although Will thinks to himself "that school had nothing whatever to do with life"—that school "disarm[ed]" him for the life that followed it—he is consciously choosing once again to "arm" him-self with its ineffectual, abstract weapons, his slide rule on his side "in a scabbard like a dagger." The warrior metaphor here suggests that Will sees life as a solitary, lonely combat rather than a hopeful wayfaring with others. (He became an accomplished boxer at Princeton.) Will believes that the "best hope" he has for conquering life lies in "the books themselves" and their "orderly" abstractions, for they present comprehensible truths for the aesthete who hopes to master his life by shrinking it into comfortable, in-telligible concepts. In contrast to these truths are the "untidy" "summer past, the ruined garden, . . . [his] own life" (*LG*, 200–201). Because sum-mers, gardens, and one's life are constantly changing actualities of time and space that defy easy comprehension, they perplex and confound Will's Car-tesian *cogito* as he attempts to transform them into tidy cognitive packages. The implication is that he finds no hope in these realities.

Symbolically "blind[ed]" by the sunlight "on the glazed pages" of the books, Will cannot see where he is, distracted by his thinking from both the beauties and deficiencies of the phenomenal moment and this sacramental place. Perky "whitethroat sparrows" "scratch . . . in the sour leaves" beneath the brilliant October sunlight. It is the fall of the year and the created world is "sour" with its impending winterly ruin, but the sun continues to shine and creatures continue to search for life. Will, however, is closed off from a consciousness of this sacramental, living time and place by his absorption in the "orderly march" of the abstractions of art and science across the blinding pages of Kitty's World Literature anthology, Jamie's chemistry text, and his own *The Theory of Large Numbers* (perhaps an allusion to Kierkegaard's "Law of Large Numbers," a popular philosophical law that Kierkegaard believed informed the modern mass man that a truth is determined by the number of people who accept it as true).[21] While Will searches in the glare of the leaves of the textbooks for what he hopes will bring him knowledge and truth, he fails to see the sacramental signs of life in the garden around him and the hope and life there (*LG*, 200–201).

Oblivious to the sacramental signs of his incarnate existence right before him, Will "read[s] off cube roots and cosines" in the "window" of his slide rule, preferring "bright pretty useful objects like slide rules" (earlier, telescopes) to the "funky gardens and jaybirds crying down October." But the objects he so admires and the calculations he can perform with them apparently lose their wonder quickly, and Will chooses to retire to "a sunny corner of the garden wall" where he curls up like a lazy cat and falls asleep. While he is asleep, absolutely unconscious of the Fallen but glorious garden that he shares with the rest of creation, the sparrows continue to "hop . . . around in the dry crape myrtle leaves." It is the "death" of the year, and they, like all others in the postlapsarian ruined garden, look for what will sustain them in a sometimes dry creation where winter and death always temper the beauty and life of summer. But even in this dry season, their world intensely makes its miraculous presence known, the tiny sparrows pecking around in a place "burn[ing] with a clear flame in the sunlight" (*LG*, 201–2).

When Will awakes amid the sparrows and the sunlight from a dream of his innocent, "sweet" kiss with his high school love Alice Bocock, he lies behind a "loose screen of sasanqua" that hides him from the others in the garden. He watches Sutter, who "look[s] down into the garden" (*LG*, 205–6) from the garage balcony like Milton's Satan looks down from his tree in Eden.[22] But Sutter is "satanic" only in the sense that he is for Will, as Milton's Satan is for Adam and Eve, a source of knowledge. Satan's knowledge leads Adam and Eve to their sin and their Fall, but this defeat is paradoxically the impetus for their subsequent search for some news outside an Eden that no longer exists. Similarly, Sutter's despair encourages Will to search beyond the Vaughts' Edenic garden walls for a new life in the desert of the Fallen world. It is Sutter's Esso map (*LG*, 282) that literally shows Will the way to Santa Fe and to the revelations there. According to Percy, Sutter is the "object of Barrett's quest" (*Con*, 14), a man in Kierkegaard's "religious sphere" (*Con*, 126) who has searched for many of the same satisfactions in love and in the transcendent knowledge of art and science that Will seeks.

When Will first talks with Sutter in the doctor's garage apartment at the Vaughts' estate, Sutter challenges the value of the transcendent aesthetic pleasures of books and slide rules that Will chooses in his efforts to escape the Fallen immanent world. Sutter knows the limitations of such an interior quest. When Will insists on believing that Sutter knows the great secret he has been searching for, the secret truth he thinks will make his life perfectly meaningful and happy, Sutter strongly denies that he has any such knowledge, advising Will that he has "come to the wrong man" (*LG*, 224) if he wants to know how to return to some unfallen existential condition. He also challeges Will's belief in a sweet, romantic love that will transport him and Kitty into a storybook world of happiness. Sutter encourages Will to look again at the Fallen, ruined place that he inhabits, a place that no amount of thinking or happiness-seeking will make anything else.

Sutter has endured a failed marriage with a gnostic romantic whose goal was to achieve the kind of "self-fulfillment" (*LG*, 244) Will has been searching for since late adolescence. He knows firsthand, then, about the existential dangers and disappointments that are inevitably the consequences of adopting the romantic solipsism that drives Will's quest for personal happiness.[23] Sutter tells Will about the depressed patient he once treated whose depression resulted from his living, as Will has, "under the necessity of being happy" (*LG*, 219). Citing for Will another example of how the normal life he yearns for with Kitty can be less than Edenic, Sutter tells him about another patient, this one the stereotypical successful businessman and happy husband that Will longs to be. After showering and dressing one morning in preparation for work, this "cheerful and healthy" American was suddenly paralyzed like Edvard Munch's terrified screamer, frozen in his tracks in his living room and "screaming, his mouth a perfect O" (*LG*, 268).

After a failed medical career, Sutter also knows about the limitations of the knowledge that the transcendent "truths" of science can offer, a knowledge that has led him to a cynical carnality and despair and to his current occupation as a pathologist who uses his scientific learning only to "study . . . the dead" (*LG*, 218). He knows that scientific objectivity has its own romantic charms and that they can lure the searcher to the conclusion that there is nothing outside his own angelic knowing about human life, nothing except the finally disappointing bestial pleasures of the flesh and the death that ends those pleasures. Addressing his sister Val in the casebook that Will finds in Sutter's abandoned apartment, Sutter admits that he believes that the "purity and life" that she finds in her Catholic "sacramental system" in fact exists, but he just doesn't "*know* where it comes from" (*LG*, 281–82; emphasis added). Sutter's despair, like the despair of all romantics, results from his yearning for a "purity and life" that he can never have because it lies outside his capacity to know it, outside the self-enclosed world of his *cogito*.

But, paradoxically, this consciousness of his despair finally makes Sutter a suitable and successful guide for Will as he attempts to locate where his life can be found. Will has been trying in his search to avoid despair by discovering the great secret, omniscience, happiness—trying to discover some knowledge or feeling that will produce a bland, self-satisfied contentment that will eliminate the need for a search. He has been unwittingly seeking that static, unreflective state of consciousness that many call happiness and that Kierkegaard calls despair "unaware of being despair."[24] Sutter shows Will how such happiness can in fact be nothing but disguised despair, how "purity and life" lie elsewhere.

Will assumes that Sutter, a brilliant medical scientist, "knows something" (*LG*, 218) of importance that will assist him in his search for the secret of life, but he rejects Val and her Catholic "sacramental system" when he meets her later in the Vaughts' garden. He finds in Val a consciousness radically different from his and Sutter's aestheticism and scientism, so different that she seems to him an alien being delivering to him an irritatingly incomprehensible message. When Val talks with Will about her dying brother Jamie (*LG*, 207–13) and asks him to assume responsibility for Jamie's "salvation" (*LG*, 212), he is scandalized by her for some reason he can't articulate. He feels very uncomfortable with Val, feels he can't "get hold of her." Imagining that she may be some sort of spiritual zombie, he thinks when he first sees her among the azaleas that she might not be composed of "tendon and bone," that one might "cut through" her "white as milk" wrist and find some "homogenous nun-substance" (*LG*, 208–9). Will wonders, even asks her accusingly, if she does not "believe in other worlds and, ah, spirits" (*LG*, 211). Will believes in no other world besides the one he constructs in his aesthetic, self-enclosed consciousnesss. Therefore, Val's Good News about a salvific love from another "world" that operates in a phenomenal creation outside his thinking or need satisfactions seems to him mere "Catholic monkey business" (*LG*, 212).

Val shows Will in their brief encounter on the patio a kind of love that one person can have for another that is quite different from the love that he depends on to bring him the duty-free happiness and contentment that he seeks at the Vaughts' home. Hers is a love that makes Will's dreams of Kitty in a cottage by a waterfall seem pathetically trivial and Sutter's despair almost comical in its romantic *angst*. This love is not a secret hidden somewhere within the feelings of the lover, but a love that announces itself in the little "towhee" in its "tuxedo-black and cinnamon vest" hopping around at their feet and in the azaleas that flourish around them (*LG*, 208). And it announces itself in even the most imperfect scoundrels that prowl the incarnate garden. Val explains to Will that in her work with the impoverished children in Tyree County, she begs from all kinds of people she does not like—even, she almost boasts, accepting a 7-Up machine from the "local Klonsul of the Klan." Hers is an unsentimental, antignostic love that looks outward at a Fallen Eden where an exiled and alienated self participates with other exiles in the redemptive process that the "love of Christ" (*LG*, 211) and his suffering and death have made possible. It is love that tells her where she is and what she must do. For Val, her brother Jamie's imminent "last days . . . and death" (*LG*, 209), a death that will surely be preceded by helpless debilitation and suffering, is not an unpleasant reality to be avoided but, like her work with the children of strangers in Mississippi, an opportunity to enrich the kingdom of God.[25]

After Will's encounters with Sutter and Val, he has a strange experience that suggests that he may be on the verge of escaping his self-enclosed world and seeing anew who he is and where he is. Symbolically enclosed in the darkness of the small apartment he shares with Jamie, Will has once again been dreaming of the garden at his childhood home and of his father who, like the misanthropic and gnostic Sutter, wished to live in a world in which "every last miserable son of bitch" had been driven "out of town." In this shadowy dream world, he also sees and hears a memory-constructed father whose noble social ideals created his reputation as an idealist who, like Val, "loved niggers . . . and Catholics" (*LG*, 237). Will has always tried to locate himself in this half-remembered world with his father, believing that somewhere in these past events lay an explanation for his inability "to live his life" *(LG*, 11).

But this night he awakes from the dream and realizes that the interior experience that he has just had is indeed just a dream. He opens his eyes to the "square of moonlight . . . [that] lay across his knees," his previous "blindness" with his textbooks in the sunlight of the garden at least temporarily and partially cured. He awakes also with a mysterious intimation that there is "something abroad," a sensation that makes him choose to forget his dream of his past and leave the symbolic enclosure of the apartment. He is alarmed by the reality of this place he has opened his eyes to, but dresses and goes "outside into the moonlight" (*LG*, 238) in spite of his fears to make a search in the actual garden below him for that mysterious something that is abroad and illuminated out in the night.

The imagery Percy uses in his description of what Will sees outside in the garden suggests that Will has begun to see where he is more clearly; he is not, at this moment at least, entirely lost in his interior thoughts and calculations and oblivious, therefore, to the beauty and wonder of the place. He sees the Vaughts' home at this moment as more than just a "good place to live" because it provides him an aesthetic paradise where he can collect his thoughts and dream of Kitty's charms in his arms (*LG*, 187). Instead, Will gazes out at what seems to him a wondrous garden; the golf links in the moonlight glow as pale and tranquil "as lake water." He sees "the shrubbery . . . grown tall as trees, cast inky shadows which seemed to walk in the moonlight" (*LG*, 238). Percy is obviously alluding in this passage both to Christ's walking on the waters of the Sea of Galilee and to Mark's story of Jesus's curing the blind man (Mark 8. 23–26)—both miracles that serve as sacramental signs of the mystery and power of the Incarnation. The blind man, when Jesus applied saliva to his eyes, saw dimly when he glimpsed the phenomenal world for the first time; he saw "men as trees walking," just as Will is now seeing, albeit darkly, the miracle of the incarnate world before him. Although Will, unlike his New Testament counterpart, cannot yet read the sacramental light and water before his newly opened eyes as signs of the source of all seeing and life, he is at least outside his private dreams and thoughts and taking a look around.

Will also sees at this moment that the Vaughts' garden where he has planned to engineer his Edenic life is ruined in ways he did not earlier recognize, that there is a deadness and menace here less obvious than the vanished summer foliage. When Will first saw "Juno's temple," a mansion nearby on the golf links, he found no particular significance to it; for him it was just a reproduction of Emperor Vespasian's temple of Juno built by another eccentric Alabama millionaire (*LG*, 189). But now Will looks across the links and sees it glowing on the ridge "like a great fiery star" and wonders, "what was it?" No longer confident about what he once saw with his objective eyes, Will now sees the temple as a demonic fiery mass "transformed by the prism of dreams and memory." He associates it in this flash of vision with "Canopus, the great red star of the south" that he also saw "over the cottonfields and canebrakes" of the plantation Old South of his childhood. Canopus is the star named after the ancient, wealthy Egyptian city where worshippers gathered at the temple of Serapis, god of the underworld. Will remember[s] seeing this symbolic star of wealth and false gods when it "reared up and hung low" (*LG*, 238–39) over the Old South plantation paradise his father tried to build in the Mississippi Delta cotton fields out of his noblesse oblige and stoic ideals. And this overbearing star continues to shine this night over the secular New South Eden the resident of Juno's temple and the Vaughts have tried to construct with their money and diversions.

Half-conscious—perhaps "sleepwalking," he admits—Will, after these visions in the garden, is, for some reason he cannot understand, prompted to search the Vaughts' attic. This scene foreshadows Will's return to the attic of his childhood home in Ithaca where his father shot himself to death. But Will's eyes are not yet quite open to that painful secret of his past and to his father's own failures to see clearly. What Will does recognize in the Vaughts' attic, with the assistance of Kitty, is that he does not know now where he is, that it's possible that he has been sleepwalking, that he is afflicted and needs another to tend his wounds (*LG*, 240). Will is assuming the psychic posture appropriate for the wounded, Fallen Adam whose only hope for a fullness of being larger than what he can construct within his gnostic, aesthetic consciousness lies in the love the others in the garden can give him. Only this recognition of his homelessness and affliction in a Fallen world make it possible for Will to achieve a oneness with others under God (*LC*, 112).

Will's solitary explorations of the Vaughts' home and garden this night conclude with his seeing that he must search elsewhere for a life that is absent in this deceptively Edenic place. He returns to his dark apartment to find that the "square of moonlight" that lay across him at the beginning of this episode has "moved onto Jamie's face." As Will stands by the hospital bedside of Jamie at the end of the novel to experience his final revelations, so here he gazes down at him and sees something that makes him realize that there is more in life than the angelic knowing he has pursued and the happiness that a normal life of bestial consumption can grant. Jamie's impending death and his adolescent love of the abstract truths of science lead Will to question, as he looks down at the dying youth, the value of his spending his own life being diverted by "the Theory of Large Numbers." What is the worth of such arcane knowing in the face of death? And further, what else is there worth doing and being in the Vaughts' garden, "this queer . . . place haunted by the goddess Juno and the spirit of the great Bobby Jones?" Aspire, as they have, to middle-class affluence and a great golf score?

"Puzzled" and uncertain, but "smiling," Will decides as he looks into Jamie's closed eyes that he should "wait and watch" for "more" (*LG*, 240–41) than his science textbooks can reveal and for more than even Kitty's charms in his arms and the Vaughts can give him.[26] He does not know what it is, but he is conscious that "*something is going to happen*" that will show him what to do and how to live his life. Will has always been a watcher of life and has believed since childhood that "something else was going to happen" that would disclose "the secret of his own life" (*LG*, 10–11), but on this night he has begun to look more closely outside himself—into the vastness of the world beneath the moonlit skies and into the faces of others.

While Will gazes down into the eyes of Jamie, he is not aware that Sutter and Rita, two residents of this "queer place" who feel there is nothing to wait for, lurk in the tiny adjoining kitchenette behind him. They both believe that they have already located all that has happened and that therefore there is nothing to wait for beyond what they currently see. Sutter the scientist cynically and stoically accepts Jamie's life and death as simply a matter of the condition of his spleen and his "white count" and "red count." For Rita, the gnostic and romantic idealist, Jamie's life is measured by the amount of "self-fullfillment" and "beauty and joy" (*LG*, 243–44) that he can experience before his Keatsian death. She wants him to leave his family and spend the few months he has left in the isolation of her rustic New Mexico ranch house and among her artistic neighbors. There he can seek the aesthetic development that she equates with the "purity and life" that Val finds in her sacramental Christianity and that Sutter knows exists but knows he cannot find (*LG*, 281). Will's instinctive rejection of Sutter's and Rita's ways of seeing is suggested at the end of this scene when he closes the door to the kitchenette and "jump[s] into bed and pull[s] the pillow over his head" (*LG*, 246–47). He will search for more.

Before leaving the Vaughts to search for Sutter and Jamie (who have left for New Mexico), Will meets Kitty at "a raw new golf links" outside of town where she has arranged to show him the suburban home she plans for them to move into after they are married. She is excited by the prospect of their repeating the idyllic life of her parents in this picturesque "rockhouse" in the "ferny Episcopal woods" of the new housing development. But, as if still conscious that there might be more than the kind of love and aesthetic detachment he has enjoyed for the past few weeks at her family's home, Will rejects Kitty's vision of their future together in the suburban development that is soon to be a replica of the Vaughts' ruined garden. While they stand together in the house and look out at the scenic view, Will sees only the "doleful foothills and the snowfield of G.E. Gold Medallion homes." He imagines becoming an aging "eccentric" in this pleasant but barren "snowfield" and, like the previous owner, Cap'n Mickle, idling away his monotonous last days "feeding the chickadees" and watching through his telescope the "buzzards and crows . . . circle" omniously for the dead down below. He feels the "Episcopal ivy . . . twining itself around his ankles." When Kitty adds that the house has a "soundproof and womanproof" basement room where Will can withdraw from the world and others and "pull the hole in after" him, he says, "no, thanks," and insists that they be on their way (*LG*, 283–85). Apparently, Will no longer yearns for the detached way of seeing that the telescope gives him and no longer envies the invisibility of the secretive English detective in his burrow (*LG*, 161–62).

After they leave their future Eden in the snowfield, Will and Kitty stop by the university, the place Will once thought of as an "intersubjective paradise" (*LG*, 204) where he could acquire the education he needed to construct his normal life as a married businessman in the suburbs. But just as the Vaughts' garden no longer looks to Will as paradisiacal as it once did, so this place that he once saw as a pleasant aesthetic refuge where he could lose himself in the study of "large numbers" and in the good feelings produced by fraternity camaraderie has become as threatening as the dark garden of Central Park that he roamed a few months earlier. Clearly a postlapsarian Eden, there is gunfire in the distance, the racial rioting in New York taking a different but no less violent and divisive form here on the sleepy campus of this Southern university.[27]

On the campus, Will is again alone and dislocated in a violent and anonymous pastoral world peopled by hurrying "dark figures," one who stops briefly to cry out, "Kill him! Kill him! Kill him!" He is not now, however, as detached as he was in Central Park when he was looking through a telescope, analyzing his past, or dreaming of his future love and happiness. Instead, Will is painfully engaged with the other residents of this obviously Fallen place, accidentally caught among a group of the rioting students and knocked unconscious while he is on his way to pick up his *Theory of Large Numbers*. As if symbolically embracing this dark, frightening garden as his home, Will lies "down under the dark shrubbery" and falls into unconsciousness. This instinctive recognition that this place of hatred and conflict is where he lives with all others is, perhaps, the cause for his revelation immediately before he loses consciousness: "the dawn of discovery, the imminent sense of coming at last upon those secrets closest to one and therefore most inaccessible, broke over him" (*LG*, 288–89). Kitty and the garden of love and happiness she offers and the university and the Eden of angelic knowing that it promises vanish from his sight as Will sees a new light dawning in the darkness, a light that may show him that there is more beyond the campus and more beyond his future home in the bleak snowfield.

Beyond the Garden Walls

The final chapter of *The Last Gentleman* begins with Will's awaking from unconsciousness just after dawn in the cab of the Trav-L-Aire (*LG*, 291) and immediately initiating his journey away from the dark and ruined gardens of Alabama that have enclosed him in Edenic dreams of a happy and "normal" future home there. He sets out alone and uncertain but, like Huck Finn, he can say to himself that he is "not going back because I've been there" (*LG*, 294).[28] Seriously dislocated when he awakes, he wonders as he searches frantically for his lost wallet, "Where is this place?" "What is my name?" (*LG*, 293). Having utterly "forgotten" Kitty and the Vaughts and the happiness they can give him, Will is "confused" (*LG*, 294), incapable of summoning the powers of the objectivity and scientific thinking that he trusted when he began his search at the beginning of the novel. He struggles to locate himself in actual "time and space" phenomena,[29] no longer the solitary transcendent thinker dreaming up an Edenic life. Instead, Will becomes an active wayfarer on the road. Motivated only by the feeling of a "huge tug forward" (*LG*, 294) and guided only by the route marked on Sutter's Esso map, Will no longer assumes that he must know everything or be omniscient in order to know what to do.

Will's journey is a journey outward into the expanses of the Delta plains of Mississippi and the American West and a symbolic pilgrimage "forward" through these landscapes toward a consciousness larger and more open than his earlier solipsistic, enclosed way of seeing. Will begins to recognize in the landscapes along the way the Fallen world of suffering and death, the home, that he shares with others. He first descends deeper into the impoverished South, there to discover at Val Vaught's "lunar installation" (*LG*, 296) in Tyree County, a home where helpless and forgotten children rely on the life they are given by Val. Her Catholic, sacramental way of seeing and unsentimental Christian love show Will what one can do besides selfishly seek personal happiness and need satisfaction. Later, in Ithaca, Will stands beneath the dark oaks in front of the home his father built for him and his family. There, he remembers the night his father killed himself and for the first time understands the self-deceptive, death-embracing failures inherent in his father's solitary and self-absorbed search, the same kind of search that Will himself has pursued for most of his twenty-five years. He concludes at this vanished home that his father "was looking in the wrong place" (*LG*, 332) for the secret of life and subsequently found only death. At his Uncle Fannin's defunct plantation in Louisiana, Will sees another kind of ruined garden and failure. His befuddled uncle with his black servant Merriam (*LG*, 338) is an example of the kind of isolated, purposeless life and home Will could have if he chose to restore the plantation he inherited, abandoned his search for any secret, and adopted an easy life as a Southern gentleman planter.

Will's wayfaring ends in the desert—at Santa Fe (Holy Faith), the Sangre de Cristo (Blood of Christ) mountains,[30] and at Sutter's Rancho la Merced (Ranch of Mercy—perhaps an allusion to la Virgen de la Merced). These place names suggest that Will has journeyed to a place where he is surrounded by some mysteries of death, love, and redemption that he has not yet sufficiently pondered, to a home he has not been able to discover in New York, Alabama, Ithaca, or at his Uncle Fannin's plantation. This desert home, threatening but beautiful in its intimidating vastness, is where Will directly encounters the reality of physical suffering and death and learns through Father Boomer of the possibilities for life transcendent of it. In the hospital room at Santa Fe, the sickness and death of Jamie show Will the blunt fact of the "dread ultimate rot of the molecules" (LG, 401)—these molecules, and nothing else, constituting what the positivistic scientist believes is human life. Father Boomer shows Will in the sacrament of Baptism what may be larger than those finite molecules, an infinite redemptive love whose purity transforms the rot. He delivers the news of a life that is as vast and mysterious as the sacramental desert and world that stretch out around the hospital room.

Will begins his journey out of Alabama by driving his hidden Trav-L-Aire out of a "cave of myrtles" (LG, 292), out into the sunlight of the dawning new day, and out toward a confrontation with the postlapsarian world of decay and death that no thinking and no engineering of himself can alter. As he drives into the South, he discovers himself in a cold, desolate place. He sees the "old corn shucks hung like frozen rags" in the empty fields beside the road, looks out across the "sparse woodland of post oaks and spindly pines infected with tumors," and hears the "killdeer . . . crying down" the freshly plowed rows of "disced-up gobbets of earth." Finding himself in a wasteland of abandoned Southern homes and towns, Will does not retire into his interior world to think about the past that these places represent and to recall his connections with that Old South past. Instead, he is drawn to the immediate present. For example, when Will reaches the ruins of a "tall blackish building" that was once Phillips Academy, once a private school for training the sons of Old South gentlemen, he searches his memory for a clue to where he is. But his memory fails him, and he is thrust uncomfortably into the undeniable "now" (LG, 295-96) of the place.

To his disappointment, this "now" is Val Vaught's "raw settlement" (LG, 296) in Tyree County, a messy conglomeration of buildings that seem to

Will like the "crude and makeshift beginnings" of life on another planet (*LG*, 302). But this is not an alien planet. At Val's home Will has entered instead the "crude" actual world beyond the perfect Alabama golf links where golfers, lost in their pursuits of happiness, make their way mechanically from empty hole to empty hole. Val's settlement is an untidy and aesthetically disappointing place, but it is also where she, and those who support and assist her, work to transform a haphazard and unfinished garden into a place of life and joy. Will finds himself in an unattactive world standing before an unattractive woman, but he is also in the presence of the unsentimental and life-giving love that is the cause for this redemptive work.[31] Val devotes her days to teaching the impoverished black children in the area to speak; she believes they come "alive" (*LG*, 301) when they acquire the power to name who they are and where they are.

Val positions herself comfortably in the Fallen world as a participant in the redemption that Christ began on earth.[32] While Will has been encouraged by his secular, middle-class American consciousness to retreat from the imperfections of life and to dream of an Eden he has not yet experienced, Val has a consciousness that directs her into the midst of the ruin where God is continuously emerging.[33] She has no uncertainties about what to do. Hers is a sacramental consciousness that informs her that "Christ is . . . [her] lord" and that her "love [for] him" necessarily requires her participation in the redemption that Christ's death and resurrection have initiated. So, she spends her days not seeking happiness, but offering what nourishment she can to the weak and abandoned.[34] She is content to stand in a chicken coop and patiently feed entrails to the injured old chicken hawk as well as teach the mute children how to be alive in a world where God tells them that they can "be happy now and forever" if they "love one another and keep the commandments and receive the Sacrament" (*LG*, 301–2).

Val delivers this same Good News to Will in her story about her recognition of her "half-dead" condition when she was a student at Columbia and her discovery of a life beyond the angelic, transcendent attractions of the university. It is a story that Will should recognize. Val tells him about how she, at the prompting of the nun with whom she shared her carrel, left her "cubicle" in the library stacks of Columbia. Will has also left his tiny rooms at Macy's and the New York Y.M.C.A. She, like Will, returned to her home in the South where the Vaughts' "castle" and surrounding gardens offered a Southern version of modern American happiness. But unlike Will, Val has discovered another world and self. She tells him about becoming "alive" after "receiv[ing] instruction" and taking her vows in a convent in Paterson, New Jersey (*LG*, 300). She sums up her Christian discovery of herself and the world in a note that she sent Sutter: "It is only from desolation of total transcendence of self and total descent of world of immanence that a man can come who can recover himself and world under God" (*LG*, 346).

Val stands before Will while "drap[ing] two feet of gut over the perch" of the chicken hawk. She is an example of someone who has descended from the transcendence that has locked Will away from discovering himself with others under God and has located herself firmly in the not always happiness-producing actualities of immanent creation. She sees herself as someone with purpose and responsibility among the sick and the dead in her settlement, whereas Will sees only disappointment. Val chooses to feed the homely, weak chicken hawk, whereas Will prefers to direct his gaze to the transcendent world of the spectacularly powerful and beautiful falcon he tried to photograph in Central Park. Will thinks as he watches Val feed the old hawk, "I could see him [the falcon] better at one mile than this creature face to face" (*LG*, 300).

Because Will has no sacramental Christian consciousness, he, of course, fails to understand Val's Christian news. Neither does he recognize any redemptive process at work at Val's home. He sees only "some blasted planet" of "cancerous pines" that is not his home. "Life indeed," he thinks while Val shows him around, feeling so removed from any kinship with these people and their home that he imagines himself an alien visitor to a strange planet who would perish after another hour there. Will is anxious to escape (*LG*, 302) to his Trav-L-Aire and to the aesthetic isolation he enjoyed while he and Jamie were on the road south from Williamsburg. Enclosed in the truck's cabin, he was detached from the waste and clutter of the Fallen home he shares with others, but was free to descend into the immanent world whenever he pleased to sample the exquisite bits of beauty in serene savannas. Will has always preferred the tidy "jewel-like warblers" enclosed in the tiny lens of his telescope (*LG*, 161) to crippled chicken hawks.

In the fields beside the road and at Val's settlement Will has seen and heard about a world of death, decay, suffering, love, and redemption beyond the walls of the compact Trav-L-Aire and the interior Edenic gardens he has sought to inhabit. And the physical world continues to impose its undeniably threatening and immense presence as he descends further into the South toward his home in Ithaca. In the "October haze" outside the G.M.C.'s windows, "dead trees shrouded in kudzu vines rear up like old women" in the dense Delta woods. Once again dislocated and wondering where he is, Will stops the truck beside the road amid vast cotton fields that stretch out forty miles, watches the "buzzards circle," and spots "a shrike, the Negro's ghost bird," eyeing him "through its black mask" from a telephone wire (*LG*, 303–4). Will, the detached aesthetic observer who prefers to remain invisible and safe from the threats of the world he inspects, now feels that he is the one being watched by the sinister-looking shrike, a predatory and brutal bird that impales its prey on thorns.[35] He obviously feels included, and uncomfortably so, in the menacing phenomenal world that he is perceiving. He is feeling the self-conscious anxiety that Percy believes is the inevitable condition of the self that recognizes that it is a homeless exile in a place of death. It is this anxiety that can serve as an impetus for his looking for "news from across the seas" that will tell him about his real home and the life available there.

Will's developing sense of his homelessness may be the cause for his continuing his search for a home when he arrives in Ithaca.[36] He remembers as he walks the streets of his old hometown that he is, in fact, at this moment homeless—that he doesn't live anywhere and has no address (*LG*, 313). This memory of his present condition prompts him to think about the possibility for a future home with the Vaughts back in Alabama; he calls Kitty to tell her he'll be back (*LG*, 316). And he thinks about the home he has lost here in Ithaca. On his last night in his old hometown, Will returns to his family's house to look into his past for the great secret he has always thought would direct him to his true self and home. Percy, commenting in an interview on this important scene, quoted Kierkegaard, who asserts that "every man has to stand in front of the house of his childhood in order to recover himself" (*Con*, 67). And this is what Will is trying to do.

Again in another dark garden, Will stands before his house that night in the "inky darkness of the water oaks . . . amid the azaleas" (*LG*, 328) and recovers some secrets that he did not anticipate. He does not discover a memory to embrace as a home and source of truth about himself but remembers instead a self-destructive past that he must leave behind in his wayfaring in the present. Finally recalling the actual suicide of his father, even the "thunderous" blast of the "double-barrel twelve-guage," Will sees clearly for the first time the dangers of the aestheticism and angelic self-transcendence that led his father to despair. He remembers sitting on the porch steps when he was thirteen and listening to the romantic Brahms while his father talked about "good character" and "the good life and the loneliness of the galaxies." Unable to accept living in a world not always filled with the beauty of Brahms, and always peopled by immoral "fornicators" and corrupt "bribers," Will's father mounted the porch steps toward the attic and ignored Will, who was desperately begging him, "Wait. . . . Don't *leave*." Will remembers his father's announcing melodramatically, "in the last analysis, you are alone," and choosing the love of his ideals over the love of his son. And what Will remembers most is the "terror" that "pierced his very soul" while the "beautiful victorious music" played on (*LG*, 329–32).

This intense memory of the terror, cruelty, and defeat inherent in the romanticism and detachment of his father leads Will to conclude in the "inky darkness" that his father was "wrong." Rejecting the aestheticism and "solitariness" of his father—the same transcendent inwardness that has created his own detached life of mere thinking and watching—Will instinctively reaches out his fingers to the "tiny iron horsehead of the hitching post" attached to the oak immediately in front of him. The bark of the tree has grown around the horsehead, drawing it "into time and change," the realities that Will's father, and Will, have been reluctant to confront.[37] "It"— the secret he has sought for a lifetime, is, he knows now, "here, under your nose, here in the very curiousness and drollness and extraness of the iron and the bark" (*LG* 332). Becoming aware at this moment of the "concreteness of things," Will feels a "comforting revelation."[38] The oak beneath his fingertips, the "sibilant corky bark" (*LG*, 329), "hisses" and "whispers" (*LG*, 332) to him that he lives here and now—in a garden as dark as the present inky gloom but also as promising as the azaleas that are sure to blossom in the spring. The oak is a sacramental Tree of Knowledge in a Fallen but living garden that speaks to Will and provides him with the sign he needs to tell him what his predicament is.

Will's improved consciousness of where he is and his escape from the interior world of his self-constructed past is illustrated by his actions immediately after this memory in front of his house. When a "Negro . . . his own age" happens to walk down the sidewalk and into the dark garden beneath the oaks with Will, Will thinks that they are both in the same "fix" (*LG*, 332-33). He is not lost in thoughts about how to find the secret of being happy, but recognizes a kinship with others in the "grave predicament" (*MB*, 144) Percy believes all share. The past no longer interferes with his efforts to decide what to do in this fix. As if no longer awed by the past and the important secrets it might hold, Will goes into the attic of the house to take from his grandfather and his father only what he will need to continue his journey toward Santa Fe. The next morning he descends from the symbolic enclosure of the attic's "windowless interior room" and the family's deadly past with his father's portable boat and his grandfather's binoculars (now, apparently, sensing that his monocular telescope might prove inadequate for his future "seeing"). He heads out into the openness of the "sparkling day" and the "wide river" toward his Uncle Fannin Barrett's plantation near Shut Off, Louisiana (*LG*, 333–35).

When Will reaches the Louisiana shore a few miles down the river, he feels he is entering "a dim green place of swamps and shacks and Negro graveyards." Will is in another dim, half-lighted symbolic garden like the one where he stood the night before—a deadly garden with graveyards, but also a green place that nurtures and sustains life. Will also sees that, like his father's garden, this is a place where abstracted plantation builders went about their lives "removed in time and space" from a consciousness of the effects of their grand goals and noble ideals. They tried to construct a paradisiacal, polite way of life out of "small and pleasant deeds" (*LG*, 337), oblivious both to the life and the graves around them. What they succeeded in constructing instead was a small life created out of deeds that verified for them their convictions about their noble character and enclosed them in the illusion that the actual world had been reduced to the diminished, shut-off place they envisioned.

Will is attracted to such a small life. Just the day before, in the Ithaca bank, Will happened to meet some of his old friends who had chosen to remain in the Delta and to live out the Old South planter lifestyle of their ancestors. They seemed so happy and carefree that Will considered once again returning to Hampton, the abandoned plantation he inherited from his grandfather, and constructing "the same sweet life" that "these splendid fellows" seemed to be enjoying (*LG*, 311). But at his Uncle Fannin's desolate plantation Will finds instead of a sweet life a life that is isolated from time and space, a self-enclosed life of despair unaware of being despair. His uncle is as lost in immanence as his father was in transcendence. The antic but deadly old man who greets him at the plantation spends his days with his servant Merriam in the empty fields of his private world armed with the Browning automatic he uses to hunt quail (*LG*, 337–38). As the Vaughts and their country-club friends sought happiness in the artificial Eden of the golf course, so Fannin Barrett seeks the Old South gentlemanly pleasures of hunting. At night, he and Merriam excitedly watch *Gunsmoke* from their matching recliners, so lost in the fictional characters on the screen and so detached from any intersubjective communication with each other that they talk "about the Western heroes as if they are real people" (*LG*, 341–42). Each morning at breakfast the two watch *Captain Kangaroo*, "transported," Will thinks, from their actual "3-D" selves and home (*LG*, 346) into the childish merriment of the Captain's and Mr. Greenjeans's fantasy world.

When Will retires the night of his visit to the upstairs bedroom of his Uncle's home, the cold "narrow cell" and "the warm goosedown [that] flow[s] up around him" symbolically enclose him. In this symbolic setting, Will reads in Sutter's casebook about the self-enclosure in transcendence and immanence that his father and uncle represent. He reads in Sutter's notes about a "spirit of abstraction and of transcendence" that demotes the immanent world and thereby elevates the transcendent knower above it. The immanent world, demoted to an inferior status, becomes by this very designation an unsatisfying and even inappropriate place for the regal, superior transcendent self to function (*LG*, 343–45). This is the transcendent self exemplified by Will's father and Sutter, a self that can see no way to live in an immanent world that lacks the grandeur of his ghostly transcendent interior palace. Will's uncle, on the other hand, is lost in immanence, his life reduced to the stimulations provided by his daily amusements in the physical world. Paradoxically, this devotion to his immanent experience results in his being transported out of phenomenal reality and into the interior world where those stimulations exist.

In the bedroom cell, Will toys with the skull that belonged to "his namesake, Dr. Williston Barrett, the original misfit"—unconsciously identifying himself as another misfit who, like Dr. Barrett, is different from Uncle Fannin and Ed Barrett. Will has obviously not found in his uncle's violent and lonely garden, any more than he found in his father's equally violent garden the night before, the secret, the something more, that will lead him to the self that he has been trying to find. Perhaps he sees in Dr. Barrett an alternative to the self-enclosure of his father and uncle. The original Williston Barrett was a man who decided after his stint in the Civil War that he'd "had enough" of humankind, abandoned his practice, and was apparently content to take an occasional dose of laudanum and pursue a career as "a philosopher of sorts" (*LG*, 343–44).[39] Like Will and his father, Will's namesake was a man who preferred his solitary transcendent thinking to the world of men; and, like Fannin Barrett, he enjoyed the pleasures of his immanent existence. But, unlike Ed and Fannin Barrett, Dr. Barrett was a man who knew firsthand from his war experience about the suffering and death outside his thinking and ideals and outside the daily, temporary pleasures his plantation and laudanum provided. While Dr. Barrett may have failed to be entirely happy or successful, at least he did not commit suicide because he loved his abstractions more than life or spend his days with a Browning automatic and Mr. Greenjeans.

REMEMBERING EVERYTHING

By the time Will reaches New Mexico and "the sunny yellow canyon of the Rio Grande" (*LG*, 355), his transcendent eyes have at least been partially opened by his wayfaring through the Fallen landscape of the South. In the perfect garden at the Vaughts, he has seen some of the possible limitations of the future Eden of love and happiness he has been trying to "engineer" since he first spotted Kitty in Central Park. He has also seen in the Old South gardens at his childhood home in Ithaca and at his uncle's plantation the dangers of looking to the past and trying to construct an interior life separate from the wasted landscape. At Val's disappointing settlement, he encountered an unabstracted Christian self that scandalized him with its refusal to turn away from the postlapsarian "now" of itself and others and turned its eyes outward to the sacramental signs of Incarnation. It is in this garden that Val directs Will to Jamie and Sutter (*LG*, 297), points him toward the desert and the revelations that await him there.

Will's improved ability to locate himself in phenomenal creation after his visits in these gardens is demonstrated when he pulls the G.M.C. to the side of the road to take a look at the Rio Grande. Percy's sacramental imagery in this scene reveals how Will is beginning to look outside himself and develop a vague awareness of the sacramental mystery of the natural world. Alluding to Hopkins's "shook foil" image in "God's Grandeur," Percy describes how "a golden aspen rattled like foil in the sunlight," right beside an intrigued Will. Perplexed by the tree's beautiful movements, since there is no wind to cause the movement, Will looks "closer" and watches how "a single leaf danced on its pedicile, mysteriously dispensed from energy laws" (*LG*, 355). In this moment of unabstracted observation and response, Will is seeing without his telescope, anticipating no great discoveries about himself. He is turning to an examination of the beauty of the actual physical world to consider what "mysteriously" might exist that is not explained by "energy laws," what might be occurring in creation that is "dispensed from" scientific theories and principles. Although Will cannot yet read the sacramental signs of nature and continues to name his observations with scientific terms like "pediciles" and "energy laws," he is beginning to look outside himself with wonder—and finding mystery.

He feels the mystery surround him in the vastness of the New Mexico desert. Experiencing a new sense of his exile in this strange environment, Will feels like a sailor in an empty place of silence where his identity and life are problematical affairs. Having arrived at Sutter's Rancho la Merced, he believes he is in a new place "of pure possibility." He thinks now that "what a man can be the next minute bears no relation to what he is or what he was the minute before" (*LG*, 355–56). If Will believes this, he believes that the scientific understanding of himself and his future that he dreamed about achieving in New York (*LG*, 41) is impossible. Since his past ("what he was"), present ("what he is"), and future ("what . . . [he] can be") may be, he thinks, unrelated in any way intelligible to him, there in actuality might be no relation among these segments of his life. If there is no logical continuity of past, present, and future except within his subjective concepts of his movements through time, then there is no objective way for Will to engineer a life. The self, finally, is a mystery.

At Sutter's ranch, Will illustrates that he is now less confident about his ability to discover scientifically who he is and where he is and more inclined to look outside himself and wait for something more to reveal itself in the immediacy of present incarnate creation. This improved consciousness of immediate time-space phenomena may be partially the result of Will's rejection of Sutter's self-transcendence. The night before he arrived at the ranch Will decided, after he read a few pages of Sutter's casebook, that the abstracted, angelic-bestial Sutter was on the wrong track in his pursuit of the absolute truth about life. The most urgent existential problem, Will now believes, is "how to live from one ordinary minute to the next on a Wednesday afternoon"—how to have a life amid the actualities of real events in real time. Will also reads in the casebook of Val's "Ich warte" way of knowing and being in the world. Her Catholic Christian way encourages him to see the possible wisdom of waiting in the open desert for "something better" (LG, 354) than the despair and death that the self-enclosed Sutter believes is life.

This change in Will's way of seeing is symbolically illustrated at Sutter's ranch the next day when Will chooses the open skies of the sacramental desert over the "cool cellarlike darkness" of Sutter's "chthonic" abandoned adobe house. When Will explores the deserted house, he finds that it is empty and contains "no sign[s]" of life except for discarded magazines, dirty laundry, and the "hindoo" pornography beneath one of the beds. Will, after a few minutes in the darkness of this chthonic cave, decides that there is "no good at all" in the house and walks out into the welcoming "bright hush of the desert" (LG, 355-56) to "wait." After a brief wait, Will sees the sacramental world reveal itself. The magnificent Sangre de Cristo range glows a Eucharistic red in the sunset. A sacramental "breeze . . . [springs] up," reminiscent of the breeze in Eden that brought the Word to Adam and Eve (Genesis 3.8). As the stars begin to glow in the darkness and hang "large and low as yellow lamps at a garden party," "little yellow flycatchers began to fly down from the mountain." Amid this glorious light, color, and life, Will "shiver[s]" (possibly in awe) and decides that he is "through with telescopes" (LG, 357–58).

By the time Will begins his visits with Jamie in the Santa Fe hospital, he has lost his fascination with his telescope and has begun to question the adequacy of the scientistic way of seeing it represents. His earlier scientific objectivism and Sutter's cynical philosophizing seem impotent when he looks into the face of the dying Jamie. Jamie's face is a sign of the absolute reality of death, a reminder to Will that human life exists in the actuality of segments of time and their ends, not in the lense of his aesthetic telescope, not in the future Edens he might construct within his thinking and feeling, and not in the memories he might explore for some secret about himself. No objective thinking, pursuit of happiness, or solipsistic carnality can dismiss the truth he sees in the hospital bed. It forces Will to wonder on his last visit to Jamie's bedside if all efforts at a meaningful life are defeated by the simple "ultimate rot" of bodily tissues, if this death he is witnessing is a sign of the "secret shame" at the heart of all human life, if there is, finally, just "ruin" and "abject surrender" (*LG*, 401).

When Will first sees Jamie, the "purpura" has "splotche[d]" his face with bruises the "horrid color . . . [of] oil slicks," the physical grotesqueness of the face defying Will's efforts to look at this sign objectively, scientifically, dispassionately. Unable to maintain a cool detachment, Will is "upset . . . badly" by the face. Because he is now in the presence of a sign that he has not before sufficiently acknowledged, Will feels he must "strain" his powers of "speaking" and "see[ing]" in an effort to respond to it in some adequate, satisfactory way. When he looks at Jamie, Will feels he must "peer this way and that to see him through an evil garden of flowers" (*LG*, 362). Father Smith tells Tom More in *The Thanatos Syndrome* that seeing the "horror" in life takes "some effort" (*TS*, 254), and Will is exerting this kind of effort. Will has for much of his life been looking only at his own face, searching for his own personal identity, and searching for a garden without any evil that might spoil his happiness. But now he is being challenged to look out at an evil garden where the suffering and death of another exists. Seeing this evil garden requires effort and strength (a "straining") in order to see through to where he is with others. Jamie's face is a sign of the disturbing facticity of human suffering and death that inevitably impinges on all private dreams of happiness, but, paradoxically, it is also a sign that can lead pilgrims like Will to search for what might exist in the desert that is more than the horror beneath his gaze.

Jamie's face is precisely the sign Will needs to reveal to him the sacramental world he inhabits. The sign Will is seeing, although he cannot yet read it, is what Flannery O'Connor sees in the cancer-disfigured face of Mary Ann. In her introductory essay to *A Memoir of Mary Ann*, O'Connor explains how she sees in the grotesqueness of Mary Ann's pain and death "something full of promise," "the good under construction." O'Connor's world, like Percy's, is a sacramental place full of signs, and human suffering is for her one of those signs that reveals that God has entered history in the Incarnation to redeem humankind through his love from what is otherwise

hopeless suffering. For O'Connor, the world is "created upon human imperfection," and this imperfect condition is, paradoxically, the basis for hope
for redemption.[40] This imperfection is the reason God's redemptive love
exists. The face of Mary Ann (or the face of Jamie) is a sign that points out
that all exiles live in the same garden, an evil one full of dreadful imperfection and suffering, but, simultaneously, the face is a reminder of the hope,
promise, and good that are the gifts of that very evil. The Passion of Christ,
of course, is the ultimate sacramental sign that shows how redemptive love
and life can mysteriously exist in the face of innocent suffering and death.

Will has not yet developed a sacramental way of seeing that will enable
him to locate himself in such a hope-filled mystery. He continues in the
New Mexico desert to see the world scientifically, as his observations of the
pediciles of the golden aspen and his thinking about the energy laws gov-
erning it illustrate earlier when he stops at the Rio Grande (*LG*, 355). There
is, however, some indication in his responses to nature and others in the
final scenes at the hospital that he is at least paying more attention to the
signs and subsequently finding some relief from his earlier dislocations from
time-space phenomena. Will demonstrates that he is much more conscious
of the inadequacy of a life of self-enclosure, thinking while he plays cards
with Jamie in the hospital room that an entire life could be spent "enclosed"
in a magical "golden circle" of "small tasks" and games that could prevent
anything "very serious" from "go[ing] amiss." Life, he concludes, can be
made into a "small tidy business" (*LG*, 365–66), as insignificant as an idle
afternoon at cards.

Will knows he is in the room with a dying child, a situation that precludes his life remaining either tidy or small. He knows that there is a
significance here that demands that he consider what is outside the circle
of games and pleasant diversions. Will exhibits his improved consciousness
of where he is during one of his afternoon visits to Jamie's room. He is
sitting "beside the bed in the sunny corner" (*LG*, 369), this time not asleep
as he was in the "sunny corner" (*LG*, 202) of the Vaughts' walled garden.
He looks out of the hospital window and wonders at the way "the flat
mathematical leaves of the aspens danced a Brownian dance in the sunlight, blown by a still, molecular wind" (*LG*, 369).[41] This description echoes
his scientific description of the spectacular golden aspen at the Rio Grande.
The Brownian dance is an allusion to Robert Brown, the nineteenth-century Scottish botanist whose meticulous study of plant life led to theories
of molecular motion. Will's thinking about this scientist when he looks out
the window suggests that when he looks at creation he still thinks of the
mathematical and scientific theories that explain how it works and that he
is prone to name his observations with the language of science. Such scien-

tific naming by itself, Percy says in "Naming and Being," can obscure reality from the observer and cause phenomena to vanish into the signs used to identify them. These language signs create the illusion that the world is a static "museum of name things" (*SP*, 134–35) rather than a living creation that exists in time. Furthermore, because these scientific signs obscure the particularities of existence that lie outside the abstractions they signify, the signs diminish the scientific namer's consciousness of the actual world.

Although Will's scientific naming illustrates that he continues to see with the objective eyes of the botanist, his description of the "mathematical leaves" implies that he is also capable of naming and seeing the aspens in another way. He responds imaginatively and emotionally to the mathematical leaves, finding a grace and beauty in their mysterious movements in the brilliant sunlight and in the oxymoronic "still . . . wind." He poetically and metaphorically names his sensory experience a "dance." Will's naming here is the kind of naming that Percy says in "Naming and Being " is characteristic of the sign system of literary art. Percy believes that these signs in literature name with the same "cognitive" precision as science and can potentially reveal as much information about "what it is to be human" (*SP*, 288). His insistence that literature's naming reveals a special kind of knowledge echoes O'Connor's assertion that the writer's work is essentially "the accurate naming of the things of God."[42]

Will is speaking artistically as well as scientifically in this passage and demonstrating a precision of observation and a power to name that are, for Percy, indexes to the capacity to know where we are, who we are, and what we should do in the actualities of the present incarnate world. As Will at the Rio Grande turns to the aspens that are immediately in front of him and at Rancho la Merced puts down his telescope, here at the hospital he again looks closely at the world just outside the window and strains a bit to name it. Will is responding to where he lives with much more directness and understanding. He is no longer the objective, scientific, abstracted engineer searching in Central Park with his telescope for a sign of the great secret within him or the self-enclosed romantic lover in the Vaughts' garden collecting his thoughts and pursuing some undefined interior state of happiness that he believes a future with Kitty in a cottage by a waterfall will furnish.

Will is not just more conscious of the phenomenal present after his wayfaring to New Mexico, but becomes convinced that he "remember[s] everything" (*LG*, 374, 375, 379). Will arrives at this new consciousness of his existence in time as he lies in the Trav-L-Aire bunk in Alamogordo Motor Park and reads Sutter's casebook. Sutter talks about his attempting

suicide last summer when he became depressed by Jamie's illness and imminent death and about his determination to try again after Jamie's death.
Will reads of a man, like his father, who cannot accept the imperfections
and dissatisfactions that he has decided are life itself, cannot wait for what
more might occur as time and his current consciousness of who he is and
where he is vanish into the past. Just as Will could recognize in front of his
family's house in Ithaca that his father was wrong, so now he can reject
Sutter's choice of death over life. Will steps out of the Trav-L-Aire and
tosses the casebook into the trashhburner at the motor park (*LG*, 373).
Later that day, after Will talks with Sutter at his ranch, he can conclude
firmly that Sutter is the "dismalest failure" (*LG*, 381).

Will's "remembering everything" is the kind of memory—as a middle-
aged Will Barrett realizes again twenty years later in *The Second
Coming*—that includes remembering "even ... the future" (*SC*, 91). It is an
intense consciousness of his existence as a participant in time-space events
that enables Will to direct his eyes outward to the "possibility of a happy,
useful life" with others in a real place and real time. Will tells Sutter at
Rancho la Merced that he hopes to return to Alabama after Jamie's death,
take a position at Confederate Chevrolet, marry Kitty, have a family, and
develop the "religious dimension" of his life (*LG*, 383–85). He is "remembering" that it is possible to have a life that will not lead him to his father's
attic or to Sutter's empty ranch house. Will's new memory enables him to
escape temporarily the self-enclosure and despair that he has unwittingly
been seeking in his search for the great secret. He can accept that he does
not know everything about himself and the world and that he has not acquired the omniscience that he has always desired, but he feels he knows all
he "wished to know" (*LG*, 379). He has seen where thinking led his father
and where it is leading Sutter, and so chooses the hope and possibilities
that lie out in the sacramental world with others and down the road.

Although he does not yet know how to achieve it, what Will is acknowledging with his remarkable new memory is the possibility of living the life
that Kierkegaard's "Knight of Infinite Resignation" lives in his ethical sphere.
Kierkegaard says that the Knight is the Christian who "remembers everything," everything, that is, relevant to his salvation. The Knight is by this
"memory" "reconciled with existence." He "work[s], "love[s] his wife,"
"love[s] his fellow man," and is content to wait for God to tell him "what
else" that he needs to know and do.[43] Will obviously has not achieved any
such Christian faith or reconciliation, but he does at least *hope* for the life
the Knight has remembered, hopes to "rejoin the human race" (*LG*, 386)
that Sutter and his father choose to abandon and Kierkegaard's Knight
yearns to embrace. This hope provides the impetus for his continuing search.

After Will refuses Sutter's invitation to join him in suicide at the ranch (*LG*, 389), he returns to Jamie's bedside to learn through his participation with Father Boomer in the boy's baptism about a love, hope, and life that will surely help him rejoin his fellow wayfarers in the world. When Will calls Val from the hospital, she insists that he take the "responsibility" (*LG*, 392, 393) for Jamie's baptism, asks him to become involved in a Christian sacrament that signifies how all humankind is united in the redemptive love and hope offered in the death and resurrection of Christ. Will, in his acceptance of this responsibility, is like Kierkegaard's Knight who, in the ethical realm of his life, takes responsibility for his neighbors and lives in love among them.[44] By acting for Jamie's possible salvation, Will is demonstrating a Christian love that is indeed "something better" (*LG*, 354) than his earlier detached, aesthetic love of knowledge and personal happiness. The priest names Will the "friend who loves" (*LG*, 406) Jamie, and during the baptism tells him of a world that was "made . . . so that you might enjoy its beauty"; its source, Father Boomer goes on to explain, is a God of love that "made you and loves you" and descended into creation in the form of "His only Son" to provide hope and joy and eternal life (*LG*, 403). Percy says that Father Boomer is Kierkegaard's "apostle" with the "news" (*Con*, 114) who accurately names for Will who he is and where he is. The priest is identifying for Will precisely where he is, the "whatness . . . [of] being itself"[45] that Percy believes is the only place where the wayfarer can join his fellow exiles in their home.

Will serves as an "interpreter" (*LG*, 404) during the baptism, somehow able to hear Jamie's barely audible responses to the priest's instructions and inquiries, and thereby able to function as a "mediat[or]" for "God's salvific love."[46] In this role, Will witnesses a healing love that he has never known, a love that can unite him with others under God. His deafness and aphasia mysteriously healed, Will successfully interprets Jamie's faintly whispered words for Father Boomer as the priest struggles to perform the baptismal rituals—"not knowing how he knew" (*LG*, 406) what Jamie was saying. Will's consciousness that he is knowing and acting in his communication with Jamie and the priest in a way that his solitary, objective intellect cannot understand may indicate that he is vaguely aware of participating in the supra-rational intersubjective communication that makes it possible for people, even total strangers, to love and become one with others.[47] When Will sees the priest hold Jamie's hand while he dies and assure the boy that he will not "let [him] go," he sees a love that his own father could not extend to him. When Will was a few years younger than Jamie, he also begged his father, "Don't leave," but his father did not "say . . . anything" and headed for the attic and his twelve-guage (*LG*, 331).

Will's responses to Father Boomer and Sutter after Jamie's death illustrate that he may, in fact, have acquired a new capacity for the kind of intersubjectivity that makes Father Boomer's ability to love possible. He expresses genuine and unguarded affection for the priest when, after the death, he thanks him "twice" and "wrings" his hand "warmly" (*LG*, 406–7). Will's response to Father Boomer shows that he knows that they have just been united in a significant and meaningful experience, even if he cannot yet understand it. As Percy says, Will "misses the import" of the baptism (*Con*, 14). But he knows something important has happened and is not reluctant to turn to another for an explanation. When he leaves the hospital room and finds Sutter in the streets of Santa Fe, Will calls out to him, "don't leave me," "I need you." This cry demonstrates again that Will recognizes that his solitary thinking is not adequate to discover the significances of the mystery that he has just witnessed, that he can only make the discovery with another. And Will may also be concerned with what Sutter needs. Because Sutter has told him earlier at the ranch about his suicide plans, Will knows that Sutter is going to return to Rancho la Merced and kill himself.[48] Will may be feeling the responsibility he has to help this man who is so in despair that he wants to die. As Sutter drives away, Will begs him repeatedly to "wait" (*LG*, 409).

When Sutter's Edsel pauses, Will is suddenly filled with a great "strength" that enables him to run toward the car "with great joyous ten-foot antelope bounds" (*LG*, 409), his spastic knee apparently no longer a bother. Will has been transformed at this moment into a vigorous and healthy person filled with an energy and hope, even if he cannot yet identify the source of his healing. Percy's allusion in this final image of Will's "leaping" may be to Isaiah 35.5–6, in which the prophet says that when God delivers Israel from bondage, "the lame [will] leap like a stag," the blind, deaf, and dumb will be cured, and the desert will bloom. Isaiah's prophecy is also traditionally interpreted as a prophecy of the Incarnation, when God's love descends into the human world to cure the otherwise hopelessly deaf, dumb, blind, and lame. Perhaps Will has encountered this same mysterious healing power in the desert of New Mexico.

Will has acquired a new strength and joy in the sacramental world Father Boomer names for him and a new consciousness of some dimensions of human love besides the good feelings he has hoped Kitty and the Vaughts could provide for him. He now has the power and the will to act in the Fallen world with others and is not paralyzed by what an older Will Barrett in The Second Coming calls "the great suck of self" (*SC*, 18). He is no longer trapped in a painful and puzzling interior world where he searches for a secret life that is hidden from him. Instead, Will is enthusiastically leaping into an open future with a "final question" (*LG*, 409) he hopes can be answered by another, assuming the psychic posture of a sovereign and volitional wayfarer whose search is for more than his thinking and his pursuit of need satisfactions can provide. With the help of Jamie, Sutter, Val Vaught, and Father Boomer, Will has remembered that the world Romano Guardini foresees in Percy's epigraph to *The Last Gentleman* is where he lives—a world "filled with animosity and danger" that can eventually become, however, an "open and clean" place where "precious . . . love . . . flows from one lonely person to another." If he has not yet discovered this clean place, Will has at least discovered how to wait (*LG*, 409).

4

The Second Coming: Signs of a Giver?

Tell me something, Father. Do you believe that Christ will come again
and that in fact there are certain unmistakable signs of his coming in
these very times?" (*SC*, 410–11)

The Second Coming (1980) is a sequel to *The Last Gentleman* in which Will
Barrett, after a successful career as a Wall Street lawyer and a marriage to
an immensely wealthy New York heiress, has at middle age retired to
Linwood, an exclusive resort community nestled among the tranquil "au-
tumn-postcard Carolina mountains" of North Carolina.[1] In the idyllic
Smokies, Will lives in a mansion on a ten-thousand-acre estate, spends his
days on the "immaculate emerald fairways" (*SC*, 7) of the Linwood Country Club with his many admiring friends and neighbors, and drives down
weekly in his Mercedes 450 SEL to continue the charitable work that his
wife Marion initiated a few years ago at "the nursing home ... [her] money
had built" (*SC*, 142). After his troubled and dislocated wandering in the
South and in the New Mexico desert two decades earlier, Will has constructed an American Dream life. He has ceased to be the twenty-five-year-old
confused searcher depicted in *The Last Gentleman* and has become a retired
Harvard-educated attorney who, over the past two decades, has "engineered"
(*LG*, 41) his current lifestyle: "a fairly normal life, a fairly happy marriage, a
successful career, and a triumphant early retirement to enjoy the good things
of life" (*SC*, 208–9). In short, he has made himself into "a talented agree-
able wealthy man living in as pleasant an environment as one can imagine"
(*SC*, 16), a cultivated version of Chandler Vaught, Kitty's crass and
flambouyant Chevy-selling father in *The Last Gentleman*. Will's Edenic
life of leisure and wealth in the majestic landscape of western North Carolina mirrors Mr. Vaught's life in his "castle" on the links in Alabama.

But something has "gone wrong" (*SC*, 3, 5,17) in this self-constructed

97

Eden where all of Will's physical and social needs are satisfied by the consumptions and diversions of upper-middle-class America. He has spent the last twenty years trying to discover a satisfying and fulfilling life exclusively through the appropriation and mastery of the resources in his environment, both in the busy Northeast and in Linwood. Will is an example of Percy's "autonomous," "Immanent Self" (*LC*, 113) who, in seeking physical, social, intellectual, and psychological need-satisfaction in his transactions with the world, loses consciousness of who he is outside the role-playing that those transactions require. Will's placement of himself in the world as just such an Immanent self has resulted in the financial and social achievements he now enjoys. But this self-placement has also resulted in his current sense of dislocation, the feeling that he has "missed" his life, that it has "passed like a dream" (*SC*, 144) of "golf and good works" (*SC*, 165). He now feels so dislocated that the "world and life around him" seem "senseless and farcical," so "demented" that he has decided that "this [life] is not for me" (*SC*, 3–4), that he must escape the meaningless emptiness that his golfing routine at the country club implies. After achieving the "happy, useful life" (*LG*, 385) of work, marriage, and family that he sought at age twenty-five, Will is presently so "sucked" down into himself and dissatisfied with the fatuous trivialities of his days that he, like his father before him, regularly contemplates suicide. Will at the beginning of the novel stands at the edge of a "gorge" holding his father's Luger to his temple, so estranged from the world and himself by a lifetime of consumption and role-playing that he sees in the mirror of his Mercedes only "a shadowy stranger" (*SC*, 15) whose existence has no more substance or value than the lifeless reflection that stares back at him.

Will believes that his recent sense of dislocation and suicidal depression (*SC*, 3) may have their origins in the "love of death" (*SC*, 83) he has inherited from his father, a love that he has never been able fully to reject. In *The Last Gentleman*, Will stood before his childhood home to examine within his painful memories the gnostic, romantic despair that caused his father to choose death over what he defined as a lifeless life in Ithaca, Mississippi, with his dishonorable and ignorant neighbors. At the end of the novel, Will was determined to wait for something better (LG, 354) in life than his father's despair, and he was offered some clues to that better life in his exposure to the sacramental Christianity exhibited in the actions and words of Sister Val Vaught and Father Boomer. The desperate middle-aged Will now standing at the edge of the gorge is evidence that he did not wait long enough for signs that might direct him to a better way. Instead of waiting, Will returned from Santa Fe and persisted in his efforts to construct a happy and anxiety-free life separate from his father and his past. He continued to try to find "something different [not "better"] out there ... maybe even a kind of life" at Harvard Law School and in New York City. In these places so radically different from Delta Mississippi, Will hoped, with a decent wife and honourable work (*SC*, 83–84), to engineer by himself a life-giving alternative to the deadly self he had inherited. He trusted that in a posh Manhattan apartment and amid the city's sophisticated theaters, restaurants, and people he could discover a life and a home that his father had denied him.

Will now knows that his "little Yankee life" has failed him, and he wonders as he searches for the golf ball he has sliced out-of-bounds on the Linwood course, "what ... am I doing here?" (*SC*, 84–85) Where am I and who am I? Percy says Will "has finished his life and doesn't know what to do" (*MCon*, 19),[2] exhausted the possibilities for action and self-development in Kierkegaard's ethical sphere where the individual depends on his codes of conduct and decent lifestyle for happiness and fulfillment. Will realizes at this moment that his marriage and his twenty years of trying to be happy by "making money like everyone else" was just a futile attempt to escape from his father's "death dealing" (*SC*, 84–85), rather than a discovery of a new and better life. Since his retirement, he no longer has the honorable work he depended on for happiness, and depended on for an identity different from his father's. The happy family he created has also vanished; his wife Marion died six months ago and his daughter Leslie is marrying a Californian and moving out of his Linwood mansion. Without these professional and family roles, Will has become just another stereotypical, anonymous golfer on the pretty "pink-and-green golf links" (*SC*, 70). He tries to appear politely interested while acquaintances like Jimmy Rogers tell racist jokes during the game; he tries to look forward to the pleasant camaraderie at the clubhouse after the eighteenth hole.

Will's recognition of his "failed" life prompts him to search for an understanding of his predicament. And, as in *The Last Gentleman*, he believes that through his intellectual, analytical powers he can arrive at the truth about who he is and where he is. Will once again becomes the Cartesian, detached observer and theorizer who in *The Last Gentleman* sought the truth about life with his telescope and *Theory of Large Numbers*. He again relies solely on his daily observations of phenomena and his thinking about them to tell him about his home and his life there with others. His current conclusion is that he is living a "death-in-life" (*SC*, 147, 155, 169, 172, e.g.). At this point in his life, Will's *cogito* has informed him that he exists in an absurd place, in a "ludicrous predicament" among "maniacs" who perfectly exemplify the "assholedness of people in general" (*SC*, 220, 217). This markedly uncharitable and hopeless view of his entrapment in a meaningless

world with insane and mean-spirited people encourages him to define creation as a threatening experience where love and intersubjective communion
with others is impossible. It is a self-placement in the world that precludes
any recognition of the "grave predicament" (MB, 144) that Percy believes is
the common, shared condition of Fallen humankind. Will, in his Cartesian
objectivity and reliance on the competency of his knowing, psychically removes himself as a participant in an imperfect world where all are united in
their homeless exile from the mysterious source of creation, and where all
wait for a salvation that will transform what appears to be death into a life
beyond their knowing.

Will's confidence in his capacity to know what's wrong with the world
and himself is reinforced by his conviction that he has acquired the ability
lately to "remember everything" (SC,10, 14, 56, 59, 83, 125, e.g.), "even . . .
the future." Whereas his similar "remembering everything" near the end of
The Last Gentleman (LG, 374, 375, 379) functioned to direct his eyes outward to his home in the desert with Sutter, here it effects a self-enclosure
within his memory and cognition that impairs his ability to perceive his
existence in present time-space experience. Will now believes that he has
succeeded in drawing his "entire life" into his *cogito*, and that all his experience therefore "lay[s] before him, beginning, middle, and end," waiting for
him to subject it to his analyses and to expose its secrets. Will apparently
believes that he has acquired the "omniscience" (LG, 170, 214), the complete knowledge of the self and the world, that he yearned for and tried to
develop in his youth. In the clubhouse at Linwood Country Club, he muses
with self-satisfaction on the fact that his life is now as "plain" to him "as the
mural [on the wall above him] of Jack Nicklaus blasting out of the sand
trap" (SC, 91). He believes that the same detached, aesthetic eyes that glance
nonchalantly at a simple painting on a wall can see the absolute truth about
life. Unwittingly, his faith in this omniscient way of seeing only serves to
suck him more completely into himself and prevents his locating himself as
an incarnate participant with others out in a sacramental creation beyond
the immaterial interior world of his memory and thinking. He is cut off
from a consciousness of the Now that Heidegger believes is the authentic
experience of Dasein, the experiencing self.[3]

Although repeatedly reminding himself that he has at last located himself in "the present" (SC, 83, 144, 208), Will, ironically, spends most of his
time withdrawn from the here-and-now. His confidence in his omniscience
and total memory deceives him into believing that he has finally escaped
"some dark past he could not remember" and that he no longer "cast[s]
himself forward . . . to a future which did not exist" (SC, 144). Will, in
contrast to what he thinks, habitually explores his past and projects himself

into the future in an effort to discover a way to live in a present he finds intolerably meaningless and purposeless. Percy, in an a 1984 interview, defined "Will Barrett's problem" as an inability to discover "where" he is "*here* in the present." This is a common twentieth-century psychic deficiency, Percy argued, that inclines people like Will to languish in the "guilt of their past" and miserably "worry about the future" (*Con*, 305–6). Dislocated from their present phenomenal existence, they are, obviously, estranged from a consciousness of their authentic selves existing in flesh-and-blood actuality; they usually suffer from that self-enclosure in thought and feeling that marks interiorized selves like Will.

Much of *The Second Coming* is about Will's enclosure in his analyses of his past. Besides Will's contemplations of the past life he has missed with Marion in New York and in the mountains of North Carolina, he also turns inward to remember the terrible hunt with his father in the Georgia swamp outside Thomasville.[4] His memories of the hunt lead him to conclude that he is a helpless victim of the "love of death" that he has inherited from his father, that there is no escape from the past, that he is "together after all" (*SC*, 83, 85) with the suicidal and homicidal father and his twelve-year-old son who make their way through the swamp in Will's self-constructed interior narrative. Will's absorption in these memories blinds him to all other experience. He believes that after the hunt "everything else that had happened . . . was a non-event," "nothing else had ever happened to him" (*SC*, 60). He identifies himself as "one of you" (*SC*, 198), another suicidal Barrett, and defines the world, because of this self-identity, as simply a place to endure stoically its finally unbearable burden. His memories tell him that the entire world may be a dark wood where violence and death stalk the innocent in the guise of a father's love, that his individual experience at age twelve may be a metaphor for the general existential condition of all others in a world without love or redemption from suffering and death. Will wonders if it is not in fact true that the world is a frightening place where "short of violence all is in the end impotence" (*SC*, 198).

When Will is not sucked down into this self-defeating past and the despair it provokes, he is trying to discover some knowledge of the future that will guide him in his efforts to figure out how to live in a present life that he finds meaningless and "farcical." He has learned in his explorations of his past and in his analyses of his memories of his father that a noble response to such a death-in-life is suicide, but Will decides that there must be another answer. As he did in *The Last Gentleman*, he again in this novel seeks with his scientific (*SC*, 216) intellect a "great secret of life" (*LG*, 10) that he trusts will reveal to him some ultimate existential truth and thereby show him what to do and how to live in the future. Percy maintains that this older Will is still "an absolute seeker . . . [who] insists on finding what he calls the truth; and it's that or death" (*Con*, 184).

Just as his belief in his omniscience encloses him in his thoughts and feelings about the past, so his theorizing about what to do about the future causes his withdrawal from his present phenomenal reality, this time into truly deranged fantasies in which he imagines himself becoming another Jacob (*SC*, 223), a modern secular Old Testament prophet. Convinced that he has discovered in his present existence "the total failure, fecklessness, and assholedness of people in general" (*SC*, 217), he demands that God explain to him the failure of His creation. If there is a God, he reasons, surely that God will personally disclose to him the destiny of the ineffectual and hopeless human lives that populate this dismal world where he is doomed to exist. Utterly confident in the powers of his omniscient intellect, Will plans a life-or-death search (*SC*, 220) for the final answers about that destiny. He plans a "scientific experiment" (*SC*, 222) in Lost Cove cave that he believes will show him whether or not there is any hope for a redemption from the disgusting nothingness implied by the anal imagery he uses to describe humanity. His science, he is certain, will bring God out in the open if He exists. Will foresees the possibility of his emerging from the cave with an ultimate scientific truth and proclaiming it to the benighted masses waiting for his prophetic good news.

When he is planning his descent into Lost Cove cave to make his search, Will envisions himself a heroic Jacob (Genesis 32.25–32) who will "rassle" with God in the "bowels" of the cave for an answer (*SC*, 223, 246) to his scientific inquiry. Percy calls Will "a good Southern Episcopal Jacob—the Jacob who wanted to force God to show himself" (Con, 189). Will wants to subdue God, force Him to cough up the final secrets. Is there a God of love and salvation working in human history who can conquer life's dark reality? Will is determined to make Him show his face. Will tells Sutter in the letter he writes him describing his experiment in the cave that he plans with his search to solve the so-called mystery of life by forcing God to give a sign clearly and unambiguously of His existence (*SC*, 222–23).

Ironically pursuing the kind of solitary "personal encounter" with God that he rejects in the easy, feel-good spirituality of his daughter Leslie's "born-again" (*SC*, 184) fundamentalist Christianity, Will plans to find out for sure if there is a transcendent power of love that will save him from a life that has driven him to suicidal despair. Will recognized at age twenty-five that he did not know the meaning of the words "love" and "salvation" (*LG*, 104, 212), and he still does not know their meanings. He admits in his letter to Sutter about his plans in Lost Cove cave that when he tries to understand his "shutoffness" from his daughter he realizes that he does not "really know what 'love' means" (*SC*, 227). Words like "love" and "salvation" require the language-user to entertain the possibility that there may be meanings for these words beyond the capacities of his thought. Perhaps Will feels impotent and therefore uncomfortable in the presence of these words because he assumes that there are no meanings beyond his cognition. Like Kierkegaard's objective thinker, Will must reduce life to what is intelligible to his intellect, suck all knowledge of all human experience for all time into the interior world of his scientific knowing.[5] As he assumed in *The Last Gentleman* that he "had to know everything before he could do anything" (*LG*, 4), so Will now assumes that it is possible for him to know everything.

Humorously, Will is so abstracted, so absorbed in his experiment, that he fails to reflect on the reality that other prophets, and even millions of Christians less devoted to a religious search, have already discovered the signs of God he is determined to find beneath the golf course. They have found these signs of a transcendent, redemptive life among the detritus of a human world that Will believes is built by feckless "assholes." Will does not recognize the signs that appear daily in the messy and imperfect incarnate natural world around him, signs of an infinite life and "home" transcendent of his and the world's "Last Days" (*SC*, 229) and beyond his death-in-life in Linwood. These signs are "up here" (*SC*, 378) in the incarnate world with others, not hidden in a dark cave and revealed privately to the solitary gnostic quester. And, because Will has never succeeded in his efforts "to believe in the Christian God" (*SC*, 84), he is incapable of recognizing that God has already dramatically sent a sign of love and redemption in the Incarnation. Religious faith of any kind would require his recognition that there is an infinite reality beyond his knowing and therefore require his surrendering the absolute epistemological competency he grants his intellect.

Percy explained in a 1981 interview that in *The Second Coming* he was primarily "interested in what was the matter with" Will Barrett (*Con*, 236). In the novel, Will discovers that "something might be wrong" (*SC*, 3) with the self he has become and the world he inhabits and therefore tries to find an alternative self and home beyond the Linwood Country Club golf course. His progress toward a new home begins early in the novel when he steps "out-of-bounds" (*SC*, 51) on the golf course. There in the glade (*SC*, 52) with Allie—the strange young woman he finds living there—he begins to recover not only the ball he has sliced into the woods but also begins his wayfaring toward a consciousness of himself as a homeless exile with others in a sacramental world. Unlike the symbolically enclosed landscape of the golf course, this is an incarnational world that opens up infinitely to the questing self as he makes his way to his true home "across the seas" (*MB*, 148). Percy says that in the novel Will symbolically steps "out of bounds" into a place beyond his "ordinary life" and eventually finds a "grace" (*Con*, 307) with Allie that promises the possibility of a new life. Later, when Will falls out of Lost Cove cave into Allie's greenhouse, he falls, Percy says, "into sacramental reality" (*MCon*, 50, 147).

Will's escapes from the symbolic self-enclosures of the golf course and cave initiate a series of ecapes from the living death created by the empty pleasures and need satisfactions of his wealthy immanent existence. After he recuperates from his trials in the cave, he returns to his Mercedes parked in the country club parking lot and falls asleep in the back seat of this icon of American success. Kitty, no longer the sweet Chi O cheerleader she was in *The Last Gentleman*, appears the next morning to invite him to join her in her villa at "Dun Romin'" (*SC*, 322), a place that might tempt Will to indeed stop roaming and settle down once again in the immanent comforts that Linwood has to offer. But Will manages to escape the comfort of the Mercedes and Kitty's villa. Leaving behind the country club and Kitty, Will returns to his mansion only to find it empty; he realizes Leslie "has moved . . . [him] out" (*SC*, 329–30). Now literally homeless, Will leaves the opulent home he has built after his lifetime of success and hits the highway, eventually catching a bus and heading toward the Georgia swamp and the only home he believes is available to him (*SC*, 334–39). On the bus, Will, in a sudden moment of insight, realizes that his father's home will not become his and demands that the bus driver stop the bus and let him off. Thrown from the moving bus by the irate driver, Will falls helplessly to the roadside and is knocked unconscious. He awakes only to find himself back in the clutches of Leslie and his Linwood golfing partners. "Comfortably installed in St. Mark's Convalescent Home" (*SC*, 349) by his family and friends, Will now faces a true death-in-life watching *Kojak* and playing with the toy trains with which a select group of patients are allowed to amuse themselves (*SC*, 354–59). *The Second Coming* ends after Will escapes from St. Mark's and begins his homeless wayfaring again, this time with Allie.

Percy's use of sacramental imagery and symbolism emphasizes Will's incipient escape from the artificial, enclosed gardens of Linwood and from the deadly interior worlds of his *cogito* where he sees himself waiting for the Last Days or committing suicide in Georgia.[6] In the closing scenes of the novel, Will is planning to seek the "possibilities" (*SC*, 370, 376, 378) for a life that he now believes exists only "up here" in the sacramental "scarlet and gold" (*SC*, 7, 25, 55) mountains that surround him. His opening to a consciousness of a world outside his thinking and outside the financial and social success he has counted on for self-satisfaction and self-fulfillment is implied by his determination to pursue a life of love with Allie in the open vastness of the beautiful Appalachian forests and, perhaps, on the Georgia island Allie has inherited. He is no longer devising an escape from a demented world full of "assholes," but planning to "incorporate" (*SC*, 396) with his friends from St. Mark's and others in order to build a new home in the ruins. Although he cannot yet read the signs—insisting to Father Weatherbee in the final scene that he is "not a believer" (*SC*, 409)—Will is beginning to look out to the sacramental world and into the faces of his fellow incarnate wayfarers, and he is discovering in them a "secret joy" (*SC*, 411) that gives him the energy and hope necessary for his continuing search.

FIXED, UNSEEING EYES

Until Will begins at the end of *The Second Coming* to turn his gaze toward the Appalachian wilderness around him and to the open seas that surround Allie's Georgia island, he spends most of his time wandering with "unseeing" (*SC*, 82) eyes through sacramental landscapes where he is unable to read the signs that will tell him that his home is in the here-and-now phenomenal world with his fellow wayfarers. He cannot determine the significances of the signs in incarnate creation and therefore cannot find meaning in a present life that recently seems to him a senseless (*SC*, 3–4) routine of diversions and achievements. Isolated and alone on the golf course, in his Mercedes, or at his home on his ten-thousand-acre mountain, Will exemplifies Percy's immanent self caught in "the iron grip of immanence" and lost in an "endless round of work, diversions, and consumption" (*LC*, 122). Closed off by his absorption in his daily activities from an awareness that he is a participant with others in a God-created existence larger than the "prison cell" (*SC*, 81) of his daily activities, Will is habitually abstracted and displaced from his genuine self.

In an effort to ameliorate this sense of dislocation he cannot explain, Will is inclined to place himself in past and future worlds that he constructs within his mind and to analyze these interior experiences in order to arrive at some truths about his predicament. He believes that his recently acquired capacity to remember everything enriches and even completes this inner world, but, ironically, this memory only provides him with a mode of perception that radically diminishes his cognitive abilities. This memory creates a consciousness that causes everything he perceives in his daily life to "remind him of something else" (*SC*, 10), thereby obscuring present reality from his sight. Instead of granting omniscience, this memory causes the actualities of his present perceptions to be replaced with something else. That something is a conglomeration of memory fragments, thoughts and feelings about them, musings about their possible relationships with present and future bits of sensory data. This newly acquired memory so displaces Will from a consciousness of who and where he is that he feels "he might shoot himself" (*SC*, 4).

In the opening scenes on the Linwood golf course, Percy illustrates Will's displacement from immediate time-space experience and blindness to the sacramental signs in it. These are signs that could reveal to him a way to move beyond the consciousness that now encloses him in a self-constructed world where he is a potential victim of his own suicidal depression. In the opening scene, Will, suffering from the epilepsy that Dr. Ellis at Duke later diagnoses, falls into a bunker while playing one of his routine golf games with his wealthy, successful friends. Symbolically ignoring "the earth" that he is "pressed" helplessly against, the incarnational home for all humankind, Will notices a "strange bird" fly past and a distant "cumulus cloud" that appears to "turn purple and gold at the bottom" while "the top boil[s] up higher and higher like the cloud over Hiroshima" (*SC*, 3). Similar to the way the self-transcendent younger Will at the beginning of *The Last Gentleman* lies thinking in Central Park and spots the peregrine falcon (*LG*, 3,5), Will here sees neither the bird in the sky nor the earth beneath him as signs of where he is as a flesh-spirit wayfarer between earth and heaven (*MB*, 113). Will might reflect on the regal, Christological purple and gold of the cloud and analogically associate the immense and spectacular form above him with the mysterious infinite power that can raise him and his fellow golfers from their helpless entrapment in the empty need satisfactions that they depend on for their happiness. But the cloud reminds him only of Hiroshima, a place of violence and death emblematic of the "Century of the Love of Death" (*SC*, 311) that Will feels encloses him and all creation in a senseless void. The bird and cloud are for him ominous signs of death and strangeness and nothing else. Unconscious of their possible sacramental significance, Will withdraws after his observations in the bunker into the abstractions of his interior world where he analyzes what's wrong with him and the place of death where he lives (*SC*, 5–6).

Again on the immaculate, artificially Edenic golf course of Linwood Country Club, this time on the seventeenth fairway, Will sees another sign he cannot read and illustrates once more his inclination to withdaw from the sacramental significances of time-space experience. Before he drives three hundred yards, he looks down toward the green at a "low ridge of red maples which in the sunlight looked like a tongue of fire searing the cool green fairway" (*SC*, 6–7). The red trees rising up over the golf course where these men casually live their easy lives reminds the Christian with a sacramental consciousness of the Crucifixion and Resurrection. The trees are signs of the fierce and beautiful transcendent power that will eventually enter the perfect life Will feels is a living death and "sear" it in a baptism of apocalyptic fire and blood and life. The allusion to the Pentecostal "tongues as of fire" that brought the "holy Spirit" to Peter and the other Apostles (Acts 2.3) clearly associates the world that Will sees on the horizon with the signs that the disciples believed heralded the Second Coming of Christ.

But "the bright October sunlight went dark as an eclipse [and] the scene before Will's eyes seemed to change." Instead of seeing at this moment the sacramental significance of the blazing maples and the "scarlet and gold hillsides" that hold him and his friends in their imperial embrace, Will "see[s] something else" within the private, solitary world of his memories, desires, and self-analyses. He is transported by his thoughts from this place and time to a weedy "parcel of leftover land" by the railroad tracks in his Mississippi hometown. In his memory of his adolescence, Will sees himself helplessly collapsing in this patch of land beside the utility company's tiny "fenced and locked enclosure" (*SC*, 7–8). This detail of his fantasy landscape suggests the claustrophobic self-enclosure that now afflicts Will as he returns to his adolescent self and to his hopeless love for the brilliant and beautiful Ethel Rosenblum. It was his desperate and overwhelming desire for Ethel that caused his collapse by the locked enclosure. In his memory, Will apotheosizes cheerleader Ethel into a goddess whose "beauty and grace" he might have enjoyed, an emblem of a life with the same "unity, symmetry, beauty" that she was able to create at the high school blackboard out of the most "ungainly" and "ugly" algebraic equations. Projecting himself and Ethel into a hypothetical life after high school, he fantasizes about the place that they might have found together and the person he would have become "had he not succeeded" and become the man he now is. Perhaps, he daydreams wistfully, he might have become as "content as [a] cat" (*SC*, 10). Finally, connecting his memories of losing the love of this Jewish girl with the entire history of the Jews, Will is led into theorizing about the departure of the Jews from North Carolina as a "sign of God's plan working out" (*SC*, 13). He is by his contemplation of this far-fetched, ridiculous theory absurdly dislocated from a sacramental consciousness of the red maples waiting for him a few yards down the fairway.

Alone in his luxurious Mercedes as he drives toward his estate, symbolically "sunk in the fragrant German leather," Will is just as self-enclosed and oblivious to the signs in sacramental creation as he was on the country-club golf course with his friends. Driving "along a gorge" amid the "pretty reds and yellows of the countryside"—on his way home from another Sunday morning on the links—Will has one of his "spells," and the "brilliant sunlight grew dim." Half-blind to the sacramental beauty out in the gorge beyond him, barely able to see the "dark bird" winging its way through the forest's spectacle of color and light, Will tries to tune his radio to "a nonreligious program." Unconsciously, he is closing his ears as well as his eyes to the good news that is penetrating his perfect German enclosure and proclaiming itself continuously to his eyes and ears. Instead of listening and watching for what is beyond the Mercedes, Will stops immediately at a scenic overlook and chooses to look at himself, to examine his own image contained in the outside mirror of the Mercedes. He finds within the mirror's frame a tiny suicidal stranger, "a self sucking everything into itself" like Count Dracula (SC, 15–17). Will is ignoring the messages in the gorge and from the radio and looking within to find only that "nought of the self" that has tried to create a life and "inform" itself through the "possession" and "consumption of goods" (MB, 284).

At home in his five-car garage a few minutes later, Will is again symbolically enclosed in the home and life that his success has ironically provided for him. And he is psychically enclosed in his self-analyses and theorizing about the nature of the human predicament. Still toying with his Luger and thoughts of suicide, Will has an insight that he considers a "revelation" while he is contemplating the "cat nodding in the sunlight" beneath his wife's Rolls-Royce. It occurs to him that the cat, unlike modern man who is "two percent himself," is "a hundred percent" itself because it is content when its needs are satisfied. As if yearning to be a cat, as he did earlier in his rhapsodizing about his possible life with Ethel Rosenblum, Will wonders how one can "ever hope to be a fat cat dozing in the sun" and thereby escape whatever place they have chosen in their lives to occupy "uneasily." Will wants to place himself in the world as a need-satisfying organism in its environment and become by that self-placement as anxiety-free and as unconscious as the cat hidden beneath the Rolls. He feels his revelation is as brilliant as Einstein's theories (SC, 17–18).

Will's restricted, interiorized vision of himself and the world in the garage is suggested after a startling gunshot sends him diving under the Rolls and the cat flees in terror. Although Will feels at this moment in the garage that he is restored to his 100 percent authentic self, he is obviously and utterly dislocated from the here-and-now reality of himself and phenomena by his profound philosophizing about the relationship between the cat and mankind's predicament. Continuing this self-dislocation, Will imagines that he is a soldier looking out from beneath the Rolls. From the perspective of this imagined self, he sees the sacramental "sunny woods" beyond the garage as through the narrow "slot" of a "pillbox" (*SC*, 18). Will is in this scene unconscious of who he is and where he is, lost in fantasies that reduce his vision to a "slot-shaped" glimpse out into a world that he imagines is a battlefield. Ironically, like Percy's "Immanent" self in *Lost in the Cosmos*, he welcomes this sudden danger and threat from a violent and dangerous world because it releases him from the meaninglessness and boredom of his daily life of mere consumption and need satisfaction (*LC*, 122).

Although Will thinks he has finally, because of the gunshot, become "himself for the first time in years," he is deluded about his self-discovery and his restored vision. Will is in this scene seeking the same kind of aesthetic, Cartesian displacement of himself from himself and from his existence with others in the created world that he sought in *The Last Gentleman*. Then he wanted to wander about in the world and "see without being seen" (*LG*, 162), and now he again relishes from his pillbox enclave the "safe corner where . . . [he] can look out without being seen" (*SC*, 20). Here, as he looks out, no more himself than the invisible soldier he imagines himself to be, the only thing Will sees besides the tiny slot of sky and trees is the tip of Ewell McBee's "red cap disappearing into the pines." Will knows that the sniper is Ewell, a native of the area that he has known since childhood, and that Ewell is simply poaching deer on his estate. But Will quickly ignores this common-sense view of his situation and launches into an extended interior self-debate about whether or not Ewell is the "enemy" or whether he is just an "example" of how the "crazy Jutes and Celts and Angles and redneck Saxons" are replacing the Jews that are leaving North Carolina (*SC*, 19–20).

This view of Ewell that Will acquires within the enclosed world of his thinking and theorizing is no more accurate nor complete than his view of the "arc of sunlit pines" he sees from beneath the Rolls-Royce. Will concludes that Ewell is not the enemy who causes the death-in-life that has converted his successful life into suicidal despair. Such an answer is too simple, he thinks (*SC*, 23). But, in fact, Ewell may be the enemy responsible for what is wrong with Will in ways Will's thinking fails to show him. The imagery in this scene suggests that Ewell is a Jungian enemy shadow self that Will has never sufficiently acknowledged, an interior enemy who accounts for the living death that has already defeated Will's efforts to achieve the "happy, useful life" (*LG*, 385) he has tried to construct in the last twenty years.[7] Ewell is a sort of demonic, visceral double of the polite and genteel Will who has lived a life trying to do what he believed he was "supposed to do" (*Con*, 306). Will remembers that Ewell is "exactly his own age" and that when they were children and played together during the summers when he and his parents vacationed in Linwood, Ewell would, like a "heavy incubus," "throw him down and sit on him" (*SC*, 21) when they wrestled.

Ewell is an incubus who is identified in the novel with Will's father and Will's childhood past, the sources, Will believes, of the "love of death" that now threatens to defeat him in suicide.[8] Ewell, a caddy for Will's father during the Barrett family's summers in Linwood, followed Mr. Barrett around the Linwood golf course in a relationship that echoes Will's memories of his following his father into the swamp in Thomasville. Ewell, however, unlike Will, was an admiring follower of the deadly Ed Barrett, a man he regards as "the smartest man I ever knew" (*SC*, 203). Now, thirty years later, Ewell, poaching in the woods on Will's estate, is himself a potential agent of death. Ewell is another hunter in Will's life who threatens his happiness in his Linwood home the way Will's father destroyed the possibilities for love and life in his childhood home. Ewell, like Will's father, is a menacing, solitary killer roaming the dark forest who may at any moment enter Will's tranquil home and defeat him.

Both Ewell and Will's father are also embodiments of a self-love that isolates and alienates them from others, a deadly love that Will believes may hold him in its grip. In Ed Barrett, this is the "self-love of death" that Will is convinced he has inherited—the autoerotic solipsism that urged his father toward "the double Winchester come of taking oneself into oneself, the cold-steel extension of oneself into the mouth" (*SC*, 172). This is also the kind of "self-love" exhibited by the adolescent Ewell that Will remembers sitting on him. Will, in his memories, associates Ewell with a similar kind of autoerotic love, exemplified by the isolated self-satisfactions of adolescent masturbation. Ewell taught Will how to "jerk off" (*SC*, 22), just as Will's father taught him another kind of lifeless, self-absorbed psychic self-love.

Associated with the death that haunts Will in his memories of his adolescence and his father, Ewell is also a symbolic embodiment of the death that Will's successful, but "demented" life in New York and Linwood has yielded. Ewell is a "redneck" version of the wealthy adult Will who passes his days puttering about the Linwood community. Ewell, like Will, has trusted in financial achievement, a life of "making money like everyone else" (*SC*, 83), to bring him happiness. Ewell has also "c[o]me up in the world," now owning several Texaco, Exxon, and Conoco stations, a movie theater, and a videotape business. He and Will are both Rotarians and eat together regularly at the local Holiday Inn. Whereas this life of need satisfaction has made Will feel like a half-alive Count Dracula, Ewell has, ironically, become the contented "fat cat dozing in the sun" that Will a few minutes earlier in the garage envied.

Will's experiences on the country club links on Monday, the next day after these "revelations" at the golf course and in his garage, show that his vision has not improved, that he still cannot accurately recognize the sacramental signs around him nor the signs of the enemy in himself that closes him off from a consciousness of incarnate present reality. Back to one of his routine games with Lewis Peckham, Jimmy Rogers, and Vance Battle, Will continues to slice out-of-bounds, fortuitously this time into a pristine "glade in a pine forest" (*SC*, 51–52). When Will steps through the fence that separates the glade from the golf course to retrieve his ball, his country club life and his fun-loving, successful acquaintances are "blotted out" (*SC*, 58). Will for the first time sees Allie and her greenhouse, sacramental symbols of a love and a life that exist just beyond his view and that can redeem him from the death-in-life he has located on his customary side of the fence. Percy says that Allie is totally immersed in the present "ordinary things" of the "sacramental" world and that the greenhouse is a symbol of "rebirth or new life" (*MCon*, 50). But Will cannot read these sacramental signs and returns to the golf course.

Also in the glade Will sees Lost Cove cave for the first time, the place that he will soon identify as an alternative to the sacramental world around him, the solitary place of death into which he will choose to "disappear" (*SC*, 241) in an effort to discover signs of a life he believes is not available in the world "up here." And, within the memory that he now considers omniscient in scope, Will sees while in the glade the dark Georgia swamp where he hunted quail with his father thirty years earlier, another interior place of death into which Will disappears in order to search for signs of who he is and where he is.[9] Both the actual cave and the swamp of his memory are places that Will must escape before he will be able to join Allie at her home in the sacramental glade.

A few holes before Will's encounter with Allie, Lewis Peckham accompanies Will through the fence in order to show him the entrance to Lost Cove cave. Will's response illustrates his blindness to the sacramental signs in creation. Lewis directs Will "toward a flaming sassafras" with "red three-fingered leaves" that has just brilliantly "turned flourescent" in "a ray of sunlight." Lewis asks Will if he "notice[s] anything unusual about . . . [the] tree," and, even amid this spectacular Christological show of color, light, and life a few inches from his face, Will repeatedly answers no—he sees "nothing" (*SC*, 57). Will is incapable of seeing these incarnate signs before him, but he does "remember every detail" (*SC*, 57, 58) of the interior of the cave and the stories he has heard about it. As if preferring these precise memories over the reality in front of him, Will retires into his memory to reflect on the fossilized tiger caged in the stalagmites and stalactites below and to recall tales about the Confederate powder works that were hidden in the cave over a century ago (*SC*, 58). Will ignores the beauty and life (and friend Lewis) before him in the glade and descends into the solitary cave of his thinking. Will reflects on the signs of past death and violence that he believes are hidden in the cave beneath the pine forest and golf course.

The sassafras, the cave, the woods, the fence, the Hopkinsian "dagger-winged falcon" (*SC*, 81) he sees drop into the pine forest—the phenomenal "now" (*SC*, 58, 70) in the glade—vanish from Will's sight because his new omniscient memory causes him to see every present time-space sensory experience as a "sign of something else" (*SC*, 59). The signs here function to transport him to another place and to another self. In his memory, Will becomes again the twelve-year-old son of Ed Barrett in the ominous "fog" and among the "lopsided scrub oak[s] . . . [and] dead leaves" of the Thomasville swamp. Assuming that his memory of the hunt is absolutely accurate and complete, Will explores the significance of the signs he finds in this self-constructed, immaterial landscape and concludes that it was on the hunt that he discovered his father's "secret love of death." He believes, after additional analyses of these signs, that there is "no escaping" this "secret love" (*SC*, 83, 85) and that all "mystery" has been eliminated by his discovery of this truth. Will believes that in the Conradian "heart of darkness" (*SC*, 63) of the swamp he "contracted into the small core" (*SC*, 67, 68) of himself and that since that time he has known that there is nothing (*SC*, 60) outside the confined self that occupies that core.

When Will returns from the swamp and his past to "now" and to the out-of-bounds glade beside the golf course, he encounters in this living moment the sacramental gift that can release him from that small core. He sees a figure in the twilight dark of the pine forest behind a "single poplar which caught the sun." She is surrounded by "pale gold," "dappled leaves" and stands in the "cone of sunlight" created by the poplar (*SC*, 59, 82–83). As he approaches this tree of light and precious gold, Will sees the sacramental home of this strange person. It "blaze[s]" up in front of him so brilliantly that he shades his eyes and steps "into the shade of the pines" so he can see it clearly. "As big as an ark" and equipped with a "copper hood" that "shade[s] the front door like a cathedral porch" (*SC*, 85–86), the greenhouse is an obvious symbol of the redemptive divine life available in the dark forest where Will is now wandering. Noah and his descendants, because of the ark God provided, were granted the hope and life promised and delivered in the Incarnation. The cathedrals of the world are the homes for the Church that continues to provide for all Noah's children the sacraments that signify that Incarnation and its hope and life.

Will approaches Allie at the poplar with a "gaze . . . fixed . . . [but]

unseeing," lost in his memories of "everything his father said and did" (*SC*, 82–83) and therefore oblivious to the sacramental significances in this dim forest. He does not know where he is. After talking with Allie a few minutes in this beautiful place, Will reveals that he attaches no particular meaning either to the place or to her. He decides that this strange-talking girl is just another carefree, irresponsible hippie who is "on something," another sign of the deteriorating modern society that he and his gnostic father "won't have" (*SC*, 90). Will walks away from her, out of the glade, and back to his death-in-life at the country club, convinced after his memory and analyses of the hunt with his father that he has discovered in his past the final truth about himself and the world. He now believes that he knows "what . . . to do" (*SC*, 91, 92) back in his life in the "demented" world of Linwood.

FINDING A PLACE

After these brief, unseeing glimpses of the sacramental landscapes beyond the golf course and his mansion, Will returns temporarily to the daily routine he has lived for the last three years at Linwood and to his memories of his failed life with his family there. He resumes his weekly visits (*SC*, 142) with the elderly patients at St. Mark's and returns to memories of the roles he has played in his marriage with Marion. While at the nursing home, he recalls being recruited as a pallbearer for the endless funerals Marion loved to attend and dining in the Holiday Inns she loved to frequent after the funerals (*SC*, 144, 151). Will, in these memories, sees himself as Marion's amiable and obliging servant who pushed her wheelchair down the aisles of the nursing home where she did her good works and down the aisles of the A&P's where she shopped for pizzas and cream pies—her pleasant attendant in her life of "sanctity and gluttony" that ended when she finally drowned in her own "ocherous fat" (*SC*, 182–83).

At his mansion home later in the day, Will finds himself in another place that reminds him of his past and his current alienation from the Linwood world where he has tried to construct his life. When he arrives there after his visit to St. Mark's, he discovers that Leslie and his future in-laws have gathered with several of his neighbors and friends—including Kitty, his fiancée twenty years ago, and her husband Walter. Perhaps because these people who have gathered in his home remind him of the past he now feels defines him, the "demented" present that sucks him into its nothingness, and his hopeless future, Will decides for certain that his father's gnostic despair and suicide are appropriate responses to his own life. As he listens to the inane chatter of his guests, Will, in an interior dialogue with his father, tells him, "You win" (SC, 188, 198).

It is only after his "Great Discovery" (SC, 211) later in the day, once more in his garage with Ewell McBee, that Will sees the possibility of "another way" (SC, 153) besides his father's suicide. After this discovery, Will assumes the role of objective, scientific "see-er" (LG, 37) and becomes the detached searcher that he imagined himself to be twenty years earlier in The Last Gentleman. He climbs the stairs to his upstairs bedroom to plan an "ultimate scientific experiment" (SC, 216) that he believes will tell him for sure whether or not there is a transcendent life beyond his knowing that can defeat the death his father embraced and the life-in-death he has lived in Linwood. This new scientific, Cartesian way, unfortunately, will lead him further into the enclosure of his memories, theorizing, and abstractions and further away from a consciousness of himself as an incarnate being existing in the here-and-now world. It is a way that leads him away from the actual and sacramental world altogether and into Lost Cove cave for a sign of God's existence (SC, 223).

Prior to his Great Discovery in the garage and his scientific plan, Will is tempted by his guests to adopt other ways of seeing and other ideas about what to do in his life. While he is upstairs alone in his bedroom, lost in his reflections on his father's love of death and suicide, Lewis Peckham, a golfing friend, arrives at his bedroom door. Will has taken his father's Greener shotgun from the closet and is "sight[ing] at the windows through the barrels" as the "white light from the cloud ... spin[s] down the mirrored bore" (SC, 169). The deadly gun barrels provide Will with a narrow way of seeing and enclose the light and life beyond the windowsill the way his scientific telescope restricted his vision of the landscapes that surrounded him in The Last Gentleman. Lewis—a romantic who writes poetry, raises goats, and listens to Beethoven—offers Will another way of seeing, albeit an equally narrow and self-enclosed one. A modern version of the "goatherd-poet" (SC, 176) of Greek pastoral idylls, Lewis suggests that Will join him in the pristine alpine meadows out at his farm for the aesthetic joys of music and verse. He wants Will to join him on the angst-ridden "lonely road" where those who are aesthetically enlightened must heroically make their journey through life. He believes that he and Will are among "the one-eyed in the land of the blind" (SC, 175), among those rare, clear-seeing elect whose "one-eyed," aesthetic way of seeing can reveal to them a beautiful private world others cannot see with both eyes open.

Kitty suggests to Will that he consider a less cerebral view of himself and his future, appealing to those bestial carnal desires that tormented him in The Last Gentleman when he tried to be an honorable Southern gentleman with the often sexually aggressive young Kitty (*LG*, 167–68). Whereas Lewis would have Will choose self-enclosure in his pleasant aesthetic sensations, Kitty suggests he choose his bestial sensations. She reminds him of their past romantic relationship, lets him know that she is once again available, and convinces him for a moment that he could find himself not in self-analyses, Beethoven, or in a gun barrel, but "in her" (*SC*, 199). As Will talks with her in the sun parlor, he feels that "the room was closed up in a cloud" (*SC*, 189); the sacramental "scarlet oak" in the gorge beyond the windows begins to grow "dimmer"(*SC*, 163, 189). These images illustrate how she causes Will to feel removed from the phenomenal world outside his desires, how his consciousness of the world beyond the room is dimmed by her flirtatious words and touches. His vision of the gorge is progressively eclipsed as his focus narrows on the sexual needs she stimulates within him. Kitty awakens in him a memory of those bestial passions that he has forgotten, and he is tempted by her into believing that what he wants is not a solution to the "mystery of life" (*SC*, 222) but "Kitty's ass." At the moment, he simply wants "to fuck her" (*SC*, 199), and all that he sees out the window fades from his sight.

Later, on his way from his bedroom to rendezvous with Kitty in the "summerhouse," Will has one of his epileptic spells and falls down the dark stairwell and into his garage (*SC*, 199–200). Ewell McBee unexpectedly appears in the garage to tempt Will with a third way into his future and a third suggestion about what he should do. Ewell proposes that Will join him at his villa that night for a party with Cheryl Lee, "a little armful of heaven" from Chapel Hill (and "as smart as she can be") who aspires to be a concert violinist but who is now starring in Ewell's latest "erotic movie" just "for the money" (*SC*, 202). Cheryl, combination musician and porn star, is a symbol of the "musical-erotic" that Kierkegaard designates as the "highest state of the aesthetic sphere" (*Con*, 47). With her sophisticated music, she appeals to the "angelism" of the transcendent, aesthetic self that pursues pleasant mental experience, and with her exuberant sexuality she promises to satisfy the needs of the bestial immanent self. Art Immelmann in *Love in the Ruins* tempts Tom More in a similar way (*LR*, 213–18) when he advises Tom to place his faith in a love in which a man loves a woman "as one loves music ... abstractly" (*LR*, 213). Both Art and Ewell are trying to convince their preys to turn their eyes away from incarnate creation and turn to their inner worlds of cognitive, aesthetic, and physical stimulations.

In the garage, Will is again, as he was at the beginning of the novel when he was pinned down by Ewell's gunfire, lying on the floor where he "could ... see ... without being seen" (*SC*, 20, 200). Will's position on the floor is symbolic of the kind of detached, aesthetic self-placement that he has always preferred, a self-placement in which he imagines that he is an invisible Cartesian observer peering out at a world that does not include him. This psychic posture makes him particularly vulnerable to Ewell's temptations, as Ewell is advising him to become just that kind of "angelic-bestial," detached self whose physical sensations and thoughts and feelings are the only reality. Will listens to his demonic alter ego (Ewell's head and "snoutish" nose look like Will's [*SC*, 199, 201, 202, 205]) once again remind him that he is the same as everyone else in the insane modern world, merely an immanent, bestial lover of money and the comforts and pleasures it can bring. Ewell also reminds Will that he is smart like his angelic, intellectual father, who believed that he knew absolutely the origin, the purpose, and the worth of all human life. The essence of Will's father's philosophical brilliance, Ewell argues, lay in his belief that "man is born between an asshole and a peehole . . . eats, sleeps, shits, fucks, works, gets old, and dies . . . that's all" (*SC*, 203–4). Ewell is advising Will to accept this angelic "truth" as a final explanation for the life beyond the garage door.

When Ewell "vanish[es]" in the "white cloud" that fills the door of the garage, Will has forgotten about Lewis Peckham, Kitty, and his present experience altogether. All present reality vanishes from his sight. "Sunk in thought" (*SC*, 208–9), Will is self-enclosed in his illusions that he is indeed, as Ewell told him, even smarter than his father and that he has finally located for sure who he is and where he is. Lying on the garage floor where he can see only the three cars, part of the floor, and the ubiquitous cat under the Rolls, Will believes that he has finally located his genuine self— "come into himself like the cat" . . . "here . . . in the real world of cats and concrete!" (*SC*, 200–201). Will's ontological blindness and aestheticism are illustrated when he sees the sun-filled white cloud, "dense and solid as a pearl" and "shot through with delicate colors," transform the dark, empty garage into a fairy-tale castle where the cars seem like "beautiful . . . birds poised for flight at any moment from the immaculate concrete." Just as the beautiful cloud "swallow[s]" up Ewell, so it also envelops all that is "here" and "real" beyond the cars, cat, and concrete. Will sees at this moment a wondrous cloud that fills this small building with a radiance and splendor, but in fact the "opalescent cloud" (*SC*, 208) is just an opaque screen that hides the sacramental world that lives just outside the empty, dark garage where Will lies injured and alone.

Will's Great Discovery immediately after his revelations in the garage is that "Ewell was right"—he is smarter than his father. This conviction about his superior intellect, coupled with his earlier discovery that he is capable of "remembering everything," results in Will's descending into himself in an angelic solipsism that, as the narrator says, borders on "madness" (*SC*,

229). As Will analyzes his predicament in his upstairs bedroom, he agrees with Ewell that he is one who can "stand . . . aside" from events and people and merely "look . . . on" and "observe" his experience analytically and from a distance while others pay little attention to their lives. He believes that after such detached observation and objective analyses, he can "figure . . . something out" that will "convert . . . a necessary evil to an ingenious good" (*SC*, 213). Because he believes he has these superior powers to understand human existence, he assumes that he has the power to make all his experience into something good. Will therefore believes that he can avoid repeating his father's wasted life and death. He concludes that his father's search was inadequate simply because it led him to no new knowledge and "did nobody good" (*SC*, 211). Will's is a cold gnostic, Utilitarian logic that evaluates all human thought and action—even his father's tortured and failed life— by the useful and good results they accomplish.

These angelic delusions about his cognitive capacities lead him to design a plan to descend into Lost Cove cave to discover some answers his father was incapable of finding. With his "scientific method," he will, like the scientist in his laboratory, withdraw from the actual world and participation in its multiplicity and simultaneity of sensory, intellectual, emotional, and aesthetic experience in order to attempt alone to locate God Himself in the cave. The sacramental world beyond his thinking hidden in a beautiful cloud just beyond his mansion, Will is so withdrawn and dislocated from reality that he sees himself as a new Jacob who, if he receives a sign in the cave, will serve as a prophet to this now insane world full of "assholes." He believes that he may come back from Lost Cove cave with prophetic answers that will once and for all eliminate all mystery (*SC*, 222) about the origin, purpose, and destiny of humankind. If, on the other hand, he receives no sign, then he will know for certain that humans are the mere organisms his father defined as souless creatures "born between an asshole and a peehole." But, whether he receives a sign or not, Will believes that he will discover finally with his remarkable intellect who he is, where he is, and what he must do.

Will's descent into the cave beneath the golf course is a symbolic descent into a radical self-enclosure, a withdrawal from his death-in-life immanent existence into the solitary darkness of his *cogito* where he believes he will find the answers that eluded his father.[10] He is confident that he knows all there is to know about the present immanent world that traps him in its meaninglessness and that he knows all about the self that makes its life there. As he walks toward the entrance to the cave and across the golf course where he spends his days, he thinks that he knows the golf links just as he knows with absolute precision "his own soul's terrain" (*SC*, 240). From this omniscient perspective, there is nothing in creation left to see and understand; one must, therefore, look elsewhere. And, because Will is a faithless Cartesian gnostic who believes in no transcendent realm of experience outside his knowing, the only other possible place to look lies in the interior world of his self.

What Will is unwittingly seeking in the cave is not a sign of God, but some new knowledge within himself that he thinks will effect a "self-salvation."[11] He vows that he will, like Percy's castaway who scans the horizon for "news from across the seas" (*MB*, 140), wait and watch for a sign, but he is choosing to remove himself from the sacramental world where the signs of a salvific God exist. Will believes he has the uncanny gnostic power to convert evil to good (*SC*, 213), and therefore sees himself as his own savior. He believes that alone in the darkness of the cave he can find out how to transform his immanent death-in-life into a pleasant and comfortable, good life—resurrect himself from the recurrent falls that leave him lying helpless in a sand trap, on the floor of his garage, or in the dark woods beyond the links.

Will's self-enclosure in his contemplations of his experiment in Lost Cove cave is illustrated when he approaches the cave's entrance. He is "pleased" by the "escape hole," the entrance to Lost Cove cave that allows him to slip through a slender "crack" in the rock by simply pushing past the branches of the sassafras that hide the opening. Instead of reflecting on immediate, present time-space experience, Will retires at this moment into thoughts of the beautiful "underground river" that flows in "sunlight through a cathedral arch of stone" (*SC*, 241–42) beneath him at the main entrance to the cave. His choice of images here shows that he associates this hidden, interior world into which he is about to descend with a holiness and redemption. Meanwhile, he ignores the sacramental "flaming" "red" (*SC*, 57) sassasfras right before his eyes and thoughtlessly steps past it in order to vanish from the created world and the people in it. Once again, Will is comfortable when he can feel that he has escaped immanence, become invisible, achieved a detached, aesthetic mode of "seeing without being seen" (*LG*, 162; *SC*, 20, 200).

Will sees his interior quest as a way to discover a new self and world, but, in fact what he discovers in the cave is merely a lifeless place of rock removed from the actual life above him. His "squeez[ing] through ... [the] crack" into the cave, crawling through rock enclosures "like a baby getting through a pelvis," and, finally, his resting comfortably in the womb-like pod (*SC*, 241–43) in the depths of the cave imply that he is engaged in some sort of dramatic rebirth. Will has not, however, been reborn into another life, but descended into lifelessness. He has not returned to a life-nurturing womb, but is trapped in the massive "bowels of Sourwood Mountain" where the only signs of life are "humpy becowled stalagmites" that look like nuns and another chunk of rock that looks like the "flattened head of a tiger." Will is also "dead"— unconscious of who he in actuality is. When he reclines in the pod where he plans to wait for a sign from God, he "feel[s] so good" as he imagines himself a Faustian "puttering scientist" discovering in the cave a knowledge that mankind has forever sought. And he projects himself forward into a vision of the "Last Days" when he and Sutter will become the prophets who greet the "Stranger from the East" at Megiddo. Meanwhile, above him and his fantasies about himself as scientist and prophet are the signs he has chosen to escape in the sacramental world. Above the dark bowels "normal" folk play golf and   barbecue amid "the mountains [that] glow . . . like rubies and amethysts" (*SC*, 244–46) in the Appalachian sunlight.

But something goes wrong that interrupts Will's grand experiment, something that disturbs his comfortable withdrawal into his angelic fantasy constructions of the future and himself. Will is assaulted by a toothache that with his "every heartbeat feels like a hot ice pick shoved straight up into the brain" (*SC*, 246–47). This is a sign that Will has not expected, a sign that will, ironically, return him to the glorious mountains and to the light he needs to cure his blindness. During his "rassling" (*SC*, 223), Jacob was wounded in the hip before he got his blessing from God. So Will's toothache reminds him that he is a corporeal being who has not entirely disappeared from phenomenal creation. This "engineer" and "scientist," who has always relied on the competency of his brain in his efforts to understand life, needs this reminder that he has a body before he re-enters the sacramental world where God is revealed and can "be known."[12]

Like a bolt of divine "forked . . . lightning" striking up "into his head" (*SC*, 257), the searing pain causes Will a Sartrean "nausea"[13] that, paradoxically, cures him of his "grandiose ideas about God, man, death, suicide" (*SC*, 247). It is only after this nausea compels him to abandon the recesses of his brain that Will can recognize that he is an incarnate creature with imperfect teeth whose life is above him in a Fallen place of pain and suffering. Will decides that the only life and home that exist are up in the bejeweled mountains with "normal folk"—and dentists! There "must be a place" (*SC*, 250) for him, he decides, and it is not here with the dead tiger he sees while in his pod. In his hallucinatory encounter with this bedraggled beast, Will sees no mythic Blakean "splendid tiger," "nothing bright or fearful or symmetrical." Just dead. Concluding that there is no sign relevant to human life in the death of this animal that he has seen with his half-conscious eyes, Will vomits in pain—"everything else" "knock[ed] . . . out of . . . [his]

head." In this scene, he awakens out of an angelic, aesthetic consciousness where imaginary mystical tigers from nineteenth-century Romantic poems roam—"child's-picture-book tiger[s]"—and into the blunt facticity of who he is and where he is (SC, 255–57).

Will's return from the world of his brain to the sacramental life above him begins with another fall, this time a terrifying drop from the comfort of his isolated enclosure in the pod into a vast darkness (SC, 258) and into a recognition of the ontological illusions that have trapped him in the painful blindness he is now suffering. While his earlier fall in the stairwell in his garage led to his Great Discovery of his omniscience and enclosed his private world within a beautiful "opalescent cloud" (SC, 208), this fall opens Will to an awareness of the limitations of his intellect and his foggy way of seeing.[14] When his single flashlight is damaged, he feels "stupid" not to have brought additional "light." This recognition that he is literally and figuratively "in the dark," is followed by the fearful realization that he is "lost," that he does not know "where he . . . [is]." As later, when he escapes from the bus to Thomasville and escapes from St. Mark's (SC, 339, 366), Will now realizes that he has misplaced himself through his aesthetic detachment from the world above and that he has subsequently "lost something" in his self-isolation (SC, 258–60). What he has lost by his objective seeing, although he cannot yet see this, is the "human connection" (MCon, 75) available only in his social interactions with his family and friends in Linwood. In his removal of himself from this social interaction, Will has lost connection with the intersubjective language transactions that only other people can provide. Percy believes that all consciousness of the self and the world has its origins in these language transactions.

Will's recognition of his lost and helpless condition provides the necessary impetus for his desperate ascent toward "light" and "water" (SC, 260–61), sacramental and redemptive symbols of the new life possible when he emerges from this dark solitary enclosure he has in his self-delusions chosen. The ascent is not easy. He is very thirsty, and limps through the darkness like a drunk (SC, 259)—or, perhaps, like the lame Jacob made his way on his journey after his wrestling match. When he nears the light, he has to shed his prideful Faustian self and crawl on his hands and knees among the colonies of bats that are drizzling their excrement into his hair. But then Will sees "a shadow on the rock" in a faint glimmer of light and "turns his head toward it slowly as a sick man greeting a visitor." The shadow is caused by what he knows must be "another source of light" (SC, 260–61) besides his inadequate and undependable flashlight. The light enables him to see that the visitor he spots beside him is his own Jungian shadow, another self hidden until now from his sight.

While at the beginning of the novel he wanted to kill the "shadowy stranger" he saw in the mirror of his Mercedes (*SC*, 15), he now, with the assistance of this light source from incarnate creation, "reach[es] the shadow" (*SC*, 260) and at least acknowledges and accepts its existence. Will is realizing the existence of his shadow self, in Jungian psychology a necessary step toward self-knowledge.[15] From the perspective of sacramental Christianity, Will is seeing in the shadow, if seeing darkly, that he actually has a corporeal existence and that he is a participant in phenomenal existence. In order to see the shadow, Will must literally recognize that there is a body causing the shadow and that it exists in the context of the physical rock beside and beneath him and the sun above.

What Will sees when he falls out of the cave illustrates that his escape from the darkness is only a step toward a precise understanding of who he is and where he is. He is conscious of his physical presence in the immediacy of creation, feels the light breeze against his skin and "smell[s] leaves and bitter bark and . . . lichened rock warming in the sunlight." But he still withdraws from this incarnate self into his interior world of thought and feeling. He thinks of himself as a Confederate or a World War II Japanese soldier who has just come out of hiding after the war. As he plummets out of the cave toward Allie's greenhouse floor and unconsciousness, Will thinks it will not be "much of a fall." He is analyzing and evaluating his situation and obviously failing to see at this moment the sacramental significance of the world into which he has just been delivered. As he descends "through . . . air and color, brilliant greens and violet and vermilion and a blue unlike any sky," he "wonder[s]" if he has died and ascended into some "tacky heaven" or has come face to face with "the great black beast of the apocalypse" (*SC*, 261–62). Will does not see that he has returned to a flesh-and-blood, Fallen place indeed very much "unlike any sky" or transcendent heaven. His aesthetic and Cartesian inclination to envision himself in other times and places interferes with his perception of where he is.

Will cannot yet read the sacramental signs in the incarnational world into which he just fallen, and therefore he cannot see that he has arrived in the only home where the life-giving water and light he was seeking in the cave (*SC*, 260–61) are available. He does not know where he is when he "open[s] his eyes" after his fall in the greenhouse and sees someone offering him a Eucharistic-like cup of water. Will thinks he is in some sort of strange church because of the stained-glass window Allie has installed (*SC*, 262), incapable of locating himself as an inhabitant and participant in these actual postlapsarian ruins where another "sick" person is providing him with water and life. Allie also gives Will a baptismal bath while he is unconscious, using the water that has been warmed in the water reservoir of the

Grand Crown stove she raised from the ruins of her aunt's home. When Will opens his eyes again after a brief sleep and "follow[s]" Allie's "gaze," he finds himself looking at the "transformed, reborn" stove with its "immaculate white and turquoise enamel glow[ing] like snowy peaks against a blue sky." "Glitter[ing] in the sunlight" (*SC*, 264), it is an obvious Christological symbol that associates Allie and the resurrection she effects for the nearly dead Will with the redemptive life provided by Christ and symbolized in the Sacraments he instituted. Earlier in the novel, the Grand Crown is called "a cathedral of a stove" (*SC*, 235), a metaphor that identifies it with the Church and the sacramental system that offers redemption from the thirst and darkness that Will has just suffered in the cave. The significance that Percy attached to the stove is implied by the fact that he rewrote the chapter about Allie's resurrection of the stove (*SC*, 230–38) while *The Second Coming* was in proofs.[16]

Will draws none of these sacramental analogies between his existential predicament and the greenhouse where he now finds himself, nor does he see Allie as an incarnational sign of a divine life, in spite of the symbolic drink and bath she gives him. Percy says that she is just such a sign, that he was thinking about Hopkins's "Glory be to God for dappled things" and the poet's "talk about block and tackle and trim" (*MCon*, 50) when he wrote about Allie's raising the stove (and the fallen Will) with her "pulleys and rope" (*SC*, 269, 230, 234, 238). She "gets back into the world," he says, through these "ordinary," "sacramental" "kind[s] of things" (*MCon*, 50). She is pictured as living among the other sacramental signs in the forest around her, the "yellow sunlight" glowing through the "spokes of the pines" (*SC*, 272) and illuminating her life in the ruins. When she finds Will lying on the cold forest path after another fall, Allie takes him into her bed in the greenhouse and serves as the nurturing "sun's warmth" for his apparently lifeless body, described here as a "cold dead planet" (*SC*, 293).[17]

While they lie together during the electrical storm that night, Allie becomes aware of an intersubjective union with Will and realizes for the first time a love (*SC*, 300, 303) that is in Percy's fiction the great earthly delight analagous to the "infinite delight" (*SP*, 417) available in union with God. Their bodies make "a diamond" as they touch "foreheads," and the spectacular cosmic light and power of the "continuous" lightning causes their home to light up like a brilliant "blue and white" "diamond" (*SC*, 300, 302–3). In his discussions of his language theory (see particularly *MB*, 40; *LC*, 98; *SP*, 124–25), Percy uses a double triadic, diamond-shaped diagram to describe how language-users are united intersubjectively when they use word signs to identify a world of meaning that they inhabit together. Allie can now see how "one plus one equals one" (*SC*, 301) in this intersubjective union and recognize a possibility for "an opening out" that she describes as "like the signs you recognize when you are getting near the ocean for the first time." In a vivid and dramatic image reminiscent of Wordsworth's "children sporting on the shore" in "Intimations of Immortality," Allie compares her new psychic opening to an entrance into a mysterious and beautiful world beyond her terrifying self-enclosure and mental illness. The experience, she thinks, is like a first visit to the seashore when signs in the changing landscape along the way mark "the beginning of the end of land and the beginning of the old uproar and the going away of the endless sea" (*SC*, 296–97).[18]

Unfortunately, Will does not recognize yet the signs of love and life available with Allie in the light-filled "diamond" house and decides during the storm to return to his home on the other side of the fence in Linwood. He says he does not know what answer he got in his cave experiment, but he now knows what he has to do (*SC*, 282) and where it must be done. Before he leaves the greenhouse for his Mercedes parked in the country club lot, Will tells Allie that he is returning to the life and the self that he has constructed on the golf course and in his marriage and career—the life he earlier defined as a death-in-life. As he and Allie talk, Will "absently" eats the steak Allie prepares for him, no longer very "interest[ed]," he tells her, in "me." He is indeed absent from himself as he casts ahead to contemplate the revivified self he will once more become and to the deeds that that self will perform in his future world. Will plans to return to a pursuit of ethical action as a way to self-realization and self-satisfaction, plans to resume his old life of doing "what is expected of" him and "tak[ing] care of people." His plans include Allie, for whom he will become a "legal guardian" in a "fiduciary relationship" (*SC*, 303–4). Allie will be just "another good work," Percy observes in his notes for the novel (WPP, series 1, E:1A:ii). Will is incapable of experiencing the intersubjective "opening out" that Allie discovers beneath the lightning-filled skies—still capable only of assuming roles that he feels will be useful and good. As a result of his failure to read the signs this night beside the Grand Crown and in the sun's warmth of Allie's body, Will turns away from the possibility for love and a new life that is now present and chooses his solitary 4 A.M. return to his Mercedes in the cold and darkness.

GOING HOME?

Will's return to the other side of the fence with his plans for a future that will be filled with good works is also a return to the self-displacement and resulting sense of dislocation that, at the beginning of the novel, provoked in him the urge to kill the "stranger" he saw in the mirror of his Mercedes (*SC*, 15). In the country club parking lot the night of his return, Will settles into the back seat of his "perfect German machine" after an exhausting two weeks in the cave and at Allie's greenhouse and again sees a stranger staring at him from the rearview mirror (*SC*, 308). Later, at home, he sees the same stranger lurking in the mirror attached to his bedroom door (*SC*, 330). As well as suffering the self-estrangement suggested by these scenes, Will is again alienated from his friends and family, those people who earlier led him to conclude that his world was a farcical and meaningless place. He learns that Leslie has "closed . . . [his] house" (*SC*, 330) and is plotting with his friends to take over the Peabody fortune he has inherited from Marion. They have other plans for his future, the matter that he has told Allie is now his only concern.

Will fails in his attempts to resume his previous life of good works in Linwood. He finds himself literally homeless and among people who no longer recognize his sovereignty over his own life. Will remains at first confident that he can with his pragmatic, rational powers of "knowing and choosing" discover a life and a home in Linwood (*SC*, 314) in spite of these obstacles, or at least exist pleasantly while playing out the roles he has assumed in the last twenty years. But he finally returns to his conviction that "this [Linwood life] is not for me" (*SC*, 4) and that his only home is in the Georgia swamp with his father. Only a moment of clear vision on his aborted bus journey south to that home awakens him to the realization that there is a "something" of great value in the "dark forest" beyond the bus window that he is, in his blindness, "losing" (*SC*, 339).

Will's search for a home begins in the parking lot the night he leaves the greenhouse. Symbolically enclosed in the dark Mercedes, beneath Marion's lap robe (*SC*, 307), Will once again searches his memories and tries to imagine a future different from, if not better than, his past. Once again solipsistically exploring and analyzing scientifically and objectively the stranger in the rearview mirror, Will sees that he is the same person he was when he was thirteen, the year after the hunting trip with his father (*SC*, 309). He concludes, as he did a few weeks earlier as he stood in the glade looking for the ball he had driven out of bounds, that nothing changes (*SC*, 60, 309), that he has inherited the love of death (*SC*, 83) that led his father to his true home. But this time, he believes, he has discovered with his keen powers of knowing a "solution to the problem" (*SC*, 311). Defining himself once again as a heroic "truth seeker" (*SC*, 313) equipped with superior analytical skills, Will imagines that he has uncovered all the sources for the living death that plagues him and his culture. In an exuberant "litany," he "names" for himself these sources: Christianity, atheism, "marriage and family," and all the other hypocritical and self-deceiving loves people embrace. He believes that he can now simply, logically, "choose life" instead of these "deaths" (*SC*, 312–14) and thereby avoid the homes that his father and all others in this "Century of the Love of Death" (*SC*, 311) have chosen to occupy. As his confidence in his omniscient intellect led him into Lost Cove cave for answers, so it now leads the gnostic Will to believe that he can choose a life, place himself in a home outside the death-filled Fallen world where all others live their lives. Will rejects the disappointing actualities of his Fallen home with the rest of humanity, denying his existence in phenomenal creation and his mortality when he vows after his litany that "death in none of its guises shall prevail over him" (*SC*, 314).

Will, in his abstraction and self-enclosure, returns to his faith in his ability to remember everything and again constructs selves and worlds within that omniscient memory. He believes he knows "what had happened and what was going to happen." This assumption of omniscience is illustrated when he falls asleep in the back of the Mercedes and experiences what he thinks is a "presentiment" (*SC*, 314–15). In this prophetic vision, Will sees himself playing out a variety of roles as he makes his way through memory-inspired past and imaginary future interior landscapes. First, he sees himself as the "special" child left alone in the kitchen with his family's cook D'Lo in a home made desolate by his parents' deaths. Then, equally alone and homeless, Will finds himself at the "bunker on number-six fairway" where he spends twenty years striking at "thousands of golf balls" with his displaced fellow golfers. After watching his Edenic country club home dissolve into a subdivision and then into a deserted mall after forty or fifty years, Will sees himself in his presentiment lying in the ruins of a mall between an abandoned Orange Julius stand and the entrance to H&R Block. In these apocalyptic suburban ruins, Will senses a presence and hears someone speak: "The ocean was not far away," he thinks (*SC*, 316–17). Will's allusion is to the ocean metaphor Allie used to describe her consciousness of the psychic opening out she experienced when she first recognized in the greenhouse her love and union with Will (*SC*, 296–97).

When Will turns to see who is approaching him in the ruins, he does not find the Incarnate Word speaking to him of a redemptive love and a new home on the ocean's horizon, but instead awakes to a "dark eclipsed face" looking down out at him from the open front door of the Mercedes. Kitty, with her "bright corona of hair" (*SC*, 318), appears in the country club parking lot in the blinding afternoon sun like a false goddess that he has worshipped in the past. In *The Last Gentleman*, a naive and often bestial Will did, in fact, spend much of his time worshipping the happiness that he thought her love could provide for him. Now Kitty is an even more lustful (*SC*, 322) goddess who reminds Will that he has just awakened from a dream, that what he thinks was a presentiment that revealed his entire existence to him is merely fantasy. Awake and feeling "a thousand miles from his dreams" about his past and future, he listens to Kitty's version of his real present life and future (*SC*, 320–28). She tells him about Leslie's taking possession of his mansion home and about the plans Leslie and Jack Curl have to acquire the fortune that he has used to construct his New York/Linwood life. Kitty also has her plans for his future. Having just separated from her husband Walter, she sees him as a future companion who should settle down with her at Dun Romin'. As if indeed awake now in the parking lot to his present loveless and homeless reality, Will "absently" interrupts Kitty's vision of their future together at Dun Romin' and mutters, "Ah, I've got to go. . . Home" (*SC*, 328).

Because Will is convinced that he can with his intellect know and with his will choose a life separate from the death he sees in his father's life and in Linwood, he is not inclined to look outside himself in his search for a new life. His blindness to the sacramental signs of his true home out in incarnate creation is illustrated after he leaves Kitty at the country club and returns to the mansion where he once made his home. Entering the house, Will notices that it "did not breathe," and from this solitary dead place he looks out at the living landscape stretching beyond it. From the empty garage of his now lifeless, "unlived-in" house, Will gazes at the "eastern sky" and watches it "turn violet" while a "small rainbow" appears on the horizon. Strangely, as if distrusting his vision of these beautiful cosmic signs in the vastness of the created universe, Will closes one eye and notices that the rainbow disappears. When he opens both eyes, it reappears. Again, when he is about to enter the house, he closes one eye. With both eyes open he sees two doors, and then, by shutting "his left eye," he sees clearly that there is a single door (*SC*, 329). Will apparently thinks he sees better with one eye. The reality is that with his monocular half-sight he is able to see how to get into the house where he has by his own estimation lived a death-in-life. But at the same time this monocular partial blindness he chooses makes the rainbow and other sacramental signs of life and hope on the horizon disappear from his sight.

Upstairs in his bedroom, also empty except for the ominous Greener shotgun and the Luger that Leslie for some reason has chosen to leave behind for her father, Will again looks out at the spectacular Appalachian wilderness and sees the "sun rest[ing] on the rim of the gorge like a copper plate on a shelf." It is fall, the end of the year, and the day is dying in the west, but a halo-like plate peacefully rests in the midst of this death and "fill[s] the empty room" of this house that does not breathe with a beautiful "rosy light." The setting sun and the fading but beautiful light in the autumn afternoon are Christological signs in death-filled incarnate creation of the redemptive love and life that have radiated continuously in the Fallen world since the Crucifixion and Resurrection. But Will cannot read the significances of what he sees and turns away from the window to gaze uncomfortably at his father's self-destructive weapons and the bare room. He wonders briefly if there is in the room "someone present or someone absent," but dismisses this fleeting sensation that there might be something present in this place other than what he sees and collapses to the floor in one of his spells. From his symbolically defeated position, Will notices a "bar of sunlight [that] seem[s] significant," but he decides quickly that "things do not have significances." From Will's perspective, then, the world is a place without meaning, without significance, where "one place is like any other place" (*SC*, 329)—all homes, then, just like this empty bedroom where he used to rest after his daily encounters with the living death of "golf and good works" (*SC*, 165) with Marion and their friends.

Because Will presently sees no significance to where he is—one place as meaningless as another—he has little interest in who he is beyond the shifting roles that are demanded in order to function pleasantly in his various environments. If all things lack significance, then by what logic is his individual self an exception to this universal truth? As Will told Allie before he left her at the greenhouse, he no longer finds himself "an interesting subject" (*SC*, 304). Will is adopting the kind of immanent self-placement that confuses role-playing with the authentic self, the result being an annihilation of a consciousness of self. But this self-alienation does not trouble him. When Will sees the stranger in the mirror in his bedroom he finds no importance in the fact that he is a stranger to himself. He is even mildly amused at the disheveled appearance of the "drunk bearded mountaineer" that stares back at him. He is equally amused when he dons the clothes Leslie has left for him and discovers that he has assumed the identity of "a young Dr. Marcus Welby" (*SC*, 330–31).

Dressed in this new disguise, a jaunty and almost carefree Will goes downstairs to his Mercedes and heads for Linwood to talk with Kitty, Leslie, and his brother-in-law Bertie about their plans for his future. Kitty and Dun Romin' are attractive, if selfish, possibilities. Leslie's plans to complete her "Mother's dream" by building her "love-and-faith community" (*SC*, 331–32) certainly seem worthwhile, an effective way for him to "take care of people" (*SC*, 303), as he now thinks he should. And he believes he could be happy enough with a future of playing Seniors golf with Bertie and his friends for the next thirty years and becoming an "eighty-year-old Gene Sarazen." Kitty's lover? Leslie's compliant philanthropic father? A drunken mountaineer? Marcus Welby? Gene Sarazen? "Why not?" Will muses (*SC*, 333). Unfortunately, Will's facile reasoning here about his future obscures from him the reality that his return to Linwood has become a return to an existence that has left him a homeless stranger who sees double and mindlessly accepts any identity that Kitty, Leslie, or his golfing partners for whatever reason wish to thrust upon him.

Paradoxically, Will's poor eyesight results in his escaping temporarily the living death that awaits him at his future homes in Linwood and his finding another way. Driving toward the town, he sees "two roads instead of one" and literally does not know where he is; he thinks he's on an interstate. He awakes to where he is, however, as he crashes into the tops of the trees by the road and sees that he has landed in a "deep empty dark." He sees also, as he does in the empty dark of Lost Cove cave, that he needs the daylight and the life that waits for him there, and, therefore, he decides to wait in the car until morning. A psychically elevated and abstracted Will "drop[s] . . . to the soft earth" (*SC*, 334–35) from the "airborne" Mercedes when he awakes and descends from the symbolic self-enclosure of his beautiful German machine to the firm earth and the new light of a new day.

Back on the earth and on the highway, Will now continues his wayfaring in a different direction and, although he has not yet developed a sacramental consciousness that can show him his true home, Will does recognize that he does not know where he is or what to do. This is a recognition that Percy's castaways must achieve before they have any impetus to look to the open seas for some signs of life beyond their current exile. Will knows as he walks along the shoulder of this mountain road that he does not know where he is, that he is indeed homeless. It is only by the many North Carolina plates on the cars that pass that he is able to deduce that he is somewhere in that state. He is unsure of his location here on the "soft earth," and wonders as he watches the strangers pass him in their speeding cars, "What am I doing here?" The answer to his question is in the sacramental signs around him—the "sun . . . warm[ing] his back," the delicate yellow "jewelweed . . . bloom[ing] in the ditches," the "bright yellow birds flutter[ing] in the trees." But Will is blind to these signs, and even to the Good News announced less subtly by a bumper sticker on a speeding Mazda that reads, "YOUR GOD MAY BE DEAD BUT I TALKED WITH MINE THIS MORNING." Although now alert to his immediate time-space experience and not entirely lost in his visions of himself as a future

Gene Sarazen, Will continues to be "somewhat abstracted, like a man who is looking at something without seeing it" (*SC*, 334–35).

It is "the Associate," another wayfarer that Will meets at the bus station, who inadvertently directs the dazed and half-blind Will toward a new way of seeing. Bernadette Prochaska believes that the Associate is a Guardian Angel for Will, one who protects him from the living death he is leaving behind on the Linwood golf course and saves him from the deadly attraction of the Georgia swamp.[19] Through his "listening" (*SC*, 336,339) to the Associate at the bus station and on the bus to Atlanta, Will achieves a power to see that enables him to resist his father's temptations and momentarily opens him to the possibility of a life and love and home not available in Linwood. In Percy's epistemology and ontology, all consciousness is accomplished by talking and listening with others in language exchanges that intersubjectively unite the language users in a shared world of meaning. The kind of Cartesian solitary knowing that Will has attempted in the cave and in his analyses of his memories is, from Percy's perspective, futile (*MB*, 282–83, 293, 295, e.g.).

The Associate, whose "flashing" glasses (*SC*, 335, 336, 338, 340) suggest he has the capacity for a special kind of illuminating vision, tells Will of his last twenty years of work at a loan company in Atlanta and about his plans for his retirement in Emerald Isle Estates. His story is similar but also very different from Will's. The Associate, like Will, has for the last twenty years counted on a successful career in business and a traditional middle-class family life to make him happy. But the Associate's life has been a "pleasure" and a joy; he has tried, like Will, to serve others with his work—and actually "enjoyed" it. In his life beyond the office, the Associate is a man who has stayed "in shape" both physically and psychically without the golf that Will has depended on for his enjoyment. He tells Will that he never played. Evidence of the efficacy of the Associate's vigorous life is illustrated by the fact that he stands "tall" and "hearty" (*SC*, 335–38), while Will falls down a lot after twenty years of trying to divert himself with golf. The Associate, like Kierkegaard's Christian, has been "glad" in his work and "rejoice[s] in life."[20] He has achieved the ethical life Will dreamed of acquiring at the end of *The Last Gentleman* (*LG*, 382–86) when he made his plans to marry Kitty and take a position as personnel manager at her father's Chevrolet dealership.

But the Associate's inspiring story does not at first open Will's eyes. On the bus, "side by side," the Associate and Will journey together through the spectacular beauty of the "sunlight and shade" of the Blue Ridge Mountains, Will sunk down in his thoughts of his past, the Associate animated by his reflections on his work in Atlanta and his new life. Listening to the

Associate's story of retirement and his past life in Georgia has reminded Will of his own deceptively "triumphant life" since the hunt with his father in the Thomasville swamp and has, at least initially, exacerbated his blindness to the world outside his thoughts and feelings. He decides that he has failed in the last thirty years to escape the death that waits for him in Georgia, that his only home is in those dark woods. Will's inability to see beyond the suicidal despair that grips him is illustrated when he looks out the window and "watch[es] a low ridge which ran just above the tree line." He thinks the ridge looks "like a levee" (*SC*, 338-39). The actual ridge that stretches across the horizon of this immense and beautiful landscape disappears from Will's sight—and any sacramental significances it might have also disappear—as he thinks of a levee, a conspicuous topographical feature of his childhood hometown on the banks of the Mississippi (*LG*, 327). Obviously, any memory of his home in Ithaca woud be accompanied by his memory of the house where his father shot himself to death in the attic.

As Will continues to listen to the Associate talk about his work and as the bus rolls on through the vast and imposing landscape outside the window, Will's "eye traveled along the ridge" to a "notch" in the "darkness" of the endless mountain forests, and he sees something whose wondrous beauty, for reasons he cannot identify, jolts him out of his memory, self-analysis, and contemplations of death. He sees amid the shadowy "pine and spruce" "a single gold poplar which caught the sun like a yellow-haired girl coming out of a dark forest" (*SC*, 339). Although the omniscient memory and intellect he has had so much faith in cannot make the connections, this light-filled poplar is similar to the one he saw when he first ventured "out of bounds" to discover Allie and her greenhouse (*SC*, 59, 82). It is a sign of Allie and the love that he is leaving behind, a sacramental sign that, in the next few minutes, saves him from the suicide he is on his way to face.[21]

Instead of viewing the poplar through the eyes of his analytical *cogito*, he responds sensuously, viscerally, imaginatively, and emotionally with great precision and intensity to this sacramental sign. It demands his attention, compels his eye to "travel" farther across the horizon, challenges his belief that "things do not have significances." He involuntarily and unconsciously asserts its significance as something more than just a tree. With a vivid simile, he imaginatively endows the tree with the beauty and life of a "yellow-haired girl." The single tree of gold and sun brilliantly projecting its light in the vast and empty darkness of what appears from the bus window to be a lifeless wilderness causes Will's heart to be "flooded" with a baptismal "sweetness." In turn, this sudden, inexplicable emotion provokes in him "a sharp sweet urgency, a need to act, to run and catch" (*SC*, 339). For Will at this moment of revelation, time and space experience beyond his passive, detached consciousness becomes alive in its immediacy, and he instinctively feels the need to place himself in the context of this immediacy—"to act," and act now, in order to "catch" whatever life reveals itself on the horizon.

The tree of light in the "dark forest" is a sign that leads Will to the immediate recognition that he is by choosing the death that awaits him in the Thomasville swamp losing something, "something of his as solid and heavy and sweet as a pot of honey in his lap." The sexual imagery here emphasizes that Will is losing the possibility of a pleasurable carnal union with Allie. But the single golden tree also associates her with a precious and redemptive spiritual love brought into the darkness of Fallen creation by Christ. Percy says that the "sunlight shining on" her when Will first spots her at the greenhouse (*SC*, 82) is a symbol of "grace" (*Con*, 307). Will makes none of these metaphorical connections. Since he has the inclination to abstract himself from flesh-and-blood reality and has no belief in transcendent spiritual experience, he is unable to make either these sexual or spiritual analogies. Will, does, however, know at this moment that the "something" he is leaving behind is "his" and that this private "thing" is somehow inextricably engaged with what lies outside the bus window.

Although he cannot name the sense of loss, he does act on his recognition of it. Will rises from his seat beside the Associate and announces to his fellow wayfarers, "I'm not going back to Georgia" (*SC*, 339). He chooses to act with a sense of urgency against the gnostic solipsism and living death that have enclosed him in an interior world of suicidal despair, even though he does not know why. Will's vision may not be perfect, but at least he is not seeing double now or choosing to close one eye in order to get into an empty home, as he did back in Linwood. Will can see well enough to know that he wants out of the bus, and, with the assistance of the vigorous and happy Associate, demands that the driver stop to let him re-enter the world where the tree proclaims its promise. When the irate driver throws him painfully back into that "dark" place, Will still can vow to himself before he loses consciousness beside the road that leads back to his home in Linwood, "it's not going to end like this or in a Georgia swamp" (*SC*, 340–41).

LIFE UP HERE: IN OTHER HANDS

Will awakes at Duke hospital "strapped" helplessly to a table "like a mummy" and asks, "Where am I?" His daughter Leslie, an ingratiating Jack Curl at her side, takes "him by a strong hand" and tells him he's at Duke hospital. After the "scientists" take care of him, she says, she wants to talk with him about his future role in her "faith-and-love" project (*SC*, 341–43) in Linwood.

In the "skillful" "hands" of the hospital attendant (*SC*, 341, 342, 343), Will is also having his future foretold by the Duke physician who is examining him. Dr. Ellis delivers to Will the prophetic, scientific "good news" (*SC*, 347) that explains what has "gone wrong" (*SC*, 3) in Will's life, answering scientifically once and for all those troubling ontological questions that have sent Will into Lost Cove cave, into his terrifying and self-defeating memories, and, almost, to Thomasville, Georgia, in search of himself.

Dr. Ellis's single and simple piece of news is revealed in the window where Will sees before him the X-rays of "his own brain." It is within the chemical workings of his Hausmann's Syndrome- afflicted brain, Dr. Ellis explains, that the sources of Will's self can be discovered. It is an unfortunate and rare chemical malfunction in his brain that accounts for the "inappropriate longings" (*SC*, 346–47) that have interfered with his ability to adjust normally to his empty and loveless life. And, he's told, Dr. Ellis can lay hands on him and cure him! The cure, however, will require his abandoning his former identity as a successful and active citizen of Linwood and becoming a permanent patient at St. Mark's Convalescent Home. The "good news" is that he can now spend the rest of his days watching *Hollywood Squares* with the other homeless old men at St. Mark's and playing an occasional round of Senior's golf with his aging golf partners. The pH level in his brain has been adjusted to a normal level by the scientists at his side, and Leslie and Jack are anxious to take him back to Linwood where he will be expected to adapt happily to his new roles as invalid and geriatric golfer. Lying in a state of "dazed content" in the examination room, Will assents to Dr. Ellis's diagnosis of what is wrong and accepts that "his life . . . [is] out of his hands" (*SC*, 348). He knows that it is in the hands of Leslie and the scientists she has employed to care for him.

Ironically, by ceasing to believe that his life is entirely in his hands alone and by giving up the illusion that he can by his solitary thinking and will create his life, Will arrives at a salutary recognition while he is at St. Mark's. There he begins to see that other hands than his may be involved in his life. At age twenty-five, Will placed himself in the world as an autonomous self capable of discovering and engineering a life of love and happiness with Kitty. Later, he believed that he could construct a life of his own design made out of his emotional and psychological experiences with Marion and his private ethical codes, financial achievement, and diversions. Still suffering now from the illusion that it is with his hands alone that he can make his life, Will has for the last few months since Marion's death depended on his memory and intellect in his efforts to locate within himself a life he has missed (*SC*, 144). But as he listens to the stories of some of the homeless and sick patients at St. Mark's—listens to others like himself who have also "finished" their lives and now wonder what to do (*MCon*, 19)—he realizes that there is beyond his interior self-constructions a world where he lives with others who have found a way to escape the living death he has for a lifetime endured.

Placed among the infirm and dying at St. Mark's, Will shares a home with aged wayfarers who must depend on the compassion and kindness of each other and the hospital staff for whatever life they have in their homeless condition. St. Mark's is a metaphor for a Fallen world where Will and all the other homeless exiles must rely on the mysterious impulse that impels human beings to extend love to the suffering and dying around them. It is this impulse toward good that not only makes Fallen human existence bearable, but provides the only joy possible in an otherwise lonely and hopeless place. Will's fellow residents at St. Mark's function as sacramental signs of this universal condition. Sick and dying, they serve as signs of an aboriginal defeat that unites Will with others in a world where neither he nor anyone else is capable of "prevail[ing] over death" (*SC*, 312). But they are also signs of the power of love incarnate in all humans, a power that can redeem humankind from that defeat. They are the signs that can show Will his true predicament: where he is, who he is, and what he must do.

At St. Mark's, Will once again is inspired with the sense of urgency to act that he felt earlier on the bus. It is this urgency that, at the end of the novel, sends him to Allie and to Father Weatherbee, into other hands in search of signs of a love that does prevail over death. With Allie at her greenhouse and at the Linwood Holiday Inn, and with Father Weatherbee in Jack Curl's office at St. Mark's, Will discovers after his life among the St. Mark's patients the possibility (*SC*, 376, 390) that the redemptive love he sees in Allie and the priest might offer him the life that he has so far failed to discover in his solitary lifelong search. Percy, commenting on Will's epiphany at the end of *The Second Coming*, says that he "sees the possibility of achieving love" (*Con*, 190) and "join[ing] the human race" (*Con*, 235; the youthful Will was also determined to "rejoin the human race" [*LG*, 386]). In addition, Percy explains, Will has escaped the autonomous, closed self that tried to find signs of God "alone in the cave," and now is committed to "finding . . . God through . . . human connection" (*MCon*, 75).

It is primarily through his intersubjective listening and talking at St. Mark's with Mr. Eberhart, a retired professional gardener, and Mr. Arnold and Mr. Ryan, both retired carpenters, that Will begins making these connections. Their Christological professions imply that they are teachers who can show Will a life that he has missed. In them, Will sees men, like the Associate, who have been able to escape the living death he has lived and who have, when they discovered life's imperfect, "demented" condition, re-sisted the temptation to head for a Georgia swamp. When Will first sees Lionel Eberhart watering a pine tree in front of St. Mark's, the old man seems to him just a "part of the scenery," an invisible object in an unre-markable landscape. But Will, after a brief conversation with him, sees that he is a man very much like himself. He, like Will, has been successful in his career and, after his success and the death of his wife, has been placed at St. Mark's by a loveless family and the family's physician. Will, after these discoveries, looks down at Mr. Eberhart from the porch of the nursing home, seeing him after their brief conversation as a man who has suffered but who has endured patiently and is still full of life, still "quick and wiry" enough to "live another thirty years" (*SC*, 351–52). Mr. Arnold, a paralyzed stroke victim, and his roommate Mr. Ryan, a double amputee, are passion-ate men, as vigorous as Mr. Eberhart in spite of their infirmities. Having suffered much more than Will after they finished their lives of doing what was expected of them (*SC*, 303), they still exhibit a kindness, good humor, and vibrance that are a sharp, life-affirming contrast to Will's own existen-tial deadness (*SC*, 370).

Mr. Ryan and Mr. Arnold are the immediate sources for a series of revela-tions that convince Will that others' hands can assist him in locating in himself and the world a life he has so far missed. While he is watching *Hollywood Squares* with them one morning in the room the men share, he rises too quickly from his bed and nearly falls. Mr. Arnold "grab[s] him with his good hand"—a "surprisingly strong" one—and both he and Mr. Ryan joke good-naturedly with Will about his youth, his good health, his imminent release from St. Mark's and return to an active life. These are instinctive, seemingly insignificant, acts and words of charity and sympa-thy that two crippled but undefeated men offer to Will without any apparent rational motive or purpose. Will, alone in the hospital corridor a few min-utes later, illustrates that their gifts have had an impact: "His head was clear but there was a sharp sweet something under his heart, a sense of loss, a going away" (*SC*, 366). Just as a similar "sense of loss" in Lost Cove cave (*SC*, 259) and on the bus to Georgia (*SC*, 339) encouraged Will to consider the possibilities of a life outside the dark interior world of his mind, so these signs of the human capacities for unmotivated kindness remind him that there is something that can stimulate a "sharp sweet" response in some region of his being outside his "clear head."

Will sees in Mr. Ryan's and Mr. Arnold's kindness and inexplicable con-cern for him the same "mysterious love" that he sees exhibited later in the same room when two orderlies take away a frightened and dying old woman.[22] Will is uncertain about the sincerity of the love that these two orderlies express toward the woman in their actions and words, but he can't deny that with their "gentle" but "strong hands" they act—act in the face of death—to deliver to her a great gift that brings her peace. In their hands, she stops her desperate fretting about her damaged heart that "rumble[s] so hard" that it shakes "her thick body," closes her eyes, and relaxes on the stretcher like a "baby." Standing at the bedside, Will wonders about the orderlies' motives; he is mystified in the presence of this obvious example of human goodness that has "no reason" he can understand. How is it possible that strangers, with so little effort, do so much for another? How can "2 c[ents] = $5?" Will sees a moral mystery here that makes him wonder further about the source of that mystery. Is God also "tricked out" (*SC*, 398–99), disguised and hidden from his powers of calculation in the same way that the orderlies' moral and volitional capacities for good are hidden in this room? Is there a life and self utterly beyond his rational knowing?

Mr. Arnold and Mr. Ryan encourage Will to consider the possibility that there may be such a moral and spiritual life. While talking with the two men in the game room as they all watch the Morning Movie, Will is again encouraged to look at himself and his connections with others anew. As he listens to these two fellow Southerners talk about their pasts, he returns to his memories of his father's attempt to kill him and realizes that he has since then been dead. But he is consoled by the subsequent conclusion that there is for him now, with this knowledge of his death, the "possibility of feeling alive though dead" (*SC*, 370–71). Percy, commenting in "Novel Writing in an Apocalyptic Time" on the necessity of the recognition Will has here achieved, says that "there is something worse than being deprived of life: it is being deprived of life and not knowing it" (*SP*, 163). Will, after listening to Mr. Ryan and Mr. Arnold talk of their pasts, knows his deprivation. As a result of this knowledge, it occurs suddenly to him that there is a semiotic "whole world of meaning, of talking and listening, which took place everywhere and all the time" (*SC*, 372), a world that has been obscured from him by a lifetime of self-enclosure in his need-satisfaction, memories, and cognition. Will's discovery of this public language world of meaning in which he lives rescues him from that meaningless landscape without "significances" (*SC*, 329) that he saw earlier at his empty mansion. Now "things . . . [take] on significance" (*SC*, 372) as he locates himself in the semiotic world that Percy believes is the only place humans can find out about who they are and where they are.

In his new knowledge of the possibility for a life beyond his solitary death-like existence, Will, as he does on the bus to Georgia, decides there is "something he ha[s] to do," and that he must do it in the world of significances where he now locates himself. When he rises a little too quickly from his chair in the game room in order to act on this sudden decision, he almost falls again. And he is again "caught" by the "strong hands" of Mr. Arnold and Mr. Ryan, who symbolically assist him as he attempts to leave the movie and resume his search out in the new world of meaning they have helped him see. As they take him in their hands, Will once more wonders at the concern of these friends, amazed at "what delicacy and gentleness they had!" He "look[s] into their faces" and then "look[s] down" at himself dressed in the dressing gown Leslie gave him and the "pajamas and . . . Bean's moose-hide slippers" his dead wife gave him a few Christmases ago. In the hands of these old men and in their faces he sees the world and the life he has missed, "paid [little] attention to" (*SC*, 372–73) in his life-long efforts to discover a genuine self and meaningful life. Will sees that the stranger in the stylish dressing gown watching Deborah Kerr in *King Solomon's Mines* is the dead man his family, friends, and Duke scientists believe is the real Will Barrett.

Less than an hour later, Will, appropriately dressed in his "street clothes" (*SC*, 372), returns to his Mercedes and to the open road to renew his search for the life and home he has failed to find in Mississippi, Georgia, New York, or Linwood. He knows where he must go if he is to have any "possibility" (*SC*, 374, 378) of entering that world of significances that he has discovered at St. Mark's. He knows that that place is beyond the Linwood golf course fence on the eighteenth fairway where Allie waits in the "cold dripping woods" (*SC*, 404) like the single gold poplar he saw from the bus window (*SC*, 339). Percy says Allie's world, the world Will is choosing, is a symbolic "sacramental" (*MCon*, 50,147) place where Will can find with her "a kind of grace" (*Con*, 307). It is where Will learns the possibility of experiencing an intersubjective love and union with another incarnate being in a relationship that is simultaneously and mysteriously both physical and spiritual, immanent and transcendent.[23] It is a relationship that serves as a sign of the Spirit made Flesh. Will has the possibility of discovering in his relationship with Allie that the union of infinite spirit with finite flesh occurred not only in the mystery of *the* Incarnation, but that it has continued to occur in the entire incarnate history of creation and humankind. And it is occurring now in his daily life. As if finally locating himself in this incarnational here-and-now where these revelations can be achieved, Will tells Allie at the greenhouse that he "think[s]" he is "in love" with her (*SC*, 374) and that he believes a new life for them is possible "up here" in the actual world with others. At least tentatively and hesitantly, Will is beginning to locate himself in the home he shares with all humankind for all time.

The sacramental imagery Percy uses to describe Will's return to Allie emphasizes Will's incipient revelations about who he is and where he is. As he strides across the golf course toward the greenhouse, Will notices with pleasure the "fresh cold air" against his face, perhaps an allusion to the breeze that brought the Word to Adam and Eve in God's recently incarnate and ruined garden (Genesis 3.8). At the greenhouse, Will talks with Allie in a "sunny warm corner" (*SC*, 373) of the "cathedral porch" (*SC*, 86). A few days later, after planning his incorporation with Mr. Arnold, Mr. Ryan, and Mr. Eberhart at St. Mark's, Will arrives at Allie's ark-like home in the ruins (*SC*, 86) to find her working beneath "bars of yellow sunlight" that gleam through the "wet spokes of the pines." In this spectacularly radiant setting, Allie is planting avocado pits in her new garden where "Mesozoic ferns" are sprouting in a delicate show of life and beauty. She sings "bell-like . . . and plangent" "Love's Message." And, apparently receiving her message, Will realizes at this moment that what he wants more than anything else in his life is "to lie down .. by the Grand Crown" with Allie in his arms. His desire is for the love, the eros, he sees incarnate in Allie's "dearest heart" and "dear ass" (*SC*, 403–5) and, unwittingly, for the agape symbolized by her sacramental "immaculate white and turquoise" (*SC*, 264) stove.

At the end of the novel, Allie joins Will on the road, where he discovers after a couple of days with her "up here" at the Linwood Holiday Inn that, although he is now homeless, that there is surely a place for him besides his father's dark woods. Will realizes at the motel that he doesn't "have an address" and doesn't "live anywhere" (*SC*, 380, 383).[24] But this sudden recognition of his dislocation and homelessness does not now cause him to seek, as he did earlier, a way out of a world he considered "farcical" and "demented." Instead, Will refuses to accept that he is an utterly "placeless person in a placeless place" and rejects his father's way. He looks out of the window of the second-floor Holiday Inn room and sees the vast openness of the Great Smokies, "the sun . . . touch[ing] the top of the violet mountains . . . [and] glitter[ing] as if it had struck sparks from rock" (*SC*, 384). It is a place where the transcendent world descends to immanent rock to spark to life the wondrous incarnate creation he has seen signified by Allie and by his love for her. That night he throws his father's Greener and Luger into the gorge just down the road from the motel (*SC*, 385–86). Will's casting from him that night the past and the death that his father's guns represent may have been prompted by his somehow intuiting earlier at the motel window that the immense creation on the horizon—electric with life—is his true home.

The next morning Will awakes with Allie, the "morning light pour[ing] in" (*SC*, 387) the room. The same sun that "sparks" life out in the vastness of the mountain landscape now bathes them in its life-giving radiance. The two lovers spend "all day and all night" in the hands of each other, Allie examining every inch of Will's body and he "marveling at how she was made." Will is free this day of the interior world of his Cartesian *cogito* and literally in touch with his incarnate existence. Through his here-and-now, flesh-and-blood union with another being, he becomes intensely conscious of his bodily existence among the actualities of the world that is his home. In Allie and in this union he finds a sign of this home, thinking to himself, "entering her was like turning a corner and coming home" (*SC*, 388, 390).

Perhaps it is this physical human connection that makes it possible for Will to realize that there may be other signs that will tell him about his home and that they may be waiting just outside the window. A sign that he sees through the drapes the next morning shows him another level of that home he has found signified in his relationship with Allie. Will sees on the horizon, the "Smoky Mountains . . . humped up like a blue whale in the clear sky" (*SC*, 391). The allusion is to the Old Testament prophet Jonah, whose escape after three days from the belly of a whale, Jesus tells a group of unbelieving scribes and Pharisees, is a sign of the Son of Man's Resurrection (Matthew 12. 38–40). It is because of this Resurrection that the home that Will has found signified in the body of Allie is filled with the life and love of the Holy Spirit, just as this room at the Linwood Holiday Inn is filled with the morning light of a new day.

Will has discovered in the hands of Allie a love and a home that has saved him from actual death in the Thomasville swamp and may save him from the living death on the other side of the fence in Linwood. And he has seen at St. Mark's in the hands of Mr. Arnold, Mr. Ryan, and the orderlies signs of a similar kind of love at work among strangers. Will's intimate experiences with Allie and the residents of the nursing home illustrate that he is now more willing to look out at the sacramental world and its inhabitants—and able to see significances (*SC*, 372) there. It may be because of this new inclination to direct his eyes outward that he goes to Father Weatherbee at the end of the novel in search for clues to the mysterious source of the love he has witnessed recently at the greenhouse, the Holiday Inn, and St. Mark's. He has learned in an earlier meeting with Father Weatherbee at St. Mark's that the old Episopalian priest believes in Apostolic Succession and the laying on of hands (*SC*, 355), and he therefore believes that he may know something about the God who sends his love through such sacramental rituals. Will assumes that because Father Weatherbee believes in the "laying on of hands" that Jesus used to cure the sick (Matthew 6.5), he knows how such sacramental acts and signs make present the salvific power of the Holy Spirit (Acts 8.17). Will apparently also believes that the priest is a modern "apostle" of the faith who can deliver this divine curative power through his hands. Will obviously wants these sacramental hands at work in his life, since he asks Father Weatherbee for the sacrament of marriage.

But Father Weatherbee does not have the knowledge and sacramental priestly powers Will is seeking. Will believes the priest "knows something" that he does not know and may have the "authority" to tell him what it is (*SC*, 409), but Will does not adequately see that Father Weatherbee is also a "senile" (*Con*, 205) believer who does not himself sufficiently understand the Good News of "salvation" (*SC*, 408) Will wants to hear. Father Weatherbee's spiritual deficiencies are suggested when the two first meet in the attic at St. Mark's (*SC*, 354–56), a place where the priest and a few other patients divert themselves for hours each day in the "waist-high landscape" of toy trains and tracks that fill the room. Enclosed in this "nostalgic" fantasy "landscape," they are as lost in romanticized versions of reality as Will's father, who also finally chose an attic escape over participation with others in real landscapes. Removed in the attic and at St. Mark's from the incarnational world and the God revealed in it, Father Weatherbee is an atrophied pastor no longer spiritually healthy enough to direct and care for his flock. Half-blind and deaf (*SC*, 335, 408), this "ancient emaciated priest" in his railroader's cap greets Will in the attic landscape with hands that are like "two dry hot whispering banyan leaves." The banyan tree is a fig tree. Percy may be alluding in this image to the parable of the barren fig tree, the parable that Jesus used to condemn the spiritual ignorance of Israel (Mark 11.14). Father Weatherbee's dry hands do not whisper the Word, but offer only a barren and lifeless communion.

Father Weatherbee tells Will in the attic that he believes firmly that the original laying on of hands "occurred" (*SC*, 355). His use of the past tense suggests that he does not acknowledge that the sacramental gesture is still occurring in his church and still offering life. Instead of expressing a faith in a church that can offer its believers such spiritual life, Father Weatherbee tacitly accepts the spiritual authority of an Episcopalian church in which the leaders are exemplified by Jack Curl, who, he tells Will, reminds him "of a Kumongakvaikvai." He explains that this is the Mindanaoan "dung bird" who follows behind cattle to feed on their manure. Unintentionally, Father Weatherbee symbolically identifies himself with this parasitic bird when he imitates its call, "*kvai kvai*" (*SC*, 356). Later, in Jack Curl's office with Will, he again unconsciously imitates the dung bird when he rhapsodizes about his idyllic life as a missionary on the island of Mindanao and excitedly "crane[s] up his neck like a Philippine bird" (*SC*, 409). As self-absorbed as a Kumongakvaikvai feeding on manure, Father Weatherbee feeds his imagination with his lifeless but, to him, beautiful memories. The priest is so lost in his feeding that he forgets about Will's request for the sacrament of marriage and this penitent's plea for knowledge about the "salvation that comes from the Jews" (*SC*, 408–10). Father Weatherbee offers no healing hands.

Father Weatherbee withdraws from the incarnational world and his spiritual duties in it and prefers his solitary, pleasant oblivion in the attic at St. Mark's to the trials of life down below. He is no Father Boomer, the muscular and healthy Catholic priest at the end of *The Last Gentleman*. This vigorous young priest confidently took the dying Jamie in his "big ruddy American League paws" (*LG* 396, 405) to administer the sacrament of baptism, knowing that his hands were capable of redeeming this innocent child from his suffering and death. Nor is Father Weatherbee willing to accept the "offensive burden" of love[25] that Father Smith in *The Thanatos Syndrome* welcomes in his work among the sick and dying outcasts at his hospice in Feliciana Parish. Instead of recognizing any power of salvation in his or his church's hands, Father Weatherbee believes no redemption is possible for the "unhappy," "worried," "pleasure-loving," "selfish," "cruel," shameless and godless people (*SC*, 409–10) who populate the hopelessly sinful America where he lives.

He tells Will in Curl's office at St. Mark's that he does not know why America is like this and goes on to tell him about an Edenic village of "gentle and loving" innocent primitives he visited regularly when he was a missionary in the Philippines. Father Weatherbee demonstrates in this celebration of the perfectly virtuous and happy lives of the Mindanaoans and in his condemnation of the sins of Americans that he does not believe in the Fall, a universal existential defeat and exile from paradise. He thinks some are Fallen and some not. Jay Tolson argues that Father Weatherbee's denial of such a universal defeat is theologically opposite from Percy's own strong Catholic conviction that there can be no belief in salvation without a belief in the blunt fact of Original Sin and its consequences in human history.[26] From Percy's perspective, Father Weatherbee's gnostic idealization of the man-made new Eden in Mindanoa has its roots in the popular twentieth-century romantic, scientistic faith in mankind's ability to build a utopian society. This is a secular faith, Percy believes, based on the assumption that humans are naturally good creatures with unlimited intellectual and moral capacities. Because of these capacities, they have the power to effect their own salvation from the unpleasant imperfections of their environment and life (*SP*, 394–96).[27] In *The Thanatos Syndrome*, Percy shows the dangers of political ideologies based on this assumption that it is possible both to conceive of a perfect life and to construct a utopian society made in the image of those conceptions. Stalin's Russia and Hitler's Germany are the most conspicuous examples in this century of such ideologies.

Because Father Weatherbee cannot accept the universal reality that sin and suffering exist in *all* the landscapes beyond his attic hideaway, he does not have the authority to give Will the news about salvation. His lack of authority does not lie simply in the fact that he is not Catholic. Percy says in "The Message in the Bottle" that only someone who accurately understands the castaway's predicament can serve as a "newsbearer" for him (*MB*, 135). Only someone who knows that the castaway is in exile from his true home with God—and in exile with all the other islanders—is capable of telling the amnesiac castaway where he is, who he is, and what he should do. Only such a newsbearer has the authority to tell him of a salvation that waits for him across the seas. Father Boomer, Percy says, is a Kierkegaardian "Apostle" who has the authority in his hands to deliver the news (*Con*, 113), but the "timid" and "fearful" Father Weatherbee does not. He does not recognize that the Rousseauean innocents in Naga-Naga and the pathetically immoral sinners of America are exiles on the same island. And Father Weatherbee does not want to be on the shore with these depressing Americans to tell them about salvation. At the very end of his meeting with Will, he tries to "sidle past" Will and "get back to the Atchinson, Topeka and the Santa Fe and the lonesome whistle of the Seaboard Air Line, the only things in all of America he recognized" (*SC*, 411).

Will does not hear any Good News from Father Weatherbee that transforms his uncertain present situation with Allie and his family into the "happy and useful" life he dreamed of at the end of *The Last Gentleman* (*LG*, 385).[28] Because Will has learned of no Christian faith that can serve as a guide as he continues his wayfaring into the future, he faces a menacing complexity of problems without the comforting Christian assurance that there is, finally, a redemption from the often painful difficulties of finite existence. Will can only hope that the love and life he has discovered with Allie can be his in the future and that the home he plans with her and his friends from St. Mark's can actually be built. The fact that Will and Allie are literally separated at the end of the novel—she at the Linwood Holiday Inn with her dog, he at St. Mark's trying to arrange a way to get someone to signify through a church sacrament he does not believe in that their union is a holy one—suggests that their future life of love together is problematical. Allie's family is trying to acquire the real estate she has inherited. It is on this property in the North Carolina mountains and on the Georgia coast that Allie and Will plan to build their new home. In addition, Kitty has vowed to make sure Will never sees Allie again and plans for her mentally ill daughter to spend the rest of her life under professional psychiatric care. Will's daughter, Jack Curl, and Vance Battle are well on their way to acquiring Will's sizeable fortune, and they also expect Will to live out the rest of his days in a convalescent home where he will not trouble them.

Father Weatherbee lacks the authority to tell Will of a Christian faith that would enable him to rejoice in a life that threatens his happiness in such overwhelming ways. But in the final scene of the novel in Jack Curl's office the priest is, ironically, responsible for Will's achieving a new hope and energy that may assist him in his future search for love and God. In the midst of his excited questioning of the priest about signs of Christ's Second Coming "in these very times," Will realizes suddenly that he is tightly gripping the wrists of Father Weatherbee. As he releases the tiny, lifeless wrists "like dry sticks," he sees something "odd" in the man's emaciated face, something that makes him "let go and f[a]ll back." In the terribly bruised face of the dying Jamie at the end of *The Last Gentleman*, Will sees a sign that makes him wonder if human life finally amounts only to the ruin and "abject surrender" of death, if finally it is just a mere "ultimate rot" of tissue (*LG*, 401). Here, in a fearful face ravaged by age and defeat, Will again sees a sign that makes him wonder if there is anything in life other than the suffering and imminent death he sees before him. In this case, the sign reminds him of Allie's face and her "strong quick hands" and the love, life, and home that he has recently discovered is possibly in them. It is this recognition that causes his heart to "leap . . . with a secret joy."

This emotional revelation causes him to wonder further if her gift of love is "a sign of a giver," makes him wonder if the "Lord is here" at this very place and in this very moment in Father Weatherbee's "simple silly holy face." Is he, he wonders as he looks into the face, "crazy" to "want" the "joy" (*SC*, 411) that is in the hands of Allie and to want also a knowledge of the God that "sparks" to life the love he finds with her and fills their home with light. "Wait" was Will's refrain after his experience twenty years ago in the hospital at Santa Fe (*LG*, 407–9). But now he realizes that he may not have to wait for the Second Coming for this "joy."[29] Will knows that it is possible that the redemptive love that made its descent into flesh in the Incarnation, the First Coming, may be continuously announcing its presence here and now in the sacramental world, even in the impotent but possibly holy faces of suffering and homeless men like Father Weatherbee.

Dr. Thomas More:
In the Ruins and at the Fire Tower

5

Love in the Ruins: Signs of the End?

> This morning, hauling up a great unclassified beast of a fish, I thought
> of Christ coming again at the end of the world. . . .
> —Love in the Ruins, 387

A few weeks before the publication of *Love in the Ruins* (1971), Walker
Percy delivered a short address to the National Book Award press conference in New York (published as "Concerning *Love in the Ruins,*" *SP*, 247–50)
in which he commented on his latest work. He began his speech by talking
about the political and social satire of his new novel and how this element
differentiates it from *The Moviegoer* (1961) and *The Last Gentleman* (1966).
But the address is less about this point of differentiation than it is about the
intricate connections between the novel's satire and its presentation of the
themes that constitute Percy's imaginative and philosophical vision, not
only in *Love in the Ruins* but in the body of his work. *Love in the Ruins,*
Percy asserts in the speech, explores some of the problems of self-placement resulting from the pervasive scientistic mind-set of twentieth-century
America. Dr. Thomas More's solipsistic messiah complex, his frustrating
search for love and happiness, and his suicidal despair are all results of his
self-placement as either transcendent, scientific "knower" or happiness-seeking, need-satisfying organism. As scientist, Tom sets himself apart from
phenomenal creation in his solitary search for the "truth" about America's
and mankind's problems, and as need satisfier he seeks those stimulations
of the *cogito* or body that he thinks will bring him happiness.

These ontological problems, Percy says in his address, are the result of
the devaluation of language in the society where Tom attempts to name the
"truth" about himself, the world, and others and tries to discover happiness
in his love for his family and friends. In the language world of Fedville and

Paradise Estates in which Tom struggles with his self-placement, most language-users identify some kind of interior state of happiness as the only reasonable existential goal and assume that consumption and need satisfaction are the only ways for the self to achieve that goal. "Love" in the language of the residents of Paradise Estates is a word used loosely to refer to the pleasant emotional condition or to the happiness one accomplishes by satisfying one's private desires. "Truths" transcendent of these desires is in the knowing of science and, peripherally, in the aesthetic pleasures of art. It is in this deprived semiotic that Tom searches for love, happiness, and knowledge about himself and the world. The result is that he becomes trapped in a closed, Cartesian concept of himself in which he cannot see any significance to his experience beyond his mental activity and the stimulations provided by his body.

As Dr. Thomas More himself diagnoses in *Love in the Ruins*, he and his neighbors in Paradise Estates suffer from a "chronic angelism-bestialism that rives soul from the body and sets it orbiting the great world as the spirit of abstraction."[1] This is a "hermaphroditism of the spirit" (*LR*, 383) that functions to enclose Tom within the knowing of his "angelic" intellect and within the satisfactions of his "bestial" desires. In this interior world, he probes into his memory for explanations for his loss of the love and happiness he enjoyed with Doris and Samantha and "cast[s] ahead" (*LR*, 382) to a self-constructed apocalyptic future where he imagines himself as a scientific messiah for his sick society and a happy lover of Lola, Moira, and/or Ellen. When not lost in his analyses of his past and dreams of the future, Tom's "bestial" self seeks the happiness that the stimulations of physical pleasure can provide—in his case, primarily the pleasures of illicit sex and heavy drinking. Percy says Tom More is an example of the Pascalian man who, in his confusing of his self with his *cogito* , "tries to be an angel" in his pursuit of transcendent ideas and ideals, only to descend to the indifferent carnality of his body and behave like a "beast" (*Con*, 140).

Finally, Percy maintained in his NBA press conference speech, he wanted to show in the novel that there is a "center" (*SP*, 248) of human existence, a language "center" that offers the "best hope" (*SP*, 250) for wayfarers who are looking for a new consciousness of where they are, who they are, and what they must do in this world. *Love in the Ruins* emphasizes that the best hope modern wayfarers like Tom have for the development of such a consciousness depends on their being able to place themselves accurately in time and space, immanent reality. They can accomplish this accurate self-placement only through language transactions with others in which they name a self and existence different from the ones they currently know. In Percy's sacramental Christianity, the self is "neither angel [transcendent

knower] nor organism [need satisfier] but . . . wayfaring creature somewhere between" (*MB*, 113).

Love in the Ruins is about Tom's professional, political, psychological,
emotional, and spiritual engagement with a scientistic culture that leads
him into the enclosure of the angelic-bestial self. Tom does not live in a
society that will provide him with a sacramental consciousness that will
open him to phenomenal creation in its here-and-now literalness and that
will simultaneously show him how to see and read the particularities there
as signs of a transcendent dimension of being. Consequently, he is displaced from the world and his genuine self. Only at the end of *Love in the
Ruins*, in the Slave Quarters, does Tom begin to learn how to see his finite
time-space experience—the "fish" he caught just "this morning" (*LR*, 387),
for example—as signifying a love and happiness larger than what he can
discover in his pleasure-seeking and knowing. Tom sees a possible mysterious significance to the fish and associates it with Christ, the Logos incarnate
in flesh; he is therefore "reading" his actual, immediate experience as a sign
of a world and self beyond his current angelism-bestialism. He begins to
assume a "waiting and watching" psychic posture, a consciousness that assents to the possibility that a true messiah will come "again at the end of
the world" in a sacred and final apocalypse (*LR*, 387) to unite the divided
bestial flesh with the angelic spirit. Tom's incipient new consciousness of
himself as a participant in this open fullness of time is the way of seeing
that Percy believes is the best hope for those interiorized, closed selves like
Tom who find themselves prisoners of their desires and mental constructions of reality.

WHAT'S GONE WRONG: PARADISE ESTATES,
SELF-PLACEMENT, LANGUAGE

As the discussion above shows, *Love in the Ruins* presents essentially the
same Catholic sacramental vision of the self and the world that Percy develops in his other novels. But, as Percy pointed out in his speech at the
NBA press conference, the comic tone and obvious social and political satire do make his third novel quite different. In his earlier *The Moviegoer* and
The Last Gentleman, Percy focuses on the personal existential quests of his
introspective and troubled wayfarers, but he is obviously more interested in
Love in the Ruins in satirically attacking various kinds of philosophical and
theological fatuousness in twentieth-century American culture. Percy reveals the mindless consumerism of the upper middle-class in his depiction
of the Paradise Estates lifestyles, exposes the inhumanity of the modern

medical science responsible for the Love Clinic and the euthanasists' Happy Isles Separation Center in Georgia, and pokes fun at the relativistic, complacent moral and spiritual climate responsible for the establishment of the American Catholic Church (based in Cicero, Illinois). Percy, commenting wryly on the novel's humor and satire in a 1971 letter to his friend Robert Daniel, says the book is "an outrageous hodgepodge . . . with a little something to offend everybody" (WPP, series 3, folder 22)—that is, everybody who does not understand the inhumanity and immorality inherent in the scientific and social scientific mind-set that is the source of the medical, artistic, economic, and political institutions the novel ridicules.[2]

This satiric attack is made through the often hilarious events and characters that Percy uses to construct his narrative; in fact, Percy was worried, Jay Tolson maintains, that the comical action in *Love in the Ruins* might cause readers to miss his serious point about the dehumanization in modern America.[3] *Love in the Ruins* is indeed funnier than *The Moviegoer* and *The Last Gentleman* and can provoke the most dour reader to laugh out loud in a way that Percy's first two novels cannot. For example, what reader of the novel could ever see an Ohio license plate or hear even the most tragic news story about the Buckeye state without involuntarily smirking and thinking of Mr. Ives's invectives aimed at the "chickenshit Ohioans," who he says "pestered" (*LR*, 231–32) him so intolerably during his forced retirement at the Golden Years Senior Citizen Settlement in Tampa (*LR*, 222)? At the old folks' home, Mr. Ives's refused to participate with these Ohioans in their inane "Guys and Gals a go-go" and "grandaddy golf," activities obviously instituted by the staff at the Settlement in order to create some kind of contrived sense of geriatric community among the strangers housed there. In his defecating twice on "flirtation Walk during the Merry Widow's promenade" and his "urinat[ing] on Ohio in the Garden of the Fifty States," Mr. Ives graphically expressed his understanding of the motives behind the social activities at the Settlement and registered his disapproval of the attempts by the staff to modify and control his behavior by their subjecting him to "extensive reconditioning in the Skinner box" (*LR*, 222–23).

The clippings and notes from current magazines and newspapers that Percy gathered as source material for the novel (WPP, series 1.C.1b) are evidence of his specific satiric intentions in *Love in the Ruins* and also provide clues to some of his serious philosophical purposes. He was, apparently, particularly impatient with some of the romantic and idealistic concepts of the self popular in 1960s America. For example, there are many clippings about the youthful counterculture and its doctrines of "free love." One article recommends that the American government pass a "sexual bill of rights" for the "sexually handicapped" and create agencies that would provide for the needs of exhibitionists and other "deviant groups." The essay promises that all sex crimes would be eliminated by such government action, a moral utopia being the result! Another article from *Time* (1966) predicts that chemical and electrical treatments of the brain will in the future make the retarded "normal," improve the memory of the senile, transform depression into elation. Science, in short, we are told, "can accomplish anything," even make the citizenry intellectually and morally palatable to the sensibilities of the scientists and the government bureaucrats who finance their research.

In his discussion of the satire in *Love in the Ruins*, Percy further explained to his audience at the NBA press conference that the novel is "futuristic satire," dealing with political events in America around 1983, and that in it he did indeed intend to deride groups like the love and peace advocates who proposed that America turn its back on the science, technology, and Judeo-Christian thought of the last two thousand years (*SP*, 249). But *Love in the Ruins* is not, he emphasized, the kind of political satire represented by Orwell's *1984* or Huxley's *Brave New World*. Instead, he argued, the novel is a more general statement about the American "pursuit of happiness" and the malaise and anxiety that ironically result from that pursuit. Unlike Orwell's and Huxley's novels, then, *Love in the Ruins* is not directly ideological satire, even though it does show the polarization of left and right, young and old, black and white, rich and poor, Southerners and Ohioans. Percy insisted in his speech that he wanted his novel to be a more general kind of diagnostic satire that examines the painful symptoms of a society that appears free, pluralistic, and democratic but is plagued by a pervading and indefinite dread, a common sense that "something has gone wrong" (*SP*, 248).

In his interviews, Percy maintained that Dr. Thomas More functions as a spokesman for and example of what "has gone wrong" and that this role differentiates Tom from his earlier protagonists. He was less interested in this novel than in *The Moviegoer* or *The Last Gentleman*, he said, in depicting an alienated quester on a pilgrimage and search for existential identity and belief. Tom, Percy argued, is quite different from Binx and Will in that he has "no doubt" and "knows exactly who he is and what he needs" (*Con*, 48); he "has no philosophical problems" and "knows what he believes" (*Con*, 74–75). Percy told Bradley Dewey in 1974 that in *Love in the Ruins*, he "was less interested in a search" than he was in writing a novel that was both "comic" and "religious" (*Con*, 115). In a 1973 interview with Zoltan Abadi-Nagy, Percy explained that in *Love in the Ruins* he wanted to create a hero through whose eyes he could satirize American culture. Because Tom More, he says, is more "involved" than Binx and Will in the "contemporary issues" and the "sociological reality" of modern American culture, he is more capable of presenting the kind of satire Percy intended (*Con*, 74).

Love in the Ruins, while clearly social satire of the sort Percy explains, is also an examination of the modern scientistic concepts of the self, society, and physical phenomena that cause the individual in such a society to suffer a dislocation from himself and reality. He says *Love in the Ruins* is about a "deranged" twentieth-century culture, "an exercise in Cartesianism" meant to show how Descartes's division of the self into *cogito* and body has become for most twentieth-century Americans an unconscious epistemological and ontological assumption. This pervading Cartesianism frustrates their attempts to place themselves "into this world in . . . [a] mode of being" (*MCon*, 233) that will provide them a satisfying sense of who they are, where they are, and what they should do as they make their way through their lives.

Dr. Thomas More in *Love in the Ruins* has been seduced by his scientistic culture into such a Cartesian self-placement. Existentially isolated and enclosed, Tom alternately places himself in the world as either an "angelic" scientist seeking satisfaction in "knowing" (*LR*, 383, 214, e.g.) or as organism "longing" (*LR*, 21, 23, 95, 157, 265, 366, 393) achingly for "happiness" (*LR*, 214, e.g.) through need satisfactions. In the four days of his life chronicled in the novel (July 1–4), Tom spends much of his time trying to convince Max Gottlieb, the director of the Fedville hospital, and any others who will listen that he has discovered through his scientific research a device that can save mankind from destruction. In his role as knower, Tom is self-absorbed in his ideas about the truth of human existence and in his personal scientific goals. He wants to achieve fame equal to Newton's and Einstein's and be recognized as one of the three greatest scientific minds "of the Christian era" (*LR*, 90)—and win a Nobel Prize. At the same time, as a longing, desire-filled organism, he yearns desperately for happiness. He believes love will provide that emotional condition and conceives of his past life with Doris and Samantha as a time when he enjoyed such an Edenic emotional and psychological state of being. Now that he has lost that happiness, he plans to regain it through his love of Moira, Ellen, and/or Lola in the Howard Johnson's. In these self-centered contemplations about his personal love and happiness, Tom is enclosed in his memories of paradise lost and in his dreams of a future paradise regained. Present time and phenomena vanish from his sight. In both roles, scientific savior and Don Juan, he is closed off from the created world and its signs in an interiorized self devoted to its private stimulations and goals.

Tom may be confident about "exactly who he is and what he needs"

(*Con*, 48), as Percy says of him, but because he has misplaced himself, he does not know where he is or what to do. The allusion to Dante's *Inferno* in the opening scene of the novel identifies Tom with another middle-aged wayfarer who "comes to [him]self" (*LR*, 3) in a forest and realizes that he does not know where he is and therefore does not know what path in life to take. Tom's impaired ability to locate himself accurately in time and space is ironically suggested by his first word in the novel, "Now." The "now" of this opening scene is, as the title of the first chapter indicates, "5 p.m./July 4" (*LR*, 3). But Tom is oblivious to this moment of actual experience; instead, he is thinking about the imminent apocalypse that he in his role as scientist-savior has prophesied—the catastrophe that will end the history of his culture. Of course, he learns in the next few hours that there is no such apocalypse. Because of this dislocation in time, Tom is also disoriented in spatial reality. Tom is indeed a lost wayfarer who cannot accurately name where he is. He looks out from his bunker at the strange world below him, and he can see nothing but threat and ruins; from his perspective, this is not his home but the place where social and political life as he knows it is coming to an end. All that he is capable of seeing in the created world is decaying buildings and crumbling interstates; the only signs that he can see to read are the ones that signify to him the hopeless demise of American society.

"What to do?" (*LR*, 73,168) is inevitably the crucial question for modern castaways like Tom who are attempting to place themselves in the world. Displaced from time and space, Tom is, on the one hand, a representative of the angelic self that habitually chooses to withdraw into the narrow, interiorized world of its own memory, theories, and "dreams of the future" (*SP*, 165) in order to locate what to do. This is Tom the scientist-savior with his lapsometer. On the other hand, as bestial organism-in-an-environment, Tom fights for his physical safety and need satisfactions against the political revolutionaries in Paradise Estates who threaten to deny him his life in the Howard Johnson rooms with his women and Early Times. But Tom's efforts at need satisfaction can only lead him to a "death in life" (*LR*, 199), the same kind of psychic death Will Barrett in *The Second Coming* discovers in Linwood, North Carolina. Tom's faith that he can live happily in the rooms of the ruined Howard Johnson's as long as the Campbell Soup, Viennas, and Early Times last (*LR*, 7) indicates that he is paradoxically and blindly striving toward this kind of living death.

The incipient change in Tom's crippling angelic-bestial vision of the world and himself is suggested at the end of *Love in the Ruins* by his defeating Art Immelmann and his abandoning his plans for his future at

Howard Johnson's. When Tom banishes Art and the angelism he represents with his prayer to St. Thomas More, Tom is in his prayer recognizing
a knowledge beyond his own angelic intellect and assenting to the possibility of a source of information about life beyond his *cogito* and desires. His
"two little popsies" (*LR*, 364), Moira and Lola, have abandoned him, and
therefore his future bestial happiness with them at Howard Johnson's is no
longer an existential option. And he does in fact give up his dreams of the
future with them and choose instead the sacrament of marriage with Ellen.

Tom is beginning at the end of the novel to name himself and his world
in a different way, and it is this change in language that may enable him to
escape the angelic-bestial consciousness that afflicts him and his society. In
his reference to the language themes in the novel, Percy implied in his 1971
NBA press conference speech (*SP*, 248) that he wanted the reader of *Love
in the Ruins* to consider the relationship between the language "degradation" in the society depicted in the novel and Yeats's famous statement about
the "center not holding" (*LR*, 18, 138). In fact, Percy considered a title for
the novel that would echo Yeats's phrase.[4] While acknowledging that *Love
in the Ruins* is, on one level, obviously a satire about the political and social
upheavals of 1960's America, Percy went on to say in his speech that when
he used Yeats's "the center does not hold," he was not referring to a political
center but "had a different center in mind" (SP, 248). Provocatively, he did
not go on to explain what he meant by this statement and left his audience
with the task of discerning what different center he wanted them to see.

In *Love in the Ruins*, Tom More uses Yeats's phrase precisely as Percy
says he does not intend it—that is, to refer to the dissolution of stable social
instutution in his society. Tom, early in the novel, when he is explaining
what he sees as the hopeless political divisions of the country, announces:
"The center did not hold" (*LR*, 18). Later, analyzing the religious divisions
and confusions in his community, Tom again says in reference to this religious problem, "the center did not hold" (*LR*, 138). Since Tom, unlike Percy,
does identify the unraveling center as a political/social one, he reveals that
he does not have a language that will enable him to locate the different
center Percy encourages the reader to discover.

For Percy, the different center that Tom fails to locate lies in human
language, the center that makes possible whatever consciousness of the self
and the world human beings have.[5] The language of Paradise Estates and
Fedville, the language of the semiotic world in which Tom lives, is, unfortunately, the language center that is the source for his consciousness of his
world and his knowledge of how to place himself in it. This is a deprived
semiotic that accounts for Tom's detached consciousness of himself as or-

biting knower and bestial happiness-seeker. In Tom's society, the meanings of words have "slipped," Percy says (*SP*, 248), the result being that in Paradise Estates words like "freedom," "dignity of the individual," and "quality of life" have become cliché abstractions drained of meaning. Or worse, they have become words that obscure the political injustice and the medical inhumanity practiced by the racist citizens and Fedville euthanasists who use them. These are the kinds of words used by Tom's fellow scientists to describe from their detached orbits the reality they see in social and individual experience.

Tom, then, functions with a language center that will not enable him to arrive at a full consciousness of himself and his world. His society's scientistic semiotic is the center that accounts for his incomplete understanding about what constitutes an ideal society and a satisfying personal life. But instead of understanding that he might have such an inadequate knowledge of his existential predicament, Tom believes that the crumbling center that is not holding involves merely the social, political, and religious problems that he can observe, analyze, and solve. The different center that Percy sees lies in the impoverished language of Tom's community, a semiotic that prevents its citizens from accurately naming their experience and therefore psychically encloses them in narrow concepts of what constitutes human happiness and consciousness.

Tom More is both an example and victim of the language "degradation" (*Con*, 140) and subsequent deprived consciousness that is endemic to such a culture. He has a language that makes it difficult for him to name his experience. Tom says, as he wanders around the abandoned Howard Johnson's with Moira reading the obscene graffiti on the walls, that his "desire for her had blown ... [his] speech center." He is suffering from the same kind of aphasia as his society, a language impairment that is at the center of a maimed consciousness. It is a naming disorder that makes it difficult for language users to name any reality outside their immanent environment and their desires and need satisfactions in it. The effects of Tom's aphasia are illustrated in this scene at the motel when he struggles to tell Moira he loves her but comes out with a syntactically garbled "Love, I, you." He is in the next moment locked in a passionate embrace with her, "kissing ... , [her]mouth open, gold eyes open" (*LR*, 136). Tom has trouble speaking about love, but is quite successful in his physical relationship with Moira, as this ardent embrace implies. Tom can engage with her in his physical need satisfaction, but has a limited semiotic that makes it difficult for him to name his love experience in any satisfactory or complete way. Such a semiotic and the resulting fragmentary consciousness make it impossible for him here to experience with Moira that intersubjective union that Percy believes language can reveal to us, that awareness of being one with others under God (*LC*, 112).

Tom's blown language center prevents his connecting the word "love" with any phenomena beyond his immediate experience with Moira's body, and therefore in his relationship with her he is limited to the satisfactions provided by his own carnal pleasure. Percy makes it clear that these two lovers are typical of love in the ruins. The graffiti on the motel walls surrounding Tom and Moira shows that their estrangement from each other is not a unique existential condition for lovers in their culture. In the graffiti, Tom and Moira read the lonely words of others who have occupied these rooms before them, lovers whose deprived language also cut them off from intersubjective union. These messengers from the past also attempted to name in their degraded language the desire and love they were experiencing. Their pathetic expressions on the walls reveal that they were, like Tom, locked in the closed selfhood of isolated physical desire: "*For a free suck call room 208*"; "*The Laughing Cavalier: Room 204 has a cutout on her pussy*" (*LR*, 136).

Percy told Marcus Smith in a 1976 interview that he wanted to show in the novel how "words can wear out," especially, in the case of twentieth-century American culture, the words of religious language (*Con*, 140). For example, when Tom tries to use the word "love" to identify his experience with another, he is using a word that is used indiscriminately in his society to signify a broad range of emotionally satisfying experiences—from the stimulus-response behavior of the couples that are studied at the Love Clinic to the desires for "women," "whiskey," "science," and "God" (*LR*, 6). The inability of Tom and the residents of Paradise Estates to name accurately with their language any kind of love beyond mere desire and need satisfactions—the Love incarnate in Christ, for example—is implied in the banner they erect for the Pro-Am golf tournament. It proclaims, "Jesus Christ Greatest Pro of Them All" (*LR*, 289). Humorously, of course, the motto reveals a writer and a reader of its message who cannot conceive of a Christ whose being is a sign of a *caritas* transcendent of their consciousness. The words on the banner imply that in the country club semiotic of Paradise Estates the word "Jesus" carries the same signification as the words "golf Pro." The motto shows that the language users here do not have a language developed enough so that they can distinguish the Christian charity signified by Christ from their other immanent loves. Percy's point is that Christ, the Word—and the love incarnate in Him—is unknowable in a world of signs like the one in Paradise Estates, a semiotic so deprived of meaning that it cannot distinguish between Sam Snead and Jesus Christ.

At the end of his address at the NBA press conference, Percy stated that he wanted in *Love in the Ruins* "to investigate the best hope of the survivors" (*SP*, 250) like Tom as they strive for consciousness in the detritus of twentieth-century America. Percy in a 1971 interview with Charles Bunting says, "if the center holds, I'm hopeful" (*Con*, 51–52). In a later interview, Percy implies that the hope in *Love in the Ruins* is indicated by the emerging "new community" (*Con*, 74) described in the final chapter, "Five Years Later." In that chapter, Tom is beginning to escape the solitary quest for happiness and knowing that has in the past isolated him from Doris and Samantha, from his neighbors in Paradise Estates, and from his colleagues at the Fedville complex. He has moved out of Paradise Estates to join another more cohesive community in the Slave Quarters, started a new family with Ellen Oglethorpe and their two children, returned to Father Smith's church, and is even thinking about joining his old friend Victor Charles in a political campaign that will unite the disaffected racial and political factions in their district. He is beginning to place himself in Gabriel Marcel's intersubjective world of "we are" (*MB*, 295).

Until his move to the Slave Quarters, Tom is closed off from a consciousness of the "plenitude of personal being" that lies beyond the roles he has adopted in his society.[6] Tom's interiorized vision has blinded him to the signs in the sacramental, sensible world. In the final chapter, he is becoming more attentive to immediate time-space events and naming his experience with more precision. This naming will take place with others in his intersubjective language transactions with his new family, the church, and his new community in the Slave Quarters. In this naming lies Will's hope for a way of seeing that will encourage him to continue his sign-reading in the mysterious world that is beginning to reveal itself to him.

MEMORY: LOVE AND HAPPINESS LOST

Tom has always placed himself apart from others and has felt little sense of community with them. Five years before his move to the Quarters he reflected on his "solitary life" (*LR*, 23). He has been known by his friends for his inwardness; Victor Charles says to him when they are talking of their past together, "You were always . . . to yourself" (*LR*, 148). Tom, early in the novel, without remorse recognizes the absence of charity in his character; he defines himself as a man who loves his "fellow man hardly at all" and does as he pleases (*LR*, 6). This cynical self-analysis indicates that he, like most in his society, is cut off from a knowledge of the kind of love represented by Christian charity. This is a love expressed by the Word in incarnate creation, a love that acts to unite all who live there. Tom's ignorance about this kind of intersubjective love is the primary cause for his past failures to find joy and satisfaction in his love for his first wife Doris, his daughter Samantha, and the Church.

During most of the action described in *Love in the Ruins* Tom looks inward to his memories and reflections on life, preferring the solitary self and life he constructs in his mind to the actual events and people immediately before him. William Godshalk explains how Tom "mythologizes" the past and thereby psychically removes himself from "immediate experience."[7] Tom's exploration of the past is primarily motivated by his desire to find an explanation for his current "unhappiness" (*LR*, 20), and he finds those explanations mostly in his past family relationships. His mother, father, wife, and daughter are transformed in his memories of them into symbolic agents that operate either to satisfy or deny his physical, emotional, or psychological needs. In these self-constructed narratives, Tom removes himself from actual experience and people and positions himself as a detached, aesthetic self who observes the world and discovers the truth about it. In this case, he sees his family experiences in the past as events that have functioned to provide him with good feelings, or events that have impinged on that happiness.

During the events of July 1 through July 4 Tom is shown repeatedly escaping the immediacy of present time and finite sacramental reality and retreating into a past where he theorizes about his personal history as it is embedded in the history of America and universal human history. He sees himself, places himself, in relation to history as an analytical observer who is trapped in its cyclical events, both an insightful witness to an end and a potential savior of society with his science and lapsometer.[8] Percy's depiction of Tom's apocalyptic theories may have been influenced by Eric Voegelin. Lewis Lawson notes that Percy in a 1967 interiew expressed his interest in Voegelin's theories about the influences of gnosticism in the development of human civilizations. Voegelin argues that throughout political history gnosticism has been a pervasive mind-set that has encouraged the founders of the great cultures to view themselves as messiahs building new utopias out of the apocalyptic ruins of their societies. He explains that such apocalyptic thinking is a function of the gnostic concept of history as endless cycles of destruction and rebuilding. This gnostic, closed, cyclical concept of human experience is in dramatic contrast to the Judaic understanding of time as a linear series of events that will end in a mysterious cosmic perfection.[9] Tom, at least during the four days of events that precede the novel's epilogue, exhibits that he does not have the hope inherent in this Judeo-Christian view of time and the self, but is more like Voegelin's gnostic, closed up in the endless cycles of history and lost in his theories about how to "save" himself and his society.

Tom's enclosure in his abstractions about history and his subsequent isolation from actual time-space experience and the people in it are illustrated throughout *Love in the Ruins*. This self-enclosure is symbolically emphasized in the novel by his frequent retreats into small, enclosed spaces where he contemplates his and his culture's history. For example, on July 4, after Tom escapes from St. Michael's where the Bantus have him imprisoned, he returns with Lola to the Howard Johnson's. There he is symbolically closed off from the world in the air-conditioner-produced "cold fogs" (*LR*, 318) that fill the tiny room. In the motel room, he sees himself as Arnold Toynbee explaining to Lola, Moira, and Ellen the dangers of what he believes is the impending political apocalypse. J. Gerald Kennedy notes the similarities between Toynbee's theories of historical cycles of cultural apocalypse and rebirth in *A Study of History* and Tom's views.[10] In a similar scene earlier that same day, Tom is alone in the bedroom of his house reading Stedmann's *History of World War I*, which he considers an accurate description of the beginning of the "suicide of the old Western world," the suicide that he believes is reaching its completion in his own day and the suicide he believes America can escape through his scientific knowledge and his lapsometer. Again in this scene in his bedroom, Tom is lost in his theories about the past and in his dreams of a paradasiacal future of his own making. He is blind to the grandeur of the sacramental present moment right outside his window, where "a sinking yellow moon shatters in the ripples" (*LR*, 47) out on the tranquil tropical waters behind his house.

In the opening scene of the novel, Tom looks out from his enclosed hideout above the interstate at the phenomenal world before him, seeing dimly through eyes swollen nearly shut by his allergic reaction to a number of gin fizzes he has recently consumed. What he is able to see he interprets incompletetely or inaccurately. He sees no mystery or beauty in the world before him and finds no significance to the Hopkinsian marsh hawk (*LR*, 4) that soars above him. He sees only a hellish ruin of death and danger. Alone "in a grove of young pines" (*LR*, 3), Tom is lost to immediacy, safely removed from the present troubles in his community by his contemplations about the demise of America and his participation in it. He talks about his political theories and America's tragic history, his self-absorption and solipsism emphasized by the fact that in this scene he is talking to himself and recording on a tape recorder his ruminations about the apocalypse he sees happening below him. Within the monologic narrative he creates, he sees himself as a citizen in an America that could have been a "new Eden" had it not been, he theorizes, for the "nigger business" and the moral failures of American Christendom in its treatment of Africans (*LR*, 57–58). He places himself in this history as one of the metaphorical riders in the roller-coaster-like saga of America: "the machinery clanks, the chain catches hold, and the cars jerk forward," he thinks, as he considers the ruins beneath his bunker in the pine grove. The United States has left "that felicitous and privileged siding," its promising frontier past and its Edenic potentiality, and is now dangerously careening through time. Now the machinery of time, he explains to himself, "carries us back into history with its ordinary catastrophes" (LR, 3–4).[11]

Tom places himself in this bleak version of American history as a middle-aged failure who is "normally . . . tolerably depressed and terrified" (LR, 25), a person whose misfortune it is to happen to live in these trying times. He explains his psychological, emotional, and spiritual discomfort by defining it as a twentieth-century paradigm. He believes that he lives in a society where many are "unhappy" (LR, 20) in the same way he is and that they therefore long, as he does, for some kind of relief from it. In such a predicament, he reasons, it is natural for the pervasive "unhappiness" to cause an incessant "longing" (LR, 21, 23, 95, 157, 265, 366, 393) for a way out of the relentless psychic malaise. The individual's existential quest, therefore, becomes a constant search for personal happiness, as is the case with Tom. He is prompted by this self-placement to seek "happiness" (LR, 214, e.g.) continuously in the self-indulgent pleasures of his science, Lola's music, drinking, and sex.

Like Camus's similarly alienated sensualist in The Fall,[12] Tom relies on his pursuit of need satisfactions to satisfy his longing, and they fail him. The result is hopelessness and despair. While talking with Max Gottlieb about his depression and attempted suicide, Tom tells Max that he wants to feel guilty about his hedonistic devotion to physical pleasure, specifically sexual pleasure, so that he can "get rid of it"—guilt—"by the sacrament of penance" (LR, 117). Although Tom is an avowed Catholic who says he is a believer, his scientistic placement of himself as a mere need-satisfying organism in an environment precludes his believing in sin. Organisms do not sin. If there is no sin, there can be no guilt. If there is no guilt, there is no repentance. And without repentance, there can be no redemption, no release from the dissatisfactions inherent in daily attempts to find satisfactions. So, Tom can only desire a way out of his suicidal despair. Tom, like Camus's Jean-Baptiste Clamence, suffers in a world that he constructs by his own misplacement in it, a world where there is no redemption from his endless longing and no release from the hopeless and fatiguing quest for moments of satisfaction.

In his analyses of his unhappiness, Tom mythologizes his own family history and the people in it. He places himself within an interior domestic drama in which he is a victim who has suffered a loss of a potentially Edenic intellectual, emotional, spiritual, and psychological happiness analogous to America's loss. He has few memories of his past with his parents and, generally, seems estranged from a parental love that could have made him happy. He places himself in his present life in the role of failed and drunken physician—a role he sees himself inheriting from his ineffectual father, whose very office he now occupies. Tom seems uncomfortably alienated from his mother in this self-scripted drama; he sees her as some sort of remote, exotic goddess, a "Catholic gnostic" with a wondrous "crystal ball." When he visits her at her home by the golf course, he admires her as if she is just some casual acquaintance, some energetic older woman in his community who is highly skilled in real estate sales and has "handsome legs" and a remarkable "bowel" (*LR*, 176–77). Noting Tom's lack of emotional intimacy with his mother, Lewis Lawson, in a psychoanalytical reading of *Love in the Ruins*, maintains that Tom's psychological problems stem largely from a psychic deprivation that results from his desire for his mother's love.[13]

Most of Tom's memories focus on his past with Doris and Samantha and the love and happiness that he experienced with them. In the opening scene in the pine grove, when Tom is reveling in his memories of his "good life" with his wife and daughter twenty years earlier—a time when he was a promising medical researcher and happily married to the lusty Doris (*LR*, 24)—Percy emphasizes once more how narrowly and partially Tom sees the actual world around him and how this dim seeing is accompanied by a turning inward to his memories. Tom, half blinded by the gin fizzes, says he sees the world as through a "turret slit." A few moments later, he abandons altogether his observations of the natural world around him, ignores "the globy oaks" and "fat grayish clouds" (*LR*, 21), and looks within to discover in his memory the causes for his tragic fall in middle age into the unhappiness of his "irregular life" (*LR*, 11). In this scene, Tom turns his eyes away from the sacramental signs in the created world and the knowledge they have the power to reveal. Instead, he locates himself within his private version of his past life, where he was a stereotypical carefree, successful American suburbanite in an idyllic life who "watch[ed] Barbara Walters talk about sexual intercourse on the *Today* show" in his "enclosed patio" with his goddess-like wife.

Tom believes that his melodramatic life story has become a tragedy. After the deaths of Doris and Samantha, his idyllic life vanished, leaving him languishing in the loneliness of his present existence, with its "morning terror," anxiety, and "large-bowel complaints" (*LR*, 24). The causes for his present condition lie, he theorizes, in the facts that his wife deserted him for some "heathen Englishman" and that his daughter Samantha died of

cancer. In this interior drama, he again places himself in the role of innocent victim who has simply been unlucky in losing his happiness (*LR*, 20).
He believes that his current psychological and professional problems are
simply a result of this past bad fortune in his love relationships.

Tom's memories of his life with Doris occur in three other major scenes
in *Love in the Ruins*, and in all these Tom is shown isolated from actual
time-space phenomena and the sacramental signs there. The first of these
scenes (*LR*, 61–72) takes place on the morning of July 1 while Tom is
pinned down by sniper fire in the enclosed patio of his Paradise Estates
home. On the floor in a corner of the patio, he recalls his daily life at home
with Doris and their debates about the meaning of love. In his next memory
of Doris (*LR*, 253–54), Tom lounges on the bed in the Howard Johnson's
room—"a dim cool grotto" (*LR*, 253)—waiting for Moira to finish her
shower. On this July 4 morning he remembers the glorious days with Doris
before the birth of Samantha, when they roamed the highways of a then
inviting America. Tom soon leaves Moira at the motel and returns to his
decaying home; there, in his final memory of Doris (*LR*, 269–73), he recalls her seduction by Alistair's aestheticism and her death.

In all three scenes, the settings emphasize Tom's angelic withdrawal from
the present and his enclosure in his memories about the happiness and love
he once had with Doris. Tom, in these memories, repeatedly confuses love
with the happiness he experienced in his marriage. He identifies the pleasures of his sexual relationship with Doris with happiness, and, by extension,
with love itself. He objectifies her as the source of pleasure-producing feelings and mythologizes her as a goddess who once provided him with love
and happiness and then, as fate would have it, punished him by withhold-
ing her gifts. In her abandonment of him came the demise of the bestial
good feelings she provided for him in bed, and therefore the end of his
happiness. Tom cannot see well enough with his angelic-bestial eyes to
find in his relationship with Doris an intersubjective union of two flesh-
and-blood humans who are incarnations of God. Tom does not have a
Christian sacramental consciousness that will help him identify Doris as
someone united with him both in flesh and spirit in an incarnational world.

On the morning of July 1, when Tom is pinned down in his house by a
sniper (*LR*, 61–72), he recalls his past with Doris. He looks out from his
patio at the rich profusion of nature just beyond his patio—the "creeper
and anise with its star-shaped funky smelling flower," the "honeysuckles,"
"azaleas," the "purplish-green heron." But he does not see sacramental signs
of the richness and beauty of an incarnational creation. Instead, he sees

only a ruined, frightening, and even disgusting garden where the "malig-
nant" vines are "evil serpents" that threaten to choke the "bird-limed head"
of St. Francis; the majestic heron he spots is to him only a "gloomy," "frowsty"
bird, no more real or significant than an "ill-conceived" bird "drawn by a
child" (*LR*, 63). Tom's interpretation of nature here shows once more that
he cannot read the sacramental signs in the created world, and that he
cannot, therefore, see himself in communion with others as a participant in
a postlapsarian garden. The statue of St. Francis should remind the Catholic Tom that there have been others who *could* read the signs.

In his memories of Doris that follow his attempts to see nature in this
scene, Tom exhibits his inability to see in his marriage with Doris signs of
the love celebrated by the Catholic sacrament of marriage. He doesn't see
Doris any more clearly than he sees the garden in front of him. She is, in
his memories and interpretations of them, merely a source of his personal
happiness, which he equates with love. He remembers another morning on
this same patio seven years earlier, shortly after the death of Samantha. On
the enclosed patio, Doris was clad in "royal green," a splendid "long-thighed
Mercury, god of the morning," with "flesh ... [of] gold" and hair "flaming
like the sun's corolla." This is his view of the woman he says he "loved ...
dearly *and* loved to lie with" (*LR*, 64–65; emphasis added). He is attempting to express his understanding of his love in this sentence; the coordination
in the sentence suggests that he has a language that equates love with sex—
"lying with." The sentence emphasizes that the Doris Tom loves is a
construction in his angelic-bestial consciousness, a mythic goddess who is
a beautiful source of pleasure. Tom concludes this nostalgic scene from his
mythic past with his goddess by remembering their rambunctious sexual
intercourse on the same brick patio where he now stares out at the "evil
vines." In his escapist memory, he sees himself and his goddess descending
from their orbits to re-enter the immanent world, join bodies, and find love
and happiness in their bestial desires.

Later, on July 4, holed up in the foggy grotto of Howard Johnson's (*LR*,
253–54) with Moira, Tom once more reminisces about his life with Doris,
this time recalling their years together before the birth of Samantha. And
again in this scene Tom retreats from the threatening reality outside the
grotto-like room, withdraws from a world he once more sees as a ruined
garden of death and evil that is "quiet as a tomb," a place where snakes lie
out by the motel pool (*LR*, 252). He revels in his memories of his carefree
travel with Doris, his "lusty Shenandoah Valley Girl" (*LR*, 13), and indulges himself in his sweet recollections of the pleasures of eating, drinking,
and lying with her in "some glittering lost motel." He also remembers leav-

ing Doris at that motel on Sunday morning to attend mass at a nearby church, where, he says, he was exhilarated by another kind of pleasure (*LR*, 254). At that time, he believed that the Church served to remind him through the Eucharist that he was "a mortal man," that he was a being incarnate in flesh. Because the Church and its sacraments seemed to Tom to sanctify the physical world and the flesh, Tom felt then that he was saved "from the spirit world," saved "from orbiting the earth like Lucifer and the angels" in the abstraction that then afflicted him. He was exhilarated by the Church's approbation of the world of the flesh where he sought with Doris his love and happiness. The celebration of mass, he believes, allowed him to "inhabit" his "own flesh," while he loved his goddess Doris (*LR*, 254).

Tom's analyses here of his past responses to Catholic sacramentalism show that he did not then, nor does he now, understand how that sacramentalism can reveal to him a created world in which his "own flesh," "the spirit world," and others are mysteriously united in a divine love made flesh in the Incarnation. Mass only furnished Tom with an interior spiritual stimulation ("exhilaration"), analagous to the kind of physical need satisfaction he enjoyed with Doris at the motel; it did not awaken him to a Christian love larger than the personal happiness that the satisfaction of his desires produced. Tom misinterpreted the sign of the Eucharist as simply "news" about the physicality of his God-created mortal existence; it only reminded him of the pleasures that he could enjoy with his body and Doris's. He did not understand how the Eucharist celebrates the union of flesh and spirit and the love incarnate in Christ. The Eucharist instead told Tom that he was a physical being who should enjoy carnal pleasures and emphasized to him that he and Doris were not purely spiritual creatures in an atemporal, transcendent existence. During mass, he did not hear the Word in the Eucharist tell him about the possibility of a love richer than the love he thinks he has with Doris back at the "glittering" motel.

Tom's description of his participation in the masses he attended while on the road with Doris suggests that his hearing the Gospel, the Good News, did not effect in him a comfortable sense of communion with the world and others, but instead made him feel as alien as a visitor from another planet who had "descended" onto a "moonscape." He remembers these masses as "the strangest exercise" in which he descended "through a moonscape countryside" and "touched the thread in the labyrinth" (*LR*, 254). These images of Tom as an alien space traveler in an alien world imply that he was as detached then from others and phenomenal creation as he is now. Unable to locate himself as a Christian self—one who is a wayfarer at home with others in a ruined but redeemable garden—Tom sees himself in his memories of these masses as a solitary spaceman venturing into a strange landscape or as a mythic solitary quester like Theseus in the labyrinth.

Tom's response to these masses and the Eucharist was a Kierkegaardian aesthetic response; that is, he valued these celebrations of Christ's sacrifice not because they reminded him of his brotherhood with all humanity in the suffering and death that all wait to be redeemed from, but because the rituals made him feel good. Kierkegaard warns that Christ is "not for consolation."[14] But Tom was consoled, and enjoyed in these "strangest exercises" the self-transcendence and "orbiting" that Percy explains in *Lost in the Cosmos* are the exhilarating (*LC*, 121) but temporary pleasures of art. Tom did not locate an authentic self in his experience at mass, but left behind the actualities of the self and phenomena to "orbit" in the regions within the *cogito* where all aesthetic "exhilarations" occur. This pleasure is similar to the pleasures experienced by Kierkegaard's aesthetic observer who enjoys the momentary loss of self in his transcendence into the beautiful world of the artwork—Keats's admirer of the Grecian urn.

Tom's aesthetic response to the masses is a sign of a general aestheticism that influences his understanding of who he is, where he is, and what he ought to do in life. Percy, in a 1971 interview with Charles Bunting, says Tom suffers from "aesthetic damnation," this mode of perception illustrated by his desire for "the highest state of the [Kierkegaard's] aesthetic sphere." That "highest state" is precisely what Art Immelmann later tempts him with when he offers him "the musical-erotic" (*Con*, 47).[15] Gary Ciuba notes that Tom's love for Doris is marked by the same kind of "aestheticism and abstraction" that Art recommends.[16] Whether at mass or in bed with Doris, Tom is inclined to place himself in the world as a detached, aesthetic observer of experience and acts to acquire and consume those experiences he thinks are most exhilarating or pleasurable.

When Tom recalls his visits to the churches, he locates himself in the scene as just such an aesthetic, aloof, curious visitor in a foreign moonscape. Tom compares himself to Theseus, an imaginary hero in a mythic land who descends into the labyrinth to do combat with the minotaur. His use of this mythic metaphor suggests that he sees life as a puzzle, riddle, or problem to be solved—like trying to find one's way out of a maze—and that he places himself in that challenging maze as a lone solver of the problems there. Tom is exhibiting the same kind of Cartesian problem-solution thinking that motivates Will Barrett in *The Last Gentleman* to seek from Sutter the absolute truth about life and in *The Second Coming* to seek God Himself in Lost Cove cave. As Will transforms his predicaments into abstract philosophical and theological questions to be answered and therefore follows false threads, so Tom frustratingly misdefines his world as a labyrinth to escape and misplaces himself as a pagan hero in it.

Gary Ciuba believes this allusion to the legend of the minotaur shows that in the past Tom's orthodox Catholicism provided him with an escape from his current bestiality; Ciuba maintains that Tom's regular taking of the Eucharist at mass indicates that he was then capable of seeing human beings as the mysterious union of flesh and spirit the sacrament signifies.[17] John Cunningham says that the Eucharist offers Tom life itself in the world of death and life-in-death presented in the novel, that it is the thread that "leads out of the maze" and "back to Christ."[18]

There is little evidence in the text that Tom is led out of his minotaur-like bestiality by the sacramental life signified by the Eucharist. His allusion to the myth instead shows how he was just as estranged then as he is now from a Catholic Christian understanding of who he is and where he is. Tom, by identifying himself as a courageous warrior-king in a maze, misplaces himself in the world, and therefore his attempts to draw analogies between his life and the mythic situation fail. Tom is unable to explore very precisely the connections between his predicament and the predicament of Theseus and the minotaur. It is not clear that he is able to interpret the myth as a symbolic statement about his redemption from bestiality or as a story emblematic of his release from his self-isolation to the openess of some new being and life. In his allusion to the myth, is he thinking of himself as some kind of half-man minotaur escaping a semihuman state of being and discovering a truly human, authentic self at mass? The minotaur is slain in this pagan myth, so that analogy does not work. Or is he identifying with the victorious Theseus (his queen waiting at the motel), who is led by the "thread" out of the labyrinth after slaying the minotaur? Maybe Tom sees himself symbolically defeating his half-man minotaur self and emerging from the maze fully human like Theseus. But Tom only "touches" the thread; he does not say he follows it out of the labyrinth.

Tom's reference to the myth reveals the problems that emanate from his placement of himself in a world that he perceives as a problem to be solved, a maze to escape. Because of this self-misplacement, he cannot see accurately the analogies between himself and the myth he tries to explore. His failure to explicate how the mythic problems of Theseus relate to his predicament shows that he has only vague ideas about how he might be somehow half-man, half-beast like the minotaur and how he might, like Theseus, be able to defeat the beast and free himself from entrapment in a symbolic existential labyrinth. He does not appear to understand that he, like all others, is neither the minotaur nor Theseus, neither beast nor heroic victor over that beasthood. More important, Tom does not understand that the Christian wayfarer's life is not a labyrinth to escape but a journey to a kingdom unknown to the pagan Theseus. Tom does not have a sacramental consciousness that will inform him that he is neither beast nor godlike hero in a labyrinth, but instead a "wayfaring creature somewhere between" (*MB*, 113) beasthood and the divine. In orbit, Tom does not see himself sacramentally as a wayfarer on his way toward a discovery of the Christian love and victory promised by the Eucharist at the masses that so exhilarated him. The Eucharistic sign should remind him of the Incarnation and his participation in it with others, but it does not. He is still half-blind to who he is and where he is —lost in the labyrinth of his problem-solving, abstractions, and memory, only half-conscious of the fullness of being that can be found with his fellow wayfarers.

Tom's final memory of his life with Doris shows him still lost in the labyrinth of his memory and thought. After Tom leaves Moira at the Howard Johnson's on July 4, he returns to his abandoned house to get his carbine to protect himself and his women during the violent political chaos that he believes is about to begin. Alone at his house, he again remembers the love and happiness the mercurial Doris provided him and laments his loss of her; he remembers losing her to Alistair and, finally, to death (*LR*, 269–73). Once more, he withdraws from the outside world, this time into the "green gloom" of what used to be his basement "'hunt' room" (*LR*, 269). As he ascends the spiral staircase toward Doris's ethereal upstairs bedroom, Tom remembers his "long-limbed and lovely" goddess of desire in her "green linen," sitting imperially in the "gold light" of her "airy," "spidery white iron" room that now "floats like a tree house in the whispering crowns of the longleaf pines" (*LR*, 270).

The imagery here suggests that Tom now sees in the irresistible Doris a sinister and threatening possibility. The kind of love she offers and the subsequent happiness she provides can be withdrawn; he can be a prey in her spidery web of desire. Tom's anxiety may be the sensualist's fear that his desires may not forever be satisfied, that there may be no hope for permanent happiness. He is remembering in this scene her departure from his world, her flight from the enclosed patio and from the nameless motels where she had granted him love and happiness. He remembers her talking with Alistair in this room, her moaning "how true!" when the Englishman quoted Wordsworth's "the world is too much with us." In his memory, he sees Doris leaving him and orbiting with Alistair in the self-transcendence of Eastern religion and Wordsworthian aestheticism, just as he himself has been habitually orbiting in his science and in his rendition of Catholicism. Doris's betrayal and death caused him such despair that he now feels that he might have been better off had he castrated himself long ago like the second-century Origen (*LR*, 271–73). Without Doris to provide satisfaction for his sexual needs, he desires to have no desire, and thereby avoid the unhappiness that is an inevitable result of thwarted need satisfaction.

Samantha is the other major figure in Tom's construction of a family past that he thinks explains how his love and happiness has turned into defeat and sorrow. Ross Labrie says Tom transfigures his past with Samantha, the memory granted such significance that it interferes with his consciousness of the present.[19] Tom sees his deceased daughter through the same Kierkegaardian aesthetic eyes that he sees Doris; Samantha was a source of pleasurable feelings for him while she was alive, but her absence now creates a contrasting hopeless emotional and psychological pain. Tom associates his daughter with that period in his life with Doris when he was lucky enough to live in psychological, emotional, and spiritual bliss. As he does in his memories of Doris, Tom connects his past love for Samantha with a cluster of memories in which his desires and their satisfactions provided him pleasure and, therefore, happiness.

His memories of Samantha, like his other memories, take place in settings that symbolize once again his enclosed selfhood and his withdrawal from present time and space. For example, on July 1, while cleaning room 203 at Howard Johnson's and preparing a place for his tryst with Moira, Tom, in one of his reveries about his past with Samantha, breaks down in tears of self-pity when he remembers the happy days with his daughter and Doris at other motels across America. "Why does desire turn to grief," he wonders sentimentally, "and memory strike at the heart?" (LR, 138). Tom is withdrawing here, as is his habit, into a self-constructed truth about life that is based purely on his personal interior experience. Like Kierkegaard's aesthete, he tries to forget the present in order to be stimulated by the private images that constitute his inner world.[20] Tom is not thinking here about his daughter, but about his own desire, grief, and memory. Again, such retreats from the present enable him to place himself in an imaginary arena of action where he is free to savor his responses to the past, here Samantha's death and his subsequent loss of happiness.

Tom has two virtually identical memories of life with Samantha (LR, 12–13 and 138). The first occurs on July 4 while he looks out from the grove of young pines (LR, 3) at the abandoned St. Michael's Church, and the other occurs earlier, on July 1, as he passes the church on his way from Howard Johnson's to town. Both memories elicit from Tom a flood of images from a period in his life that he considers "the best of times" (LR, 12) before the deaths of Doris and his daughter. In both of these memories, Tom lumps together a cluster of disparate experiences that he associates with various kinds of love and happiness. Both memories are Tom's recreations of the times that he walked home from mass at St. Michael's with Samantha, "happy as a man can be" (*LR*, 138), "feeling so good" (*LR*, 13). Feeling "like King David before the Ark" (*LR*, 13, 138) after he "ate Christ" at mass, Tom remembers returning home to "snug down Samantha" in front of *Gentle Ben*, taking "four, five, six long pulls from the quart of Early Times" (*LR*, 138), and preparing to cook out on his patio while singing excerpts from *Tantum Ergo* and *Don Giovanni* (*LR*, 13, 138). He would then seek out Doris so he could satisfy his desire for her out in the "zoysia grass" (*LR*, 13) or "under the Mobile pinks" (*LR*, 138).

These scenes from his past with Samantha reveal the "aesthetic damnation" that Percy says afflicts Tom More (*Con*, 47). Tom loved Samantha, loved attending mass with her, and loved the eating, drinking, music, and sex afterwards at home because they all produced pleasant emotions in him. Tom's memories of his life with Doris reveal that he has little understanding of any kind of love or happiness beyond the pleasures derived from his need satisfactions, and so it is with his memories of Samantha. As long as he can love an innocent, content child who has yet to be assailed by the suffering and death in a Fallen world, his love causes him no sorrow or grief, and in that love he finds, therefore, happiness. He can love this love because it makes him happy.

At mass with Samantha, he loves communion in a similar way; it makes him "rejoice" because he believes it creates "life *in*" him (*LR*, 13, 138; emphasis added). Tom is exhilarated by the Eucharist because it causes pleasant responses *within him*, not because it directs his vision outward to a more challenging kind of love. The Christian *caritas* that the Eucharist signifies demands a consciousness of the sorrow of others, their suffering being the reason that this love is needed. This Christian love seems to deny the importance of personal happiness and instead call for self-denial and self-sacrifice. Tom has little consciousness of this kind of love. In fact, he says that after mass he cared "nought for my fellow Catholics but only for myself and Samantha" (*LR*, 13). Tom has no sense of a communion with the rest of humanity through a larger kind of caring love incarnate in a suffering and self-sacrificing Christ. He is blind to the love that makes possible a redemption from the self-absorption and complacency he exhibits in these scenes.

Back at home after mass, Tom enjoys the family love and happiness he finds in the self-indulgent pleasures of eating and drinking, sex, and music. Out on his patio at the barbecue grill, Tom is emotionally overwhelmed by his sudden sensation of "joy for the beauty of the world" (*LR*, 13) and involuntarily bursts into song—the secular *Don Giovanni* (Kierkegaard's prime example of what "delights" the aesthete),[21] as well as sacred songs from the mass he has just attended. Tom, lost in the private aesthetic joy of the moment, has no consciousness that these songs represent different kinds of love and different kinds of satisfactions.

In other memories of Samantha, Tom sees the love he had in the past with his daughter as a painful source of grief and sorrow, a paradise lost. These memories prompt his thinking about the possibility of regaining this lost paradise of happiness. He reasons that by discovering another love to replace the love he no longer has with Samantha he will be able to re-enter that past emotional Eden he enjoyed with her. He believes now that by loving and marrying Moira and returning with her to Paradise Estates he can return to the happiness he had when Samantha was alive. In his memories, he repeatedly links Samantha with the beautiful, young, "perfect" (*LR*, 347) Moira, the goddess he believes will accompany him into a future of renewed love and happiness. For Tom, Samantha is a sign of the suffering and death that caused his loss, Moira a sign of the beauty and pleasure that can restore him to a paradise of good feeling.

On July 1, again alone and enclosed in room 203, he is busy cleaning the room and preparing it for the arrival of Moira. He says he found himself "thinking not of Moira but of Samantha" (*LR*, 138). He refers more than once to the twenty-two-year-old Moira's being "like a child" (*LR*, 135, 255, 256). Perhaps, unconsciously, Tom sees Moira as an adult Samantha who has not been ravaged by time and death and therefore someone he can love who will not transform his desire into grief (*LR*, 138). In the motel bed with her, his "heart lifts" with love, he says, when he looks at "her perfect oval face" (*LR*, 347). Hers is a face quite unlike Samantha's face, which he remembers as distorted as "a Picasso profile" by the "neuroblastoma ... [that] pushed one eye out and around the nosebridge" (*LR*, 373). As Tom looks over at Moira beside him in bed, he sees a child-like "face unwounded, unscarred, unlined, unmarked by sadness" (*LR*, 347), a face very different from the pudgy, "acned" (*LR*, 12) face of his daughter. As he holds Moira in his arms, he recalls spending a painful evening with an adolescent Samantha watching *Gunsmoke* and the Miss America pageant on television after her first blind date failed to arrive. He recalls how his pity for her and his helplessness in the face of her date's cruelty made him "curse God" (*LR*, 260) for a world in which the innocent and blameless like Samantha must suffer injustice and humiliation. But in Moira's perfect face Tom sees a sign of a human life that seems exempt from such suffering, and therefore he believes his loving her will not cause him this kind of despair. He lies in bed with her at the motel and shares with her dreams of their future lives together in the paradise of Paradise Estates (*LR*, 256).

The love Tom feels for the perfect Moira as he examines her flawlessness in the motel bed is an overwhelming "tenderness" that he says causes his throat to fill with emotion (*LR*, 347). The fact that he is again and again reminded of Samantha in his encounters with Moira suggests that this "tenderness" is also the kind of emotion he had for his daughter, albeit in a somewhat different way. Tom's responses to Samantha and Moira are once more the Kierkegaardian aesthete's responses to experience: both his daughter and Moira are objectified as sources of emotional gratification. Even Samantha's death, Tom finally recognizes, gave him "a secret satisfaction . . . , a delectation of tragedy, a license for drink, a taste . . . for taste's sake" (*LR*, 374)—like art for art's sake. Teilhard de Chardin also uses the word "tenderness" to define the kind of love Tom exhibits for Samantha and Moira; it is, he says, a "little closed love," hardly more than a mere detached sympathy. He contrasts this "little closed love" with Christian charity in which the individual arrives at an awareness of being united in love and Christ with all others in the world's beauties and joys, as well as in its sin, suffering, and death.[22]

In Percy's fiction, the sufferings of Samantha, Lonnie in *The Moviegoer*, Jamie in *The Last Gentleman*, and the children victimized by the German and American scientists in *The Thanatos Syndrome* are sacramental signs of a redemptive love larger than the tenderness Teilhard de Chardin discusses. But Percy's heroes are not always able to see these signs of love. Tom, for example, can only see (as Gary Ciuba says) that Samantha's "flesh [is] in ruins," and this encourages him to conclude that all of creation is a hopeless ruin and waste.[23] But Samantha's face carries other messages for those who can read them. Sue Crowley sees these children in Percy's novels as "personified hierophany," signs in a fallen world of the suffering that is in the process of being redeemed by the love God sends in the Incarnation.[24] Samantha's face, as well as Lonnie's and Jamie's, are like the cancer-ravaged face of Flannery O'Connor's Mary Ann. O'Connor sees such suffering by innocent children as a sign of a universal "human imperfection" and a sign that simultaneously and paradoxically points to the charity and "goodness of God" needed for mankind's redemption from these "grotesque" imperfections. O'Connor contrasts this charity and love of God with what she also calls a sentimental "tenderness," a "popular pity," that causes many to wish that such "human imperfection" did not exist. This "tenderness," she says, "ends in forced-labor camps and in . . . the gas chamber."[25] Echoing O'Connor, Father Smith in *The Thanatos Syndrome* explains to an older Tom More the death inherent in this "tenderness" (*TS*, 239).

In Tom's final memory of Samantha (*LR*, 373–74) on the smoldering golf course where he banishes Art, he is not seeing as clearly as O'Connor, but he is at least beginning to question his previous view of Samantha's face and what it signified. He remembers standing by her bed and looking down at her grotesquely disfigured face while she talked about the importance of his attending mass and there receiving God's grace, the gift of love that she says will grant him forgiveness and therefore redemption from sin. She is telling him about a love that will relieve the despair that earlier in his life caused him to curse God (*LR*, 260) for her, his, and the world's imperfections. After hearing her advice, he agrees with her assertions about his need for God's love; he replies, "I know." Perhaps what Tom is at least on the verge of "knowing" in his assenting to the truth of what Samantha has told him is that his love of her, as well as his love for her mother and all others in his life, have been "little closed loves." Maybe this is what he is close to recognizing when he looks down at Samantha's face and wonders if his finding in it only the source of his various emotions about her—his happiness, love, tenderness, grief, sorrow, pity, outrage, and despair—was not a discovery of life and love, but just his "feasting on death" (*LR*, 374).

This last memory of Samantha and her religious instruction leads Tom to question his aesthetic understanding of love and happiness and causes him to wonder if his dwelling on his own feelings and thoughts about her life and death has been a satisfactory response to his daughter. It is immediately after this memory on the golf course that he can summon the will to pray to St. Thomas More, an act that implies he is assenting to a knowledge of love and happiness beyond what he has been able to understand in his aestheticism. From the smoldering bunker, he prays that Art Immelmann be "driven" from him (*LR*, 376), symbolically rejecting the angelic happiness and love Art has just promised him in this scene. This memory of himself at Samantha's bedside causes him to wonder if his aesthetic self-absorption in his thoughts and feelings about his daughter caused his blindness to his actual experience with her. He wonders if his anticipation of her death, and then his "sweet remorse" after her death, didn't cause him to "miss" "present time." He feels he may have been "defeated" by his casting ahead to her future death while she was alive and by his savoring of "past time" after her death. Tom realizes that it is possible to live a life in which his anticipation of future sorrow or joy and his recollection of past happiness or grief can cause him to "miss ... ourselves, miss ... everything" in the here-and-now reality of phenomenal life beyond his feelings and thoughts about it (*LR*, 374).

Tom begins to ask the right questions about his past capacities for love and his selfish pursuit of happiness. When he thinks about his failure to take Samantha to Lourdes to be cured, he realizes he "didn't want to take her" because he was "afraid she might be cured" (*LR*, 374). Eric Link argues that Tom's fear causes him to reject the divine grace that could miraculously cure Samantha at Lourdes.[26] But Tom's fears may be more complicated. Perhaps Tom is recognizing now that he was afraid at the time because a cure would have verified that God exists—and therefore that a love and happiness exists utterly beyond his knowing of the world and his understanding of who he is. He wonders how he would "live the rest of . . . [his] life" after such a discovery (*LR*, 374). How would he live if all his thinking and feeling about his love for Samantha, Doris, science, music, sex, and Early Times were proven mere self-delusion? How could he live knowing that his quest for happiness is absurdly the cause for his despair? How could he face a world where love is not personal happiness but is inevitably accompanied by the heartbreaking sorrow of suffering and death? How could he endure a world where he has no power in his science or in his pleasure-seeking to redeem himself from its inescapable pain?

THE PURSUIT OF HAPPINESS: SOLDIER AND LOVER

Immediately after this last memory of Samantha, Tom opens his eyes to watch Art Immelmann disappear across the country club golf course and to discover Ellen Oglethorpe, who guides him home (*LR*, 376). The last chapter of *Love in the Ruins* follows this literally eye-opening experience on the golf course and describes Tom's new home in the Slave Quarters five years after his July 1– 4 adventures among the ruins and the catastrophes of Paradise Estates. In this final chapter, Tom is in the process of discovering a potentially more satisfying kind of love and happiness with Ellen and their two children, with his community, and with the Church.

But until this promising and hopeful end, Tom is a lonely and alienated man, who, after a failed first attempt at marriage and family, arrives at his forty-fifth birthday alcoholic and suicidal, wondering "Who am I?" (*LR*, 214) and "What to do?" (*LR*, 168). His analyses of his past at this point in his life have proven to him that the love and happiness he enjoyed in his relationships with Doris, Samantha, and the Church cannot be trusted, that inevitably "desire turn[s] to grief and memory strike[s] at the heart" (*LR*, 138). He will try again to find happiness, however, either by pursuing the sexual pleasure provided by women or by seeking the self-transcendence available through his science. At the Howard Johnson's he becomes the bestial Don Juan sensualist, a soldier fighting for his need satisfactions; at Fedville with his fellow scientists he becomes the angelic intellectual Dr. Faustus who believes he can make himself and the entire world happy with his lapsometer.[27] In both roles, Tom is plagued by an aesthetic self-mis-

placement that prompts him again to define personal happiness as his ultimate life goal and persuades him that pursuit of his desires is the way to
accomplish that goal.

Tom fails both as Don Juan/soldier and as Faustian scientific savior of
humankind. As Don Juan, he seeks the love of women, this time outside
the sacrament of marriage. But Tom discovers nothing more than an isolated self-stimulation and closed love in his bestial attraction to Moira,
Lola, and Ellen.[28] His mere self-gratification in these encounters is implied by the claustrophobic settings where he meets his loves—the
anonymous, shabby rooms at the Howard Johnson's. As Dr. Faustus, Tom
tries another kind of self-transcendence besides the religious exhilaration
he experienced at St. Michael's and the similar exhilarations he enjoyed
when he visited the churches he happened to discover when he and Doris
were on the road back in the "old Auto Age" (LR, 213). Now it is science
that he looks to for the larger truths that will make him happy. He believes
now that he has discovered through his scientific study the "excessive abstraction" and "alternating . . . satyriasis" that cause his and all mankind's
unhappiness— and he believes he has discovered a cure for this universal
psychic disorder. Tom believes he can use his lapsometer, a product of his
scientific knowledge, "to be happy and make others happy" (LR, 20). He
no longer needs the Church and its sacraments to make him "happy as a
man . . . [can] be" (LR, 138). Tom has at this point in his life turned away
from the sacramental signs in creation and their truths and has directed his
eyes inward to the truths about himself, others, and the world provided by
his scientific medical knowledge.

In his Don Juan/soldier role he envisions himself as a military hero in
combat for his happiness and safety in a hostile world. He recalls his military training in "the First Air Cav" during "the fifteen-year war in Ecuador"
(LR, 61) and now sees himself resuming this role during the apocalyptic
political upheavals that he foresees. Tom feels that he is engaged in a desperate solitary struggle to acquire the shelter, food, and drink he needs in
order to enjoy his isolated life at Howard Johnson's with Lola, Moira, and
Ellen. In this bestial pursuit of happiness, Tom places himself in his world
as a lonely self facing daily a Darwinian, threatening environment where
he must compete for survival and need satisfaction.

In the opening scene of the novel, Tom exemplifies this kind of "Self as
Immanent" (LC, 113), a self estranged from the world where he is trying to
be happy. He is armed with a carbine, waiting in the pine grove above the
crumbling interstate to fight for his life in the violent (LR, 3) social revolu-
tion that he believes will defeat his efforts to "live happily" (LR, 8) with

Lola, Moira, and Ellen in the ruined Howard Johnson's.[29] Paradoxically, his sense of impending catastrophe has made him "quite comfortable" (*LR*, 4), an effect that catastrophes usually have, Percy maintains, on those caught in the clutches of the endless consumption of the immanent self (*LR*, 122). Catastrophe is at least a relief from the discomforts of boredom, and comfort is always the organism's primary concern.

The oppressive enclosure of the pine grove symbolically suggests Tom's psychic detachment at this moment and his blindness to the sacramental signs in phenomena around him. Ready to respond from his defensive position to the upcoming challenges, Tom, with his sharp eye, is ironically capable of seeing only the waste in the landscape below him—the "lichen grow[ing] in the oil stain," the stagnant motel swimming pool, the "rotting top[s]" of the convertibles in the parking lot (*LR*, 8–9). He sees only disease and threat in his surroundings. He imagines that the pine tree at his back is afflicted with a "tumor" and sees the other pines rise up around him like menacing "steel knitting needles." In the stifling heat and the impending darkness, "not a breath stirs"; he is keenly aware of the suffocating "turpentine smells" that engulf him (*LR*, 4). In the distance, on the horizon, an ominous "thunderhead . . . humps over . . . like a troll," and in the skies directly above him he spots "a couple of buzzards" he thinks may be "eyeing" him "for meat" (*LR*, 6). The created world from Tom's perspective here is not a sacred place full of sacramental signs of hope and love, but a lonely place of imminent death, frightening deformity, danger.

Percy's landscape imagery in this opening scene emphasizes Tom's vision problems. Tom wonders as he sits under the pine, "What's wrong with my eyes?" (*LR*, 20). Symbolically, his vision is "narrow[ed]," and he sees the world around him from the limited point of view of a soldier fighting to survive; "the world," he says to himself, "looks as if it were seen through the slit of a gun turret" (*LR*, 21). This restricted vision prevents him from being awed by the beauty of the sacramental sun that "makes bursts and halos through the screen of pine needles" (*LR*, 8) and encloses him in a brilliant light. He worries about the threatening buzzards that circle him as if he is a potential prey, but fails to make any connections between himself and the beauty of the Christological, Hopkinsian "marsh hawk" (*LR*, 6, 8) that glides effortlessly "into the line of cypresses, which are green as paint against the purple thunderhead" (*LR*, 8).[30] For Tom, the thunderhead he sees is only a grotesque troll, but the regal purple of the cloud suggests that it is a sacramental sign. The image may be an allusion to the thunderhead that David saw as a sign of God's love and protection (2 Samuel 22.10). In the pine grove, Tom can see himself only as a dead animal, food for the buzzards, or as a soldier wedged into a tiny gun turret. The landscape imagery suggests, however, that he is in fact a participant in a vigorous and mysterious sacramental world of light and energy that is being approached by a power on the horizon that he would surely welcome were he not too blind to see.

This opening scene introduces a series of military exploits by Tom among the revolutionaries that are taking over Paradise Estates. In one of his adventures, Tom searches for the sniper that he thinks is following him and launches a guerrilla attack on the Bantus who have taken over the country club beyond the "gates of Paradise" (LR, 281). Percy's description of these events again shows how Tom is blind to the sacramental signs in nature. When Tom makes his assault on the country club, he is totally focused on the most minute details of his military strategies, lost in the mental calculations he thinks will bring victory. Consequently, he is oblivious to the possible significances of the signs in nature that are right before him. Out in the bayou behind the country club, "mullet jump," "sunlight shatters like quicksilver" on the boats, and "gold dust drifts on the black water" (LR, 290). This imagery emphasizes that outside the interior regions of Tom's calculations and plans is a vibrant, beautiful, living creation that his problem-solving, Cartesian consciousness will not allow him to see.

Tom fails in his military mission at the country club and is imprisoned by the Bantus in Monsignor Schleifkopf's former office at St. Michael's. In his imprisonment and escape, he illustrates the literal-minded consciousness that prevents him from seeing the symbolic significance of the life in the bayou behind the country club or in his own actions. Percy describes the office where Tom is held prisoner as a symbolic Miltonic hell of heat without light (LR, 305); but for Tom the darkness and heat are just problems to be solved by using his mental powers and memory of the office to figure out how to switch on the air conditioner. As he picks up Saint Michael's sword (LR, 308), the "foot-long papercutter" on Monsignor's desk, he could be reminded of Michael's escorting Adam and Eve out of Paradise into the postlapsarian world and the angel's lecturing them about the virtues of patience and moderation.[31] Tom attaches no significance to the sword, however, seeing it merely as a useful tool that can turn a Phillips-head screw and get him into the air-conditioner ductwork, out of the church, and back to the motel.

Finally, as he kicks his way out of the air-conditioner duct into the Monsignor's ruined garage, he appears to see for the first time some kind of symbolic significance to these events. But his symbolic interpretation is incomplete and inaccurate and implies that there is no change in his way of seeing himself and the world. His description of his escape indicates that he interprets it as a symbolic rebirth: he says he was "born again" out of "the womb" of the abandoned church "into the hot bright perilous world" (LR,

310–11). But, ironically, he experiences no escape from his blindness and no entrance into a new life. The world is still for him only a perilous arena for combat and survival. His way of seeing continues to be narrow and incomplete. Immediately after what he sees as his rebirth, he hides under the Monsignor's "burnt-out Buick" with "a cockroach's view" (*LR*, 311) of the world. As songs about the Nativity and the Magi ring out from the church's bell tower, Tom does not think of the Incarnation, the Word made flesh that offers him and all mankind a rebirth into a way of seeing not available to a cockroach. Instead, Tom sees himself "reborn" as "old Duke Wayne" (*LR*, 315) after Lola recues him from the garage, and he and his valiant sidekick Lola gallop back to the ruins of the motel and to their happiness. Tom does not see himself and the world anew, but returns to his interiorized selfhood and continues to seek stimulations for that self. After he escapes from St. Michael's and returns victoriously to Howard Johnson's, he expresses his old Cartesian, aesthetic view of himself as a satisfier of needs and an observer of his environment: "What does a man live for," he asks himself, "but to have a girl, use his mind, practice his trade, drink a drink, read a book, and watch the martins wing it for the Amazon . . . " (*LR*, 336–37).

Tom's military posturing and his afflicted eyesight continue throughout the novel, until his defeat of Art Immelmann on the golf course on the night of July 4. A few minutes before he meets Art, Tom awakes in the same pine grove of the novel's opening scene. Armed with his carbine, he still sees himself as a soldier in combat in a threatening, demonic world. He also continues to have trouble with his eyes. It is dusk, the "sky is still light," and on the horizon "the dark crowns of the cypress flatten out against the sky like African veldt trees." The sacramental union of the earthly and the divine in this landscape is symbolically suggested by the beautiful image of "the glimmering violet line" on the horizon "that joins dark earth to light bowl of sky." Amid this sacramental splendor, however, Tom is more attentive to the "pall of smoke" caused by the smoldering golf course beneath him and the eerie "spectral light on the fairway . . . big creeping shadows in the rough." He is not looking for sacramental signs, but a "sign of a sniper" that could end his happiness at any moment. His gaze is focused on the "three windows . . . lit at Howard Johnson's" where "the girls" and the other sources of his need satisfaction are waiting for him (*LR*, 353).

In his role as angelic scientist with his magical, happiness-producing lapsometer, Tom is as existentially blind as he is in his role as combative soldier fighting the forces of evil for his need satisfactions. He, in his angelism, again does not know where he is or who he is. He believes he is in an America that is facing imminent social and political apocalypse and believes that he can through his scientific discoveries create a future Eden out of the ruins. As scientist-savior, he pursues not only his own personal bestial happiness but also the universal happiness of mankind that he believes will arrive on earth after he has completed his scientific research and perfected his lapsometer.

The delusional consequences of this angelic self-misplacement can be seen in an important scene at the Napoleon, his favorite neighborhood bar. It is July 1, and Tom has just left the hospital where he has been talking with Max Gottlieb about funding for his research and lapsometer. Once more in a dark, enclosed space, Tom in his angelism turns away from the created world. Outside, "the martins are skimming in from the swamp, sliding down the dark glassy sky like flecks of soot" (LR, 152). Inside the "peaceable gloom" (LR, 151) of the bar, he shares drinks and boiled eggs with the owner, Leroy Ledbetter, and descends into his interior world to envision a paradasiacal future America filled with a kind of love quite different from his love of the girls in the Howard Johnson's. He imagines in the dimness of the Napoleon a universal caritas[32] that will "reconcile man with his sins" (LR, 153) and unite all in a new Eden sometime after his lapsometer has "weld[ed]" together "man and spirit" and effected an existential transformation he believes will be the prelude to "man ... reenter[ing] paradise" (LR, 36). Looking at himself in the "dark mirror" of the Napoleon, Tom sees a "hollow-eyed Spanish Christ," "the maculate Christ, the sinful Christ," the new Christ who is soon to arrive in a secular parousia to bring all together in love. He imagines that he himself is this new Christ, a modern savior who "lies drunk in a ditch" while his friends, the black Victor Charles and the racist Leroy Ledbetter, "join . . . hands" and pick him up. In this act of charity by Victor and Leroy, he imagines that the alienated men will come together; they will "love the new Christ and so they love each other" (LR, 153).

Tom's experiences with Victor and Leroy immediately before this scene have led him to these sentimental, romantic fantasies about how these two men are, like all men, essentially brothers in their capacity for caritas. It is because of their common capacity for charity, he believes, that he can, as secular Christ, bring them together and create an innocent world free from the consequences of the Fall, consequences so obviously exemplified in the racial, political, and social differences that divide Victor and Leroy. These differences, he feels, are defeated by their shared potential for goodness, and his recent experience with Victor and Leroy proves this to him. Tom remembers that just this afternoon, while he was on his way to the Napoleon, Victor rescued him from the ditch where he had fainted. Victor's selfless kindness leads Tom into speculations about the charity that Victor is capable of extending to a white person in a racist society where these same whites are responsible for his and his family's oppression and poverty. Later, talking with the racist Leroy at the Napoleon, he sees in Leroy a similar inclination toward acts of "sweet-natured"*caritas*. As the charitable Victor has literally helped Tom out of a ditch (*LR*, 142), so Leroy, Tom believes, is equally charitable, the archetypal good old Southern boy who is the first one there "if you run in a ditch or have a flat tire" (*LR*, 152).

But the two, Tom observes, are quite different in one puzzling way. While Victor is both charitable toward whites and forgiving of their cruelty and injustice, Leroy's charity exists alongside a contrasting racism and potential for violent physical attacks on blacks who violate his concepts of social propriety and order. Victor's morality makes sense—charity and forgiveness are clearly compatible virtues that one would expect to find in a "good" person. But Leroy is a mystery. How can one make sense of a moral life in which charity and goodness exist alongside pride and cruelty?

In the bar, Tom descends into his angelic *cogito* to try to explain to himself Leroy's paradoxical morality. Tom says he feels a "terror" as the amiable Leroy talks of his belief in "learn[ing] them [rebellious Bantus] . . . upside the head." Searching for a source of his sensation of terror, he concludes that it is caused by his consciousness of Leroy's "goodness and what lies beneath, some fault in the soul's terrain so deep that all is well on top, evil grins like good." From Tom's dualistic perspective, what is good about Leroy is just what is on top, the good deeds that Tom sees him affably perform for others. Tom sees Leroy as a good person because he'll help others change a flat tire (*LR*, 152). Since Leroy is a good man, Tom seems to reason, he cannot be truly and genuinely an evil man. If he were in fact an evil person, this existential fact would explain logically his propensity for violence; evil men do evil things. Such an explanation would render his violence no more terrifying than a violent act of nature and no more of a mystery than Victor's virtues. Sentimentally, Tom concludes that Leroy's evil is a sort of "piteousness," "good gone wrong and not knowing it" (*LR*, 152–53). By Tom's analysis, then, Leroy has no evil at the core of his being, but is a Rousseau innocent who is a victim of some fault he does not have the knowledge or free will to change.

Tom's angelic analyses of the nature of good and evil in Victor and Leroy illustrates that he cannot locate himself and others in a Fallen world where all are united in a way that transcends their racial and political differences. He is absorbed in his thinking about the messiah in the dark mirror (*LR*, 153) at the Napoleon and therefore incapable of seeing where he is. He cannot take his eyes away from the mirror long enough to see that all are together as children of God, albeit willfull and errant children, in a created world that is the incarnation of a mysterious divine love that is working to redeem them from their self-estrangement and show them their common home. He does not see an incarnational creation where all, including the face in the mirror, are united in a common exile from their true selves. He is not the savior of mankind, Victor is not incarnate virtue, nor is Leroy innocent, but intractable, "evil grin[ning] like good."

In Tom's attempts to understand the love and charity he sees in his old friends there is a tenderness (*LR*, 347) that isolates him from an understanding of God's love and how it operates in the world, the same tenderness that marks his love for Samantha. Unwittingly, Tom is blinded by his tender feelings for Victor, Leroy, and Samantha, either loving the kindness and innocence they radiate or savoring the sorrow and terror they can provoke as they make their way through their lives with him. It is his attention to this tenderness within him that isolates Tom from the incarnate creation outside the Napoleon and from a more profound love that can show him the way out of the interior labyrinth he has constructed with his thoughts and feelings.

Tom's angelic blindness is revealed again during his July 3 visit to the hospital to petition the "Director" for funding for his research. In their meeting, Tom explains to the Director the importance of his scientific article and lapsometer, both products of his genius (*LR*, 11), and both "epochal" (*LR*, 97), he believes, in their significance in human history. He has been very confident about the Director's support, believing that Art Immelmann's earlier offer of funding for his research is a sign that he has won acceptance in the scientific community (*LR*, 168). Tom, then, is lured to this meeting with the Director by his pride in his world-saving lapsometer and his confidence in his messianic intellect. He assumes that the Director and the rest of his colleagues will join him in his faith in his Einstein-level intellectual capacities and support him in his efforts to realize his mind's salvific potential. Instead, the Director ignores Tom's discoveries and defines him as just another mental patient who needs to get back to his ward.

Immediately after his meeting with the Director, Tom shuffles down the halls of the Fedville mental hospital and asks himself, "Where am I?" (*LR*, 207). He is so abstracted by his frustrated plans for his lapsometer and his desire for the Nobel Prize that he literally cannot locate himself in time and space. Tom wanders into the men's room down the hall and once again encounters Art Immelmann, who has been lurking there in order to tempt the defeated Tom with a gift of angelic "freedom and omniscience" (*LR*, 214). Tom's abstraction from himself and the world is made obvious when he again looks into a mirror and reports what he sees. Tom stares into the mirror over the washstand and says to himself, "I am gazing at my face in the mirror intently, like the man in Saint James's epistle." Percy's allusion is to the man who is "tempted" by his "own desire" (James 1.14). St. James says that the man who hears the word and does nothing is like "a man who looks at his own face in a mirror. He sees himself, then goes off and promptly forgets what he looks like" (James 1. 23–24). Similarly, Tom cannot see who he is.

Tom, like the man in St. James's epistle, is a Christian who has heard the Word. Tom himself says that he believes "the whole business" (*LR*, 6) that his Church, the current representative of the Word on earth, teaches. Percy insists that Tom is a firm Catholic who "knows what he believes" (*Con*, 75). But Tom has not acted in his life in response to the Word, has not allowed the Word to direct him about what to do. Instead, he has chosen to do as he pleases (*LR*, 6) and has pursued his own happiness. As a result, he, like the man in St. James's parable, has turned away from the mirror and forgotten who he is, forgotten what his true self looks like, become a stranger to himself. Tom has forgotten that he is a physical being in an incarnational, sacramental world where the particularities of physical phenomena, which include the face looking back at him, can be read as signs of another mysterious dimension of life. Tom cannot recognize the face in the mirror because he doesn't believe it is actually him. Instead, he defines himself, locates himself, not as a physical body that can be seen in a mirror but as a ghostly *cogito* whose interior abstractions and desires are the only reality.

Before turning away from his face to take two drinks from his Early Times, Tom imagines that "the image reverses on the retina and a hole opens" (*LR*, 209); his face is lost down this hole, swallowed up in the emptiness of his self-constructed inner world. Tom is the self Will Barrett in *The Second Coming* calls the "self suck[ing] everything into itself" (*SC*,15). Percy says that abstracted wayfarers like Tom experience a Sartrean nothingness, Marcel's "the aching wound of self" (*MB*, 283–84). Tom, however, cannot see in the mirror his own nothingness or his wounded self. He believes that his lapsometer can treat any "aching wound" (*LR*, 36) that the stranger in the mirror suffers. He believes, as he illustrates in his messianic delusions before the mirror in the Napoleon, that he can cure himself and the world of such self-alienation with his science and technology and deliver all to a new Eden.

Art leads Tom away from the mirror in the bathroom and over to "the shoeshine chair," where he sits as if on a "throne," talks with Tom about having "faith," and treats him with the lapsometer (*LR*, 209–18). In a sort of anti-mass, Art promises in his homily that if Tom will "drink this drink" [the lapsometer stimulations] . . . that he will "never want a drink." He preaches of a love that can be experienced if the "Brodmann 11" area of the brain (the musical-erotic area) is properly stimulated. In this mental state, he vows, Tom can experience "the abstract . . . concretely and the concrete abstractly" and love women in the same way that he enjoys music. Art explains that when the musical-erotic is properly functioning, one "loves her [an individual woman] as one loves music. A woman is the concrete experienced abstractly, as women. Music is the abstract experienced as the concrete, namely sound." Art is tempting Tom to embrace a love that he argues "has its counterpart in scientific knowledge," a "neutral[ly] moral . . . , abstractive and godlike" love that is pure "freedom and omniscience." Admonishing "Physician, heal thyself," Art turns Tom away from the sacramental signs outside the open window of the hospital bathroom. There "fat white clouds are blown by map winds," "swallows dip," and "cicadas go zreeeee" in the "gold-green" summer noon. Art wants Tom instead to look within, "look at . . . [him]self" and think about being happy through the kind of love he is defining. The anti-mass ends with Tom's signing the contract with Art and with a parodic communion—"the bottle of Early Times passes between" them.

Art convinces Tom, after he is rejected by his fellow scientists at Fedville, that his intellect and desires still have the power to grant him happiness. Until the very end of the novel, Tom persists in his belief that "Art Immelmann is right" (LR, 337)—happiness can be the only reasonable life goal. This angelic aestheticism is exhibited the next day (July 4) after his communion with Art, when Tom once again turns his eyes away from time and space and its actualities and dreams of a future self and happy life with the beautiful cellist Lola.[33] Tom lies in bed at the HoJo with Lola and day-dreams about a future with her. He romanticizes about a tranquil life on the gallery of her home—a Hollywood imitation of Tara—where they would idly "watch evening fall and lightning bugs wink in the purple meadow." The "intolerable tenderness of the past," he believes, would be "discharged" by her music, the cello providing an aesthetic musical joy that he says "ransoms us from the past."[34] He imagines himself in this future life as an affable scientist, "working on a time machine and forgetting time" (LR, 339).

It is only after Art steals Tom's lapsometers and begins to use them for his own demonic purposes that Tom begins to see the dangers of the angelism Art preaches. As the political troubles intensify near the end of the novel, Tom discovers that Art is circulating among a group of leftist student dissidents, surreptitiously treating them with the lapsometer. He rails out at Art about the dangers of the angelic abstraction that he is inducing by his treatments:

> It [the lapsometer-induced abstraction] would render him [the patient] to-
> tally abstracted from himself, totally alienated from the concrete world, and
> in such a state of angelism that he will fall prey to the first abstract notion
> proposed to him and will kill anybody who gets in his way, torture, execute,
> wipe out entire populations, all with the best possible motives and the best
> possible intentions, in fact in the name of peace and freedom, etcetera.(*LR*,
> 328)

Tom is beginning at the end of the novel to understand the terror that
O'Connor believes is the natural consequence of those who see human
experience through the angelic eye of theory and abstraction.[35]

THE BEST HOPE: WAITING, WATCHING, LISTENING

An examination of the novel's concluding chapter, "Five Years Later" (381–
403), reveals where Percy finds the "best hope" (*SP*, 250) for Tom's escaping
the angelism-bestialism that has frustrated him in his search for love and
happiness. The best hope for Tom's freedom lies in the ironically named
Slave Quarters, the new community (*Con*, 74) that he chooses for his home.
There he acquires some new languages and begins to name his world and
his place in it in new ways. He has removed himself from Paradise Estates
and its glib religious language and from Fedville and its scientific/social
scientific jargon and clichés; these are the communities and languages that
have encouraged Tom to place himself apart from the world and others in
his quest for knowing and happiness. Tom frees himself from his enslave-
ment in the language world of Paradise Estates and the Fedville medical
complex, a semiotic world in which the Church and the authority of its
language has disappeared as a source of truth about the self and creation.
The language of Paradise Estates has reduced the truths of the faith to
catchy phrases on pennants, like the one that reads "Jesus Christ Greatest
Pro of Them All." At his home in the Quarters, Tom returns, with the
assistance of Father Smith, to the sacramental language of the Church, an
alternative semiotic that speaks the Good News of a human brotherhood
and love that can heal the individual and social divisions that plague Tom
and the citizenry of Paradise Estates.

Tom's inchoate development of this sacramental naming and being enables him to begin to acquire a new sense of commmunity with his family,
his neighbors in the Slave Quarters, and his fellow Christians at Father
Smith's chapel. Tom at the end of *Love in the Ruins* has initiated a family

life with Ellen Oglethorpe and their two children that opens him once again to the possibility for the intersubjective love that he fails to achieve with Moira and Lola and that he failed to understand in his relationship with Doris and Samantha. His opportunity for a new existential spaciousness and comfort in his family life is humorously suggested in the final scene in the novel when he is settling down with Ellen in the king-size "Sears Best" that he has just purchased as a Christmas gift for her. He is now symbolically free from the cramped little "convent beds" (*LR*, 391]) he and Doris endured in his first attempt at marital love. An opportunity for Tom to open himself to social and political "community" and intersubjectivity in the Slave Quarters rests with Victor Charles, whose friendship with Tom and his family precedes the political, religious, and racial conflicts described in the novel. Victor is "running for Congress" and wants Tom to serve as the "campaign manager" for a political coalition that he has formed with the Bantus, Chuck Parker, Max Gottlieb, and Leroy Ledbetter (*LR*, 400–401). And, finally, another kind of community is made available to Tom through Father Smith. Tom returns to the Church, Father Smith administering to him at the Christmas Eve mass the sacraments of Reconciliation and Eucharist. Tom is being offered by the priest and the sacramental system of the Church a release from his enclosed consciousness and a community with all humanity for all time. If he will listen to the Word he is receiving and act in response to it, Tom can recover a consciousness of who he is and where he is and learn what he must do as he makes his journey with others toward Christ.

Tom's new openness to a Catholic Christian knowledge of the sacramental world is intimated by the fact that he begins in the Slave Quarters to acquire an improved capacity to place himself in the particularities of incarnate creation and make deductions about who he is and where he is in terms of this self-placement. It is Christmas Eve morning when this last chapter of *Love in the Ruins* opens, and Tom, in his "new boots," is "hoeing collards" in his family's "walled garden." He is now oriented toward working in the immediacy of present time and space and is no longer withdrawn into his memories and constructing a self and world in that interior landscape. Neither is he casting ahead to make plans for a return to an Edenic garden, some existential utopia created by his scientific knowledge and lapsometer. He says he continues to "believe ... [his] lapsometer can save the world," "cure the chronic angelism-bestialism that rives soul from body"(*LR*, 382–83) but he is now more interested in healing one person at a time and less obsessed with messianic illusions about his role in an imminent apocalypse. He does not fantasize about becoming a world-renowned secular savior but instead imagines himself in the future as a practicing physician who will be able to heal a single abstracted patient. Tom sees the patient walk into his office a "ghost-beast and walk out as a man." He is not dreaming of returning this man—or himself—to Paradise, but envisions them both becoming genuinely themselves: "sovereign wanderer, lordly exile, worker and waiter and watcher" (*LR*, 383).

Tom is already on his way to achieving this kind of Christian "sovereignty" as he works contentedly, open-eyed and newly awake in the confines of his postlapsarion walled garden—ready with his new boots (like Allie's in *The Second Coming*, 26) for the wayfaring ahead. He is neither grieving over a past happiness lost nor fretting about his ability to acquire a future paradasiacal bliss. Instead, Tom is in the process of developing the kind of authentic self that Kierkegaard says realizes that true existence is in the existential now of one's current becoming. He is becoming the Christian self who is not lost in memory or sucked down into dreams of the future, but "approaches [ontological issues] from the future." This is the self who looks at the future as a mysterious not-now when all human experience will reach its fulfillment.[36]

Tom is no longer stocking rooms at Howard Johnson's or planning an endless series of happiness-producing trysts with Moira, Lola, and Ellen; nor is he withdrawn into the scientific abstractions of his angelic *cogito* creating his imaginary apocalyptic scenarios. He thinks to himself as he works in his garden, "knowing, not women, said Sir Thomas [More] is man's happiness" (*LR*, 383). This statement sounds very much like the old Cartesian happiness-seeking Tom, but there is a great difference here. The "knowing" that he now thinks will make him happy is not the knowing of Fedville medical science but, as his allusion to St. Thomas More indicates, the knowing of his Catholic namesake. Tom, then, is assenting to the possible truth of More's Catholic Christian knowing. It is this knowledge that can open him to a consciousness of himself as a sovereign wanderer and exile in a sacramental world where he should "watch and listen and wait" (*LR*, 382) for signs that will direct him to his home ("Watch!" Christ warns [Mark 13:37]). Tom now is looking to the horizon for a knowledge that can, possibly, provide a happiness not available in motel rooms or in the stimulations of his other past need satisfactions.

Percy's use of sacramental imagery in this garden scene at the Slave Quarters emphasizes that Tom is beginning to see the finite world with more clarity and precision and that he is beginning to attach more meaning to the signs in the phenomena he perceives. He is developing a way of seeing that can reveal to him that he exists in a beautiful and mysterious place resplendent with being and beginning to place himself and others firmly in the particularities and wonders of that world. It is the eve of the celebration of the birth of Christ, the Incarnation, and Tom seems to sense an incarnational presence in the world around him. In his garden filled with sun, he can see Ellen through the open doorway of their simple cottage, radiant in "a swatch of sunlight." In the past he was inclined to approach Doris as if she were some remote pagan goddess orbiting physical creation, but he now sees Ellen as a more earthly "Velasquez's weaver girl." Above him, "a kingfisher goes ringing down the bayou." Even the spider in the corner of the garden wall is an unthreatening, innocent wonder, swinging in its web "like a child on a swing." He recalls how every morning at dawn he sets his trotline in the "mystical" water of the bayou nearby. The bayou in his mind's eye is a silent, serene, but gloriously alive place where his skiff seems "suspended in a new element globy and white." Below him in the water, in "the vaporish depths," float magnificent "great green turtles, blue catfish, lordly gaspergous" (*LR*, 382).[37]

Later in the morning, while he is waiting for the bus to take him to town, Tom happens to encounter one of the new Bantu residents of Paradise Estates. In this scene Percy makes clear the difference between Tom's emerging new sacramental language and sign-reading skills and the degraded semiotic he has left behind at the Fedville medical center and in Paradise Estates. Colley Wilkes, one of the Bantus who now occupy Paradise Estates and run Fedville, stops to give Tom a lift to his office. Colley and Fran, his wife, are ecstatic about their spotting last Sunday in Honey Island Swamp the rare "ivory-billed woodpecker," an achievement they feel will make them stars in the local Audubon Society. They excitedly exude, "He's alive! He's come back! After all these years!" "Who?" Tom asks, and begins to think of the "great unclassified beast of a fish" he caught this morning as a possible sign "of Christ coming again at the end of the world" (*LR*, 387). While Fran and Colley remain self-absorbed in the joys of their discovery of the woodpecker—and lost in the aesthetic raptures of Tchaikovsky playing on their Toyota's tape deck—Tom is contemplating the possibility of another kind of discovery and joy signified by the unclassified fish he has recently pulled up out of the dark waters of the bayou. Tom believes the fish may be a sign of a wonder and happiness that is indeed unclassifiable by the Linnaean science that the Wilkeses' use to classify the woodpecker. Unlike Tom, they can marvel at their discovery in nature only because the woodpecker is an example of a rare species in a taxonomic class.

At the end of this scene in the Wilkeses' Toyota, the difference between Tom's new language and the meaning it is opening to him and the language of this Bantu couple becomes obvious. Colley praises Tom for his medical research, expressing his confidence in the potential of his lapsometer to "explore . . . the motor and sensory areas of the cortex." With a phraseology very similar to that used by T. S. Eliot's frustrated Prufrock when he tries to explain to the braceleted ladies that they do not understand him, Tom responds to Colley's praise for his scientific knowledge by saying, "that's not it at all." Tom answers Colley's compliments by pointing out that he is not interested in using his lapsometer merely to stimulate brain tissue, but is more concerned with "perturbations of the soul." The linguistic and metaphysical distance between Tom and the Wilkeses is again emphasized at the end of their encounter as Tom steps out of the Toyota and wishes them a "merry Christmas"; they dismiss him with a pagan "merry Longhu6" [sic] (LR, 390).

Although he is now experiencing a more complete alienation than ever before from the Bantu-dominated political and medical community of Paradise Estates that has temporarily assumed power, Tom is finding a new community and home (LR, 386) among the other disenfranchised citizens of Paradise Estates in the Slave Quarters. After the midnight Christmas mass, Victor Charles affably wishes Tom a merry Christmas and invites him to join the political coalition of swamp hippies, Fedville liberals, "peckerwood" rednecks, and Catholics he is organizing in his efforts to win a seat in Congress (LR, 400–401). The different races, political persuasions, social classes, professions, religions, and ethnic groups represented by the members of this coalition Tom may join have the potential to create a new cohesive and harmonious society. They illustrate how such divided and conflicting social and economic groups can unite in a some shared understanding of their predicament and learn how to act to ameliorate it.

Percy implied in his 1971 National Book Award press conference address that the kind of cooperative political community the black Victor Charles is trying to form is most possible in the South (SP, 250), where there has survived to some degree a language and social fabric that makes possible the intersubjective knowing that exists in the relationship between Victor and Tom. Radically different in their racial heritage, economic and professional achievements, and social class, still they know each other in a way that impels them to act for the other's welfare. Percy, drawing some parallels between the hopeful ending of the novel and the problems in race relations in Covington, said that he saw both in the fictional world of Love in the Ruins and in his own hometown the possibility for "reconciliation" (Con, 51). In the novel, this reconciliation is possible only when individuals like Victor and Tom recognize their shared existential predicament.

In his new community, Tom is beginning to feel that his home is among these local "eccentrics who don't fit in anywhere else," beginning to see that his personal predicament may be the predicament all humankind experiences. Earlier, in the garden, Tom thinks to himself that all men are exiles and castaways that don't fit in the world, and he places himself among these exiles. In his reflections on his home after he meets Victor, he again expresses a unity with his fellow citizens and vows that only their good nature and natural inclination to help strangers— their capacity for charity, in other words—can save them from hopeless division and conflict (*LR*, 386). Although he cannot yet articulate it, Tom is on the verge of realizing that his situation in the Slave Quarters is a microcosm of the human predicament as the Catholic Percy understands it: all are misfits in exile from their home and alienated from their true selves and each other by an aboriginal Fall from innocence and goodness. This is the common condition all share, what unites all in the redemptive process now underway through the Incarnation. Tom is beginning to escape his isolation from others and creation and approaching Marcel's consciousness of "we are."

At mass with his fellow exiles this Christmas Eve night, Tom learns about the charity necessary for the communion of all mankind, primarily through the confession and penance (the sacrament of Reconciliation) administered by Father Smith (*LR*, 396–400). Tom has not been to confession in eleven years. Unlike his past experiences at mass with Samantha and on the road with Doris, Tom is not exhilarated and made happy by the sacramental experience this time. When Father Smith asks him in the confessional booth if he feels "sorry for" his sins, Tom says, "I don't feel much of anything." Percy's point is that Tom, in his sacramental dialogue with the priest, is in the process of developing a consciousness of a love and happiness larger than the good feelings that were the exclusive goals of the happiness-seeking Tom of the past.

By choosing once again to enter the confessional box after years of debilitating self-enclosure in his science and pleasure-seeking, Tom is symbolically agreeing to a sacramental confinement that will, paradoxically, open him to a new sense of oneness with the world and others. When Tom enters the confession box, he enters a place where, he says, he began "forgetting everything" (*LR*, 396), began creating a sort of metaphysical tabula rasa on which the priest can write about the "true knowledge" (*LR*, 398, 399) of his sins. In this detail of Tom's confession, Percy may be alluding to Kierkegaard's similar ideas about the importance of the Christian's forgetting. The Kierkegaardian Christian is one who must forget his personal desires in order to remember his existence in a place of universal human suffering and death. Kierkegaard, in his *Training and Christianity*, explains that confession of sin is admission "to oneself where one is" because it is the penitent's recognition that he lives in such a world of grave imperfection. His confession is a recognition of his communion with all who suffer in this world. This knowledge of a common humanity and destiny with others should provoke a humility, love, and a dedication to the service of mankind. Further, this knowledge of the human predicament— the penitent's recognition of where he is—should urge him to "remember" the redemption available for him and for all through the Incarnation of Christ.[38]

Tom's emerging consciousness of such a fellowship with other sinners is suggested by his referring to all Catholics as "we" (*LR*, 400) after he emerges from the box in the sackcloth Father Smith has instructed him to wear and in the ashes the priest has dumped in his hair. Tom has always declared his belief in the Church and the God it represents, but he has never felt a oneness with other Catholics and therefore has not been given to acts of charity. Tom, while always a believer, has never placed himself in service among God's servants and flock, but has instead pursued his own desires. St. James makes it clear that this kind of Christian has an inadequate knowledge of the human predicament: "Even the demons," says St. James, believe in God "and tremble" (James 2.19). Tom's confession and his accepting the signs of penance from Father Smith imply that he now places himself in the world as a participant with others in a sign-filled sacramental universe, sees himself as a member of the universal "we."

Although Tom is not capable of arriving at the contrition he and Father Smith agree is the ideal next step after his confession, he does promise to "pray" for "a true knowledge of . . . [his] sins and a true contrition." Father Smith tells him to "ask for sorrow. Pray for me." Tom accepts these instructions, replying, "All right." The priest is asking Tom to forget his own desires and the personal happiness that satisfying those desires can bring and to accept a true knowledge of his place among other suffering wayfarers. Father Smith is encouraging Tom to recognize that he lives in a Fallen world of sorrow where "ordinary kindness" (*LR*, 399) and the prayers of others are the only hope for its suffering inhabitants.

Tom promises Father Smith that he will pray for a knowledge of his and others' sins and for the sorrow that accompanies this consciousness. He is, with this promise, tacitly accepting to the existence of a knowledge not available through the exercise of his intellect, and he is assuming that he will be changed significantly by it. Tom is assuming that he is capable of feeling a sorrow for the condition of all humankind, and even believes this sorrow is something he should desire. This is a quite different Tom from the one who has spent the last two decades or so of his life desiring nothing but his own personal happiness and doing as he pleases (*LR*, 6). He has in his life vainly sought the loves that he believed could provide him with happiness and has lived in dread of the grief and sorrow that are the ineluctable consequences of the absence of that love and happiness. "Why does desire turn to grief?" Tom literally sobbed in room 203 of the Howard Johnson's five years earlier (LR, 137–38). Now Tom is learning at this Christmas mass, when he "eat[s] Christ" (LR, 400), that there is a love that will redeem him and all others from the despair unaware of being despair and grief that are inherent consequences of the "little closed loves" he has chosen in the past. Through the Eucharist, "the sacrament of Incarnation,"[39] he is allowing himself to "listen" (LR, 381) to the Word, and this time vowing to act out there in the incarnational world with others in order to discover whatever fullness of being this love will reveal.

At the end of Love in the Ruins, Tom does not free himself totally from "the longing, the desire that has no name," which has driven him in his solipsistic pursuit of love and happiness with Doris, Lola, Moira, and Ellen. Nor does he lose his faith in his scientific knowledge. He still longs for the good times provided by illicit sex, drinking, and scientific knowing (LR, 393), but his angelic-bestial desires are less likely now to lure him into fantasies about his future or into regrets about his past. As he sits in his office on Christmas Eve afternoon and idly stares out his back door, he is attracted by the brazen enticements of Mrs. Prouty, a Sears clerk who has come out onto the company's loading dock just across the vacant lot. He remembers that she made it clear to him when he ordered his Sears mattress from her that she was available if he needed a partner on the mattress. Although he still contemplates the pleasures of relationships like the one Mrs. Prouty is offering, he does not see her as the source of his future happiness. Tom also continues to long for the pleasures of Early Times. When he takes Ellen to bed that night, he admits that he is drunk, having just taken "six drinks in six minutes" while outside smoking the Christmas turkey (LR, 302). He is not, however, stocking his house with cases of Early Times the way he stocked the Howard Johnson's rooms five years earlier. He does not seem now so desperate to make sure that his longing for his favorite drink will be satisfied well into the future. And he still believes that his scientific knowledge and lapsometer can help mankind. Now, however, Tom does not define himself as a scientific messiah but simply as a physician who can help one patient at a time with his invention. The lapsometer, Lewis Lawson says, becomes for Tom at the end of the novel merely a "diagnostic flashlight, not . . . a metaphysical welding torch."[40]

In his final descriptions of Tom at his Slave Quarters home, Percy may be implying that Tom's changes have been subtle interior changes in psychic posture, changes in his way of seeing, rather than changes in his de-sires, personality, or social behavior. In the novel's last scene, when Tom returns home from Christmas mass in his sackcloth and ashes—and re-turns with the implied knowledge these sacramental signs signify—Percy describes him as an antic, carefree "David before the Ark"—drinking, "danc-ing around," and "cutting the fool" while he barbecues under the night skies. Tom seems here to be no different from the exhilarated aesthete who, a decade or so ago, used to "love" mass because it made him so happy. Percy uses many of the same images to describe Tom's return from mass this Christmas night that he uses to describe Tom's experiences after he and Samantha attended the masses at St. Michael's (*LR*, 12–13, 138). In the past, the masses at St. Michael's were for Tom just another happiness-pro-ducing experience that reinforced his comforting belief that he had life in him because of the Eucharist (*LR*, 13, 138) he consumed there. When he returned to his home in Paradise Estates with Doris and Samantha, he danced and sang just as he does now—"cut the fool like David" (*LR*, 13,138), took six quick drinks (*LR*, 13, 138) while he barbecued, and capped the evening off by bedding down with his wife (*LR*, 13, 138). He seems in no obvious, external way different on this Christmas night with this new fam-ily than he was in the past with Doris and Samantha.

But there are some differences, as Percy's details in this final scene subtly suggest. First of all, this time he is returning from a mass that has been preceded by his confession and a dialogue with Father Smith. The priest has asked Tom to consider what is outside his inner life of good feeling and scientific thought; he has instructed him about a world of sin, suffering, and sorrow that he shares with others and a God who can redeem all from that desperate condition. Also, this mass is a *Christmas* mass, a celebration of the Nativity, the Logos become flesh, the Incarnation. It is more likely, therefore, to remind Tom of the incarnational, sacred world beyond the pleasant life in him that he was so happy about when he and Samantha attended mass (*LR*, 13,138).

Tom's new inclination to look beyond the closed world of the feelings in him and outward to where he exists with others in incarnational time and space is indicated when he announces to himself while dancing around in the cold darkness at the barbecue grill, "It is Christmas Day and the Lord is here, a holy night and surely that is all one needs" (*LR*, 402). He is now locating something holy that is "here" in this actual moment and place, a presence that "surely" (possibly, hopefully) is mankind's single need. Tom is choosing the phenomenal world that is right here and now. He is like Kierkegaard's ideal Christian, who "work[s], . . . [and is] glad in it, love[s] his wife . . . [and is] glad in her, bring[s] up his children with joyfulness, love[s] his fellow man, rejoice[s] in life." "God will surely," Kierkegaard argues, let the Christian know what else he must "understand" and do.[41] Tom appears willing to wait and watch in the darkness of this present moment at his home for that future revelation.

Tom may in some ways still see himself as the exuberant, sovereign King David before the Ark enjoying his physical pleasures; but at the end of the novel he is also a less hysterical David who feels a unity with all others in the sovereignty of self all enjoy in incarnate creation. While he still luxuriates in the pleasures of food, drink, song (but, significantly, not now the aesthetic*Don Giovanni*), and sex, he is more conscious of the phenomenal world beyond his need satisfactions and the people in it. After mass at St. Michael's a decade earlier he would conclude his evenings by flinging himself down into the shrubberies with Doris (*LR*, 13, 138), conscious only of his own overwhelming desire (*LR*, 13, 138). Now he joins Ellen in their new Sears Best and considers how he and his wife are just like "all good folk" (*LR*, 403), placing this moment of private experience in the context of all human experience. As he felt with the congregation at this night's mass a sense of "we are," so here Tom's phrasing suggests that he is beginning to think of himself as a participant with Ellen, and with all people, in a holy place. He is beginning to see himself as a wayfarer with others who might profitably wait and watch in the sacramental world for the signs promised by the New Covenant celebrated on this Christmas night. These are signs that were not available to the Old Testament King David, signs that surely have the power to reveal a redemptive love and happiness transcendent of Tom's desires and this moment. Tom suspects that in this holy night's sky are the signs that can show him how to conquer the dread of "grief and memory" (*LR*, 138) that has until now defeated him.

6

The Thanatos Syndrome: Life or Death

> ... in this age of the lost self, lost in the desert of theory and consumption, nothing of significance remains but signs. And only two signs are of significance .... One is oneself and the other is the Jews .... By "the Jews" I mean ... the worldwide *ecclesia* instituted by one of them, God-become-man, a Jew.
>
> — "Why Are You a Catholic?" *SP,* 312

THE AGE OF THANATOS

Percy intended *The Thanatos Syndrome* (1987) to be read as a "sequel to *Love in the Ruins*" (*MCon,* 77)—more precisely, he noted, a "deranged sequel."[1] He again wanted to expose, in a comic novel that would avoid the "far out sci-fi ... futuristic gimmickry" of his earlier novel (*MCon,* 206), the problems, even the "horror" (*TS,* 254), of self-dislocation in a "demented" twentieth century (*SP,* 309). In this sequel set ten years later in Feliciana Parish, Louisiana, Dr. Thomas More is still an alcoholic, failed psychiatrist trying to treat his patients who are victims of this century. But instead of relying on gadgetry such as his ontological lapsometer, he now depends on an old-fashioned Freudian/Jungian psychiatry in his attempts to explain what he metaphorically calls the "stealing of people's selves, an invasion of body snatchers" (*TS,* 33) that is plaguing his community. Most of the novel chronicles Tom's efforts to discover the pathogen responsible for the syndrome exhibited by his patients; they demonstrate in their behavior what he diagnoses as a certain "loss" of "the old ache of self" (*TS,* 85). Much like their counterparts in the classic horror movie about the "body snatchers," they are simply not themselves, their language and social skills suggesting to Tom that they have "lost" consciousness of the "truest unique self which

191

lies within" (*TS*, 17). A letter to Shelby Foote indicates that as early as 1977 Percy had toyed with the idea of writing "a modern version of Body Snatchers."[2] Later, in a 1984 letter to Elizabeth Spencer, Percy said that his new novel would be "a metaphysical rendering of the theme of *The Invasion of the Body Snatchers*."[3]

In *The Thanatos Syndrome*, Tom returns to his role as Cartesian scientist, analyzing objectively what's "gone wrong" (*SP*, 248) in his society and searching again for "what to do" (*TS*, 5, 21, 74, 75, 88, 111, e.g.)—in this case, what to do about the frightening loss of self that he believes is transforming his patients, friends, and wife into aphasic zombies. But the social and political world of Feliciana Parish where he makes his search is a more sinister and threatening place than Paradise Estates in *Love in the Ruins*. At the end of *Love in the Ruins*, Tom finds himself in an America where there is a promise of racial and political harmony and a hope for a new sense of community (*Con*, 74). Tom imagines himself as an ebullient King David before the Ark, dancing around in celebration of the hope he has discovered in a world and cosmos that he considers holy (*LR*, 402). But Tom's Louisiana home in *The Thanatos Syndrome* is a place very similar to the small American town in the horror movie, *The Invasion of the Body Snatchers*. It is an apparently normal community where there is a secret agent of death lurking beneath its innocuous facade. In Feliciana the citizens are hopeless and helpless victims of a passionless government that employs scientists who methodically exterminate innocent children, the aged, the infirm—the very weakest and most vulnerable members of society. Tom learns, with the help of Lucy Lipscomb, his cousin and fellow research physician, that he lives in a community where the science he has depended on all his life for the "truth" about himself, his patients, and the nature of physical reality is being used to turn his patients into self-absorbed automata and his children into victims of pedophiles. He is forced to recognize that the medical profession that has provided him with his own identity and sense of self is dominated by scientists like Bob Comeaux, the director of the Feliciana Qualitarian Life Center who creates the secret Blue Boy project, and John Van Dorn, the founder and headmaster of Belle Ame school who administers the Na-24-treated water provided by Comeaux's project to his unsuspecting students. They are the "body snatchers" behind the "loss" and dehumanization that Tom discovers among his friends, family, and fellow citizens.

Percy is again in *The Thanatos Syndrome* satirically attacking the dislocation of the self in an America where scientistic, "angelic" theorizing about life places the transcendent, knowing self in "orbit" (*LC*, 116) and "bestial" consumption in the pursuit of personal happiness reduces the self to a mere organism satisfying its needs. Tom says, after he and Lucy discover that Na-24 is being dumped into the water supply in southeastern Louisiana, that the heavy sodium could produce "angelism-bestialism" (*TS*, 180), the same kind of "hermaphroditism of the spirit" (*LR*, 383) that he tries to cure with his lapsometer ten years earlier in Paradise Estates. And the Na-24 victims do indeed exhibit the same angelic-bestial sense of self. Tom finds in his patients who have ingested heavy sodium, a strange, angelic kind of "disconnectedness" (*TS*, 8), an "absence of super-ego . . . anxiety" (*TS*, 30). The old terrors that he treated them for two years earlier, before his imprisonment at Fort Pelham, have vanished, and most of the time— when they are not lost in the remote recesses of their computer-like brains—they exhibit bestial "unfocused animal good spirits." Unfortunately, the Na-24 also causes a radical loss of language competency since it affects the "posterior speech center, Wernicke's area, Brodmann 39 and 40," the part of the brain that neurologists identify as the "locus of self-conscious-ness, the 'I,' the utterer, the 'self'" (*TS*, 21–22). Perhaps the single most important idea in Percy's epistemology, expressed again and again in his essays and interviews (especially *MB*, 282), is his conviction that this kind of impoverishment in the power to name experience causes a subsequent impoverishment of consciousness and being since it is only through lan-guage transactions with others that the self locates who and where it is.[4]

It is not only the victims of Na-24 who are being impoverished in *The Thanatos Syndrome*, but also the scientists who victimize and study them. They, including Tom, are enclosed in a lifeless, self-constructed interior world of scientific abstractions that numb them to the realities of the phenomenal world and the flesh-and-blood people in it. All, Percy maintains, are casualties, of a "century of death" (*MCon*, 120–21), an "age of thanatos" (*TS*, 86). The twenti-eth century, Percy believes, is an era in the history of the Christian West in which few believe that there has been an aboriginal Fall of mankind from a primal fullness of life, a universal diminishment of being. Instead, most, par-ticularly scientists like the ones in Feliciana, suffer from an angelism that denies any inherent ontological deficiency and posits a self with potentially limitless capacity for discovery of itself and its existence. They, like Kierkegaard's aes-thetes, withdraw into their private thoughts, theories, intuitions, and feelings in their attempts to know who they are and where they are. Their angelic mind-set lures them away from actual phenomena and their own being in it and encourages them to mistake the lifeless abstractions of their impoverished *cogito* for truths about life. Their withdrawal from the actualities of human existence can only result in the loneliness, anxiety, self-delusion, and ontologi-cal inauthenticity that Marcel, Heidegger, and Jaspers point out are the defining characteristics of the modern alienated self.[5]

While *The Thanatos Syndrome* is a humorous, "futuristic novel" in which, Percy says, he continues the satirical attacks on contemporary American "politics . . . medicine and . . . science" (*MCon*, 77) that he initiated in *Love in the Ruins*, the novel is also a more somber diagnosis and indictment of this "age of thanatos." In his final novelistic expression of his imaginative and philosophical vision, Percy asserts, primarily through Father Smith's "Confession" (*TS*, 239–57) and through his diatribe at the mass at the end of the novel (*TS*, 357–63), the central dark truth that he believed was at the heart of "all his novels"—the fact that "we live in the century of death" (*MCon*, 120–21). Commenting on the deceptive nature of this existential death in "Novel Writing in an Apocalyptic Time," Percy says, "there is something worse than being deprived of life: it is being deprived of life and not knowing it" (*SP*, 163). His point is that, like the self-deceived scientists in *The Thanatos Syndrome* who are incapable of seeing their work at the Qualitarian Center as a sign in the desert, most fail to recognize this place of death where they are being deprived of a life that they cannot with their current diminished consciousness identify and name.

Percy maintained in a 1986 interview that he was "angry" about "a certain mind-set in the biological and social sciences" currently popular among many "educated folk," a mind-set responsible for the living death that so many in this century are deceived into mistaking for life. It was this anger, he said, that motivated his writing of *The Thanatos Syndrome* (*SP*, 394). In his portrayals of the Fedville scientists, Percy is attacking in the novel the scientistic assumptions about life popular in a period in human history that Binx in *The Moviegoer* calls "the very century of merde, the great shithouse of scientific humanism" (*MG*, 199). Parading itself as a secular humanism that values "free scientific inquiry," this pervading Cartesianism is, Percy argued, in fact "anti-human" and "neither free nor scientific" in its view of mankind and the phenomenal world it proposes. Instead, it is a philosophy that promotes a "widespread and ongoing devaluation of human life" by paradoxically denying that suffering and death are inevitable realities of human existence. Of course, if, as these scientists would suggest, the world can be a place without suffering and death, then that is the world we should devote ourselves to discovering, instead of trying to develop our capacity to respond with compassion and love to our suffering and dying neighbors.

This angelic mind-set that so angered Percy posits that there can be endless discovery of scientific truths that can be used to improve the "quality of life" and eliminate "pointless suffering" and "life without meaning." In anthropological studies in this century, for example, Margaret Mead and many like-minded romantic "scientists" argued that they had discovered in primitive civilizations an innocent way of life exempt from the social, political, psychological, spiritual, and moral problems of modern civilizations. The Samoans, Mayans, and the Tasaday tribe of Indonesia (Father Weatherbee's noble "Mindanoans" [SC, 410]), these anthropologists suggested, are models of the kind of "perfect" lives that we could all achieve if we would reject experience as we know it and model our lives after the primitive noble savages they and Rousseau enshrine in their theoretical constructs. Percy goes on to point out that more sinister examples of this modern romanticized, Cartesian mind-set can be found in the political ideologies of Stalin's Russia and Hitler's Germany. Because such ideologies also ignore individual experience in order to champion an abstract way of life free from the imperfections of the Fallen world, they subsequently deny the worth of any individual who might be an impediment to the realization of the ideals they endorse. The gas chamber is the logical consequence of a belief in such ideologies (SP, 394–96) since it is an effective way of eliminating the bothersome imperfections in the potential utopia the ideologue envisions.

In *The Thanatos Syndrome*, Bob Comeaux and John Van Dorn are obvious examples of the kind of angelic mind-set Percy believes is so dangerous in this century. Comeaux defends the killing at the Qualitarian Center and the humanitarian goals of his Blue Boy project on the basis that they represent efforts by the scientific community to eliminate human suffering and improve the quality of life in southeastern Louisiana. He boasts that by adding Na-24 to the water supply in the area he has dramatically reduced teenage pregnancies, lowered the crime rate, and boosted SAT scores to a record high. Van Dorn uses this same additive in the water supply at his exclusive school in order to transform the students into Teutonic academic achievers and compliant sex partners for him and the other pedophiles that work at Belle Ame. He tells Tom that the Blue Boy project is a war on crime, "teenage suicide and drug abuse," and AIDS—the "three social plagues" he theorizes will "wreck" civilization. Van Dorn sees his school as a vanguard of excellence in this war, a training center for America's youth modeled after the "old European Gymnasium-Hochschule" (*TS*, 218–19). Even after Tom confronts him about the child molestation at Belle Ame, Van Dorn tells Tom that he can see "no suffering, cruelty or abuse" in his exploitation of the children for his sexual gratification, and he even argues that he and his staff are exhibiting a special kind of "caring" in response to children who are "starved for human affection" (*TS*, 303).

Dr. Thomas More has been guilty of a similar kind of abstraction and theorizing in his posturing in *Love in the Ruins* as a lapsometer-wielding secular scientific savior and in his role as Christlike physician for individuals hopelessly estranged from themselves and others. In *The Thanatos*

Syndrome Tom is not entirely free from the scientific mind-set he exhibited in *Love in the Ruins*, the same kind of mind-set that drives Comeaux and Van Dorn to their inhumane theories about the "ultimate goal[s]" of life (*TS*, 346). Tom is still the "solitary" (*LR*, 23), inward scientist who isolates himself from friends and family in order to explore the "objective evidence" and examine "more cases" (*TS*, 23) so that he will have the data to support a theory that will explain the strange behavior of his patients. He assumes that through this scientific data-gathering and anaytical procedure, he can discover the truth. His individual patients are for him mere case studies as he proceeds in his analyses, classifications, and theorizing. Meanwhile, his devotion to these interiorized abstractions alienates him from Ellen, his children, his friends, his colleagues, and his church. In orbit like the transcendent self in *Lost in the Cosmos*, Tom chooses his theories about who he is and where he is over actual time-space events. As Chandra tells him, he is "too much up in [his] head" (*TS*, 40).

Tom does not share Chandra's view of his diminished consciousness but instead feels that he has recently developed a self-enriching mode of perception. He believes that in prison, where he served two years for selling "prescriptions of Desoxyn and Dalmane . . . at the Union 76 truckstop" (*TS*, 26–27), he had the opportunity to "learn . . . a certain detachment and cultivate . . . a mild, low-grade curiosity" (*TS*, 67). Percy explains that in Heidegger's epistemology the kind of "curious" self that Tom is so pleased about having become is one of the unauthentic roles *Dasein* can assume in its transactions with the world, a role that results in an alienation from one's genuine self and others (*LC*, 113). But Tom feels that this curiosity has helped hone his powers of perception. He believes that his perceptive powers have also been enhanced by his ignoring metaphysical experience and narrowing his vision to the sensory perceptions that he happens to gather during his daily existence. He says that in prison he became "more curious" about people and less interested in God (*TS*, 81), declaring that he has not "given religion two thoughts or been to Mass for years" (*TS*, 46). Unfortunately, what Tom has developed in prison, and what Chandra can identify, is not a new acuity of consciousness, but a typically Cartesian, enclosed way of seeing that restricts itself to the knowing possible in its narrow realm of private perception. The "small life" (compare Lance's "little view" [*L*, 1]) he feels "good" about (*TS*, 67) having achieved in prison is indeed small.

This new, curious Tom has abandoned what he calls the "Faustian" (*TS*, 67) angelism that prompted his search for the scientific achievement he pursued so desperately in *Love in the Ruins*. He has given up his search for a solution to mankind's self-alienation and anxiety and tries to find contentment in his small life of detachment and few worries (*TS*, 67). Also, although he does not seem to be entirely conscious of it, Tom has lost the intense bestial longing (*LR*, 21, e.g.) that drove his desperate search for happiness (*LR*, 214, e.g.) and love with Doris, Moira, Lola, Ellen, and Samantha in *Love in the Ruins*. He has now suspended this quest for love and happiness, a quest that prompted him to probe within himself and question his desires, a quest that led him to wonder and agonize about a world where the pursuing of love can inexplicably turn into a grief that "strike[s] at the heart" (*LR*, 138).[6] Tom has succeeded in escaping the suicidal despair that his longing caused in *Love in the Ruins*, but he has also lost the introspective temper necessary for self-development and discovery. He has reduced his life to a placid self-satisfaction that is, he says, merely "not unhappy" (*TS*, 75). Tom has given up his earlier quests and has become content with a limited way of knowing and being that Kierkegaard calls despair unaware of being despair.[7]

Tom's angelism-bestialism has now taken an attenuated form that makes him very much like the sexually uninhibited, half-conscious, lost selves who have been victimized by the Blue Boy project. Tom has lost the intense desires that used to cause him so much anxiety about how to proceed through his "disorderly life" (*LR*, 6). While Tom's desperate desire to build a happy life for himself and his society drives him into the Fedville mental ward in *Love in the Ruins*, in *The Thanatos Syndrome* he, like many of his Na-24 drugged patients, can locate no desire important enough to cause him that much emotional distress. His daily activities are limited to either casual bestial consumption of experiences that make him feel good or small bits of angelic knowing directed at the problems in his immediate environment. He spends much of his time alone on the front porch of his office idly "making little paper P51s" and sailing them toward the "martin house" (*TS*, 13, 366), waiting for the arrival of his patients so he can continue his angelic scientific probings into their problems and the "syndrome" he has observed. Or, he may choose to down a drink of Jack Daniel's from the bottle in his desk drawer or drop by the Little Napoleon, the neighborhood bar where he has been a regular for years. And there are the pleasurable sensations of "bestial" sex. The day after his release from Fort Pelham, he returns home where he mechanically performs sex with his drunken wife. Feeling that he is engaged in sexual acrobatics with a woman under "light hypnosis" (*TS*, 51–53), Tom assents with mild surprise to Ellen's newly acquired taste for sodomy. Later, at Pantherburn, he passively, literally unconsciously, submits to the aggressive sexual overtures of his cousin, Lucy Lipscomb (*TS*, 162–69). Tom, at this stage in his life, is no longer passionately seeking some permanent state of happiness in his romantic relationships nor seeking fame as a scientific savior of mankind. He now has smaller existential goals that provoke less anxiety.

Tom demonstrates that he has also lost the sacramental way of seeing he was beginning to acquire at the end of *Love in the Ruins* and has again psychically removed himself from time-space experiences that lie outside his interiorized consciousness and the incidental bestial sensations of his daily need satisfactions. At the end of *Love in the Ruins*, Tom can look out at the natural world and see the "great unclassified beast of a fish" he caught as a possible sign of "Christ coming again" (*LR*, 387). But he has now lost his ability to see the created world as divine incarnation and therefore lost the capacity to locate a sacramental "added dimension" to his experience.[8] Throughout most of *The Thanatos Syndrome*, Percy repeatedly shows Tom looking "out there" (*TS*, 121) at a wondrous and sacred natural world, but looking with the dim vision of the angelic-bestial Cartesian who can discover little significance there beyond his private sensory data.

During his conversation with Father Smith when he first visits the priest at the fire tower, Tom demonstrates his ability to "rattle off" a definition of *sacrament* that he memorized in school—"a sensible sign instituted by Christ to produce grace." In addition, he can remember the sisters telling all the children that if they did not "eat . . . [Christ's] body and drink . . . [His] blood" they would "not have life in" them (*TS*, 125). Although Tom can recall these words he memorized in his childhood, he has now rejected the Catholic faith that provided him with a sacramental understanding of sensible experience. He has at the moment, therefore, no knowledge of the mysterious life signified by the Eucharist and other sacramental signs. Ironically, Tom's knowing these words but not what they signify is evidence to prove Father Smith's earlier argument that the language of this century has been "evacuated" of meaning (*TS*, 121).

Although Tom never entirely regains the sacramental vision he exhibits in *Love in the Ruins*, by the end of *The Thanatos Syndrome* there is some hope for him. He has learned from Father Smith about the "horror" (*TS*, 254) of this "century of death" (*MCon*, 183) and has been told by the priest what to do (*TS*, 366) in response to it. Speaking of this horror Smith identifies for Tom, Percy says that an intense consciousness of it "penetrates the ordinariness of everyday life and opens one to mystery" (*MCon*, 186). Tom is, throughout most of the novel, blind to the mystery of his being in the world because he withdraws from it into the closed world of his problem-solution thinking, a mode of perception exemplified by his investigation of the "body snatching" in Feliciana. He has the kind of problem-solution consciousness that Gabriel Marcel says deceives the individual into seeing life merely as something to "lay seige to and reduce" rather than a mystery that requires involvement.[9] Father Smith's instructions at the end of the novel have the potential to open Tom's eyes to this mystery and show him, Percy says, an "opening to God" (*MCon*, 186).

PRISON AND THE SMALL LIFE: WHAT TO DO?

The Thanatos Syndrome begins with Tom More's release from prison at Fort Pelham, Alabama, and his acquiring a new freedom he says he's "glad" (*TS*, 43) to have. Now the problem is what to do in this freedom. Although free from the bars at Pelham, Tom reveals on his first day back home in Feliciana that he remains a prisoner of his enclosed consciousness, this ontological condition preventing him from developing a self that can do more than think, theorize, and explore his memories as he attempts to rejoin his family, medical colleagues, and community. He continues to be psychically imprisoned, now locked away from a knowledge of life "out there" beyond his present angelic-bestial consciousness. Tom's psychic imprisonment and lifelessness are symbolically suggested by the "Bruno Hauptmann suit" (*TS*, 24, 44, 46, 55, 103, 143) that he wears daily until, at Pantherburn, Lucy Lipscomb orders him to discard the "smelly suit" so she can burn it (*TS*, 143). Both Tom and Lucy identify the "ten-year-old double-breasted broad-stripe seersucker" suit with Bruno Hauptmann (*TS*, 24), the despised kidnapper of the Lindbergh infant who was "executed fifty years ago" (*TS*, 55) by an outraged American public. Tom's alienation from a knowledge of who he is, his alienation from others, and his psychic death are suggested by the grim identity he has unconsciously chosen to assume.

Tom apparently does not see these metaphorical connections between himself and Bruno Hauptmann, perhaps because he sees with a detached Cartesian eye that reduces the experience it observes to mere objective sensory data separate and independent of the self that does the observing. He does not, therefore, have a consciousness that is very adept at seeing symbolic or imaginative relationships between himself and what he experiences with his five senses. For example, he is not even conscious of being dressed as Bruno Hauptmann until he meets with Bob Comeaux and Max Gottlieb (his parole officers) in Bob's office at Fedville the morning he is released from Fort Pelham. It occurs to him during the meeting that he "wasn't even aware . . . [he] was wearing" the suit until it suddenly felt "dank and heavy" (*TS*, 24). Tom illustrates in his response here that he sees little symbolic significance to his dress, conscious only of the tactile sensations caused by the suit—the dankness and weight of the fabric against his skin. This literally superficial response to the suit shows that Tom has a self that is limited in its capacity for reading signs and what they signify. It is a mind-set that not only encourages him to pay little attention (*TS*, 24) to his symbolic suit, but it also cuts him off from other signs in the world that offer other kinds of knowledge about who he is and where he is.

Tom's limited ability to discover significance in his environment is again illustrated shortly before he meets with Bob and Max. From the windows of Bob's penthouse office atop the Fedville complex, Tom looks out at "a splendid panoramic view of the river" and "the wooded loess hills of St. Francisville to the north." He does not see in the magnificence of the natural world beneath him any sacramental signs that direct him to the source of the created world and himself, but instead connects the "waters all gold and rose in the sunset" with fictional scenes in Mark Twain's stories, with the technology represented by the "cooling tower of Grand Mer looming" in the midst of the beauty, and with the pollution that is fouling the river (*TS*, 23). This scene shows how Tom, when confronted with the splendid here-and-now phenomena of creation, tends to turn away from the perception and retreat into his private imaginative experience (stories by Mark Twain) or into analyses of the social problems illustrated by the phenomena (pollution in America). Such psychic withdrawal is the defining characteristic of the egoistic Kierkegaardian aesthete who is isolated from the actualities of his life and confined in the interior world of his thoughts, feelings, emotions, and imagination.

Still dressed in his prison suit, Tom leaves Bob's office and stops by Leroy Ledbetter's Little Napoleon for a drink at his favorite bar. At the bar, he once more reveals his inability to connect what he sees with what he is. It was at the Little Napoleon ten years earlier that Tom looked into its mirror and saw himself as a "maculate Christ" (*LR*, 153) who would with his lapsometer bring all people together in peace and love. This time, however, Tom glimpses in the mirror someone he can hardly recognize, somebody who looks like he's "going to a funeral." The man in the mirror is a strange person who reminds Tom of a dead criminal, "an ungainly German executed fifty years ago" (*TS*, 55). Tom cannot interpret the image metaphorically as a sign of his own existential deadness and psychic imprisonment because he is still lost in the small interior world of his thoughts and feelings. He tries to ignore the man in the mirror and dwell on how good he feels. As he sits and talks idly with James Earl Jones and Leroy, he dwells on the blessing that he feels when "the straight bourbon slides into . . . [his] stomach," how "things ease" after the drink, how the second one "feels even better, warmth overlaying warmth." He only wonders momentarily about why the face that is staring back at him reminds him of the German kidnapper. At the end of the scene, Tom simply turns away from the mirror and what the image in it might metaphorically signify to talk with Leroy about borrowing his Bluebird RV and heading out west with Ellen (*TS*, 54–55).

When Tom returns to his home and family that afternoon, he demonstrates how cut off from others he is by the enclosed selfhood that he has chosen. He is hardly welcomed with warmth and enthusiasm. His wife Ellen is asleep when he arrives. His children, Margaret and Tom, Jr., their sullen nanny, Chandra, and Hudeen, Tom's eighty-year-old cook, are obviously uncomfortable around him. He does not use language signs very well, having developed in prison the habit of avoiding conversations with other inmates. Because he is not very accomplished at the intersubjective communication that can be achieved in language transactions, he feels alienated among the members of his own household, and they feel awkward around him. Tom knows he cannot communicate with his children, and he feels that all the members of his household are trying to act as if he is not there— "step[ping] around [him] like a hole in the floor" (*TS*, 38).

Tom's response to this disorienting sense of invisibility is to descend into the basement bedroom of his Slave Quarters cottage where he sits alone and watches the "late afternoon sun off the bayou." Again, Tom indicates as he looks out at nature that he cannot read the sacramental signs there any better than he can read and use the language signs that could unite him with his family upstairs. He feels that he had never before noticed the lush tropical scene in front of him (*TS*, 43), apparently having forgotten that ten years earlier he saw this same bayou as a "mystical" place filled with a wondrous and mysterious life (*LR*, 382). The mathematical and geometrical language he uses to describe the effects of the sunlight that enters his darkening room suggests that Tom's once sacramental eyes have now become the eyes of the scientist. What he sees here are "parabolas of light on the ceiling . . . [that] intersect each other" (*TS*, 43).

Tom's developing sacramental vision at the end of *Love in the Ruins* leads him to consider anew who he is, where he is, and what he should do in the holy (*LR*, 402) world he inhabits. But now Tom turns away from the light and the bayou waters and inward to his memories of his two years at Fort Pelham prison. In his memories he can forget who he is and where he is at this moment —- Dr. Thomas More, an alcoholic, failed physician returning to a disaffected family. He can ignore both the reality of the lonely figure sitting in his basement alone in his Bruno Hauptmann suit and the reality of the mysterious sacramental world radiant before him in the bayou that invites him to a fuller life in communion with others. What Tom chooses to do instead is to construct an alternative self and world, a prisoner-self inhabiting an interior world of pleasant thoughts and feelings. He sees himself in his memory as he was in his recent past—a robust, groundskeeper driving a John Deere over the golf course at Fort Pelham and keeping "the greens like billiard tables." In a bit of self-congratulatory self-analysis, he contemplates also what he believes is the "mystery"of the penetrating new way of "listen[ing]" and "watch[ing]" that he developed in prison (*TS*, 43). This disengaged mode of perception he assumed was a way, he says, of avoiding boring participation with the other prisoners.

When Tom on his first day of freedom returns to his office to resume his psychiatric practice, he is similarly detached from time and space and enclosed in his memories, abstractions, and aesthetic stimulations. The fact that his office is his "father's old coroner's building" symbolically implies the psychic lifelessness that marks its current resident. Tom detects nothing death-like about the place or himself, however, and enjoys the "pleasant little Cajun cottage" (*TS*, 12) as he sits on the porch and waits for the arrival of Donna S_____, one of his former patients. In the beautiful sacramental world around him the "gum leaves [are] beginning to speckle" with fall color in the "Louisiana heat" of October, the sparrows are crowding into the "martin hotel" his father built, and the cicadas in "the live oaks [are] fuguing one upon the other."

Amid this spectacular symphony of color, light, and sound, Tom withdraws once more into self-analysis and theorizing about who he is. He contemplates the causes for his being the "only poor physician in town," postulating that his superior insights into the human psyche make him a physician out of step with his less enlightened colleagues. Tom considers himself a disciple of Freud who is capable of discovering "the soul's own secret" by "talking and listening" to his patients, by "venturing into the heart of darkness" to find the "very self" (*TS*, 13). The romanticized inwardness that here leads Tom to see himself as a heroic Conradian explorer of the "heart of darkness" of the self reveals that he is the type of "guru" Percy says searches exclusively and vainly within for the truth about the self and the world (*SP*, 193). Percy's Catholic Christian ontology, in contrast, posits a Kierkegaardian "inwardness that paradoxically turns outward" to phenomenal creation[10]—the world beyond the porch—as the self searches for its final home.

Continuing his withdrawn self-explorations and self-analyses, Tom considers how Freud's "science" has served as the intellectual source for his own scientific understanding of himself and others, how it was the reason for his deciding to become the "psyche-iatrist," the "old-fashioned physician of the soul," that he is. An additional major influence, he believes, "as valuable as Freud's genius," was the "psychiatric *faith*" [emphasis added] of his teacher, Dr. Harry Stack Sullivan.[11] From Sullivan, Tom recalls, he learned "an article of faith" that still guides him as he seeks solutions to his and his patients' problems: the psychiatrist has the power to help his patients in "obtaining what . . . [they] need" (*TS*, 16). Tom says later in *The Thanatos Syndrome* that he "was nuts" to try earlier in his professional life to "diagnose the madness" in the world and treat it with his lapsometer (*TS*, 67), but in his self-reflections in this scene he reveals that he continues to have a similar kind of savior complex. Tom expresses a secular humanistic faith in the knowing and intuitions of psychiatrists like himself; he believes they have the abilty to discover what their patients need. The tacit scientistic assumption behind such a belief is that human beings are organisms with needs and that the scientist is the expert who has the best information about these needs.

As Tom ponders the possible sources for the faith that he was led to by Dr. Sullivan, he admits that he doesn't know whether his teacher learned about the needs of people and how one helps them "from Ramakrishna, Dr. Jung, or Matthew 13:44" (*TS*, 16). In this passage, Tom demonstrates that he has currently assumed a scientistic mind-set that closes him off from sources of information outside the truths provided by his personal faith and science. This Cartesian consciousness leads him to a philosophical alliance with Jung and an ignoring of Matthew. Tom is convinced that Jung is right in his theories about anxiety and depression within the depths of the self being the sources of "something of value." Jung, he says, discovered that "there's gold down there in the darkness" (*TS*, 67). Matthew also comments about the experience of the self: "The kingdom of heaven is like a treasure buried in a field, which a person finds and hides again, and out of joy goes and sells all that he has and buys that field" (13.44). Were Tom to reflect a little more on this Christian view of the self, he might discover that it posits a self and world very different from the Jungian view that he endorses. The Christian self has faith that there is a treasure that can be found out there in the incarnate world beyond its interior world of private anxieties, depressions, and terrors—a joyous kingdom as different from all that he has currently as heaven is from earth. When that treasure is discovered, the searcher experiences a joy that makes him throw down everything in order to make that field and the kingdom it holds his home. While the Jungian search is in the terror and darkness of the enclosed self, the Chrisian self looks outward with hope for joy.

Tom's scientific faith and his theoretical way of seeing are revealed when he returns to the porch of his office on the next Monday morning. Tom is again alone sailing paper P-51s and "watching the sparrows flock around the martin hotel." Ignoring the sacramental signs in the natural scene before him—"the sweet-gum leaves . . . speckled with fall" and glowing in the morning sun (*TS*, 65–66)—Tom turns inward to his memories of his "two years in the clink" and what he discovered of value while he was there. The signs in nature he learned to notice while he mowed the St. Augustine grass of the Fort Pelham golf course were not sacramental signs opening him to a kingdom of being beyond his knowing and private sensations. Instead, he saw in a much smaller way and, ironically, enjoyed the blindness. He is proud that he learned to identify the "off-color spots" on the golf course "as an early sign of chinch-bug infestation," and he recalls that he "felt surprisingly good about" "saving" the golf course by his perceptive sign-reading (*TS*, 67). Tom has learned to turn his gaze to the insects beneath his feet and to find pleasure in his role as the savior of a golf course where he worked as a prisoner. The result of this atrophied seeing and sign-reading is that he is now resigned to a life that he believes is "ninety-nine percent failure," a life in which simply being "not unhappy" (*TS*, 75) is a satisfactory condition. For Percy, and Matthew, this is a life without hope.

Later in this Monday morning scene at his office—after he has talked with three more patients whose behavior he thinks validates his syndrome theory—Tom reflects on a discovery he has made by watching his patients with the detached psychic posture that he developed in prison. He believes he has discovered "a private classification of people" that is useful to him in his treatment of patients, even if it does not have the intellectual precision of a "scientific taxonomy." All people, Tom proposes in his theory, are either "bluebirds" who desperately want "to be happy" or "jaybirds" who believe that they can "do" something that will make them "happy." Neither pursuit succeeds very well (*TS*, 88–89), Tom concludes. Even worse, he laments, all the anxiety-ridden bluebirds and jaybirds he used to know have "turned into chickens," have for some reason become as complacent and unthinking as "Rhode Island Reds scratching in the barnyard" (*TS*, 90).

Tom's poultry metaphor here suggests that he sees no more similarity between himself and the patients he uses to construct his theory of happiness than he sees between himself and a chicken. "Chickens have no myths" (nor cats! [*LC*, 101]) Percy humorously asserts in his essay, "Is a Theory of Man Possible?" Unlike humans who create a semiotic world of signs and thereby attach meaning to their experiences in their environments, chickens, Percy goes on to explain, have no such unseen world of meaning. They operate solely by stimulus-response as they encounter their environment (*SP*, 126). Tom illustrates by his metaphor that he does not include himself in the pen with his Rhode Island Red patients; therefore, by extension, he does not recognize that he exists in a semiotic world of meaning with them. Tom is the Cartesian scientist who believes that he is removed from the life he is observing and analyzing, that his discoveries of truths are the result of his isolated thinking. He is therefore blind to the fact that there is nowhere to make discoveries except through naming things with one's fellow language-users within the semiotic world Percy posits. He is prevented by this epistemological perspective from any recognition that his existential predicament might be identical to the condition he observes in his specimens. His abstractions about their condition cluttering his *cogito*, Tom is removed from a consciousness of their existence as actual individual beings who create in their semiotic exchanges the world of meaning he himself inhabits. Instead, they become chickens in a barnyard and he the solitary, curious scientist peering over the fence and taking notes.

BEYOND THE PRISON WALLS: THE DEMONS IN THE DESERT

As Tom's unconscious preference for his Bruno Hauptmann suit symbolically implies, he remains after his release from Fort Pelham a prisoner of a self-definition that dislocates him from his family, colleagues, community, and the sacramental cosmos. Ironically, he seems to enjoy the small life this enclosed prisoner-self fabricates, finding in the self and world he has created an escape from the anxieties that others inevitably experience when engaged with phenomenal life. Tom says near the end of the novel when he is incarcerated at Angola that he "felt almost as good" there as he did at Fort Pelham, declaring to himself before he drops off to a peaceful sleep in his cell that "there is something to be said for having no choice in what one does" (*TS*, 262). Prison life allows him to manufacture a self that lives in a choice-free, therefore anxiety-free, inner world where he can avoid the existential complexities and mysteries that are the inescapable realities of the self that is conscious of being one with others under God (*LC*, 112). Tom is "free" in prison to withdraw from life with others into the private interior world of his memories and his thoughts and feelings about his existence.

When Tom leaves prison and the freedom from choice he enjoys there, he returns home to Feliciana Parish to resume his associations with John Van Dorn, Lucy Lipscomb, Bob Comeaux, and Father Smith. In his transactions with them, he is forced to think anew about the nature of the world "out there" (*TS*, 121) beyond the prison walls and about who he is in it. Tom, in his relationships with them, begins to understand that he is not excluded from a difficult world where evil, suffering, and death are daily actualities that demand he make choices about what to do in order to help create a meaningful and truly human life in his community. He begins to realize that because he is a participant with others in these actualities, his moral and ethical choices can have life-and-death consequences.

Van Dorn and Comeaux want Tom to join them in their Blue Boy and Belle Ame projects and make the kinds of choices they have made about who they are, where they are, and what they should do. Tom resists their temptations, however, when he begins to see in them and their choices the inhumanity and self-delusion inherent in the transcendent, angelic, "curious" selfhood that he himself has developed and values. Lucy, another scientist employed at Fedville, not only wants Tom to become a member of the social engineering "team" (TS, 189, 212) that is killing children, the aged, and AIDS patients at the Qualitarian Center in order to make a better society, but she also wants him to abandon his family, marry her, and spend the rest of his days absorbed in scientific research on her remote plantation (TS, 229). She wants him to escape with her to a life at Pantherburn, a place symbolic of that Old South plantation past when an inhumanity created by another kind of social theory went dressed not in the technology of modern science, but in the grandeur of the plantation house and "alley[s] of great oaks" (TS, 134).

Father Smith offers Tom an alternative to the temptations of Bob, Van Dorn, and Lucy. Early in the novel, before Tom's temptations at Pantherburn, the priest warns him about the dangers (TS, 127) of his colleagues' truths and, by implication, warns him also of the dangers involved in his assuming the self-identities and worldview they recommend. The priest urges Tom to reflect on the possibility that he may be more than just a discoverer of scientific truths and that the world may be more than merely his thoughts and feelings about it. Father Smith wants Tom to consider a Catholic Christian, sacramental ontology that will open him to the reality that he is a wayfarer with others in a holy place, a self in the process of becoming utterly not what it currently is (SP, 290; MB, 284) in a land that it cannot yet accurately identify.

Although Tom maintains the detached way of seeing he developed in prison during his first extended encounter with Van Dorn, he does begin to get some clues about the dangers beyond his interior world that he must eventually address. On the Sunday morning after his release from prison, Tom takes Van Dorn fishing in Pontchatolawa bayou (TS, 56–64). As always, Tom is content merely to watch while he pilots the "Arkansas Traveler" through the swamp. Tom makes small talk with Van Dorn, communicating little beyond the information he offers about the best techniques for catching bream, the most effective baits, and methods for casting. When Van Dorn asks him if he wants to fish, Tom replies with a succinct "no." But he immediately thinks, "What I want to do is watch him" (TS, 58).

Tom is also satisfied just to watch nature. Percy describes the unspoiled bayou the two men have entered as a place filled with obvious signs of the mysterious sacramental dimensions of creation. Sue Crowley says this scene is one of the many scenes in Percy's fiction in which the imagery functions to communicate his "sacramental sense of the world"[12]—"The sun is just clearing the cypresses. . . . Mullet jump. Cicadas tune up. There is a dusting of gold on the water." The cypress knees seem to have acquired a Christlike power to walk on water as they "march . . . across the bayou" (*TS*, 57). The sacramental imagery is most obvious when Percy describes the sunfish Van Dorn catches. Both men gaze in wonder at the "fine-scaled, and silvered" fish, "round as a plate," whose "amazing color spot at its throat" reflects "the sun like a topaz set in amethyst." Tom thinks that "the fish looks both perfectly alive yet metallic, handwrought in Byzantium and bejeweled beyond price" (*TS*, 59).[13] The language Tom uses here—his description of the regal colors, the light, the halo-like "plate"—shows that he is capable of turning his eyes outward to incarnate nature and its signs. But he has lost the capacity he once had to read these signs, as his failure to see the analogies here between the sunfish and Christ demonstrates.

Tom exhibits in his response to the bayou life he observes that he has not yet developed a sacramental consciousness that will open him to the information the signs in nature have about where he is and who he is. But his conversation with Van Dorn does reveal to him some information about a possible danger that demands he abandon the confines of his interiorized self and begin to think about his community and family. From Van Dorn, Tom learns that there may be a sinister evil that has entered his Feliciana Parish home while he was away at Fort Pelham, a threatening force that demands a response. As the two men return from their fishing, Tom begins to question Van Dorn about the strange incantation of bridge terms he heard Ellen muttering to herself the night before when she and Tom were in bed. Tom is a little worried about the unusual sexual behavior and language habits of his wife, behavior and habits he also sees in some of his patients. He suspects that there is some connection between Ellen's drunken mutterings and these behaviors. Tom is particularly interested in the bridge strategy that she called the "Azazel convention" (*TS*, 61).

This fishing scene with Van Dorn ends with Tom's pondering the associations between the "Azazel convention" and the mythical Azazel. He knows that in Hebrew and Canaanite belief, Azazel was "a demon who lived in the Syrian desert," a godless region—"a hell on earth" (*TS*, 64). Gary Ciuba argues that the scientists like Van Dorn in *The Thanatos Syndrome* are "lost souls," the followers of Azazel who are responsible for creating in Feliciana Parish a society that is as frightening as the "hell on earth" where Azazel lived.[14] By the end of the novel, after Tom has learned the truth about the

Blue Boy project and Belle Ame school, he can identify these lost souls and some features of the hell they have created. Now he can only suspect that Azazel is somehow related to his wife's and his patients' "unfocused" (*TS*, 21) selves. But these suspicions are enough to shake him out of his comfortable interior seclusion and compel him to consider making some choices and taking some action in response to Azazel. Van Dorn has given Tom a clue about the demons that are out there beyond the small life he has created for himself in prison, and Tom feels that he must act. He promises Van Dorn that he will "do something about this" (*TS*, 64).

Later in the day, Tom pays his first visit to Father Smith at the fire tower in order to determine the priest's mental and physical health and to talk with him about giving up his work at the hospice. It is at the fire tower that he hears a great deal more about the demons. While Tom is there, the priest launches into a rambling, impromptu homily about language being "deprived" (*TS*, 120) of meaning, the Nazi Holocaust, the Jews as a sign, and a "tenderness . . . [that] leads . . . . to the gas chamber" (*TS*, 128). Smith is trying to direct Tom's attention to some other "dangers down there" (*TS*, 131) in a world created by theorizing scientific minds like Tom's own. Unfortunately, while Tom is at the tower, instead of looking outward to the time-space experience and dangers Smith points out to him, he withdraws into the interior world of his thinking and into the abstractions of the medical science he has always depended on to explain life to him. He spends most of his time clinically observing Smith's behavior and speech, trying to arrive at a diagnosis of his mental illness and trying to decide to which "category of nut" the priest belongs. Tom rejects the priest's observations and warnings about the dangers as the delusions of someone who "has gone batty" (*TS*, 120).

Father Smith, in an effort to draw Tom out of his abstraction, first gives him a quick lesson in sign-reading, showing him how he uses his azimuth to read the "signs out there" in the "shaggy forest" beneath them (*TS*, 121). But because he is so self-absorbed, Tom finds the signs Smith points out "insignificant-looking," again in this scene revealing that he has limited success when he tries to connect his sensory data with meaning and action. He sees the smoke that Smith points out to him as no more significant than "a pile of leaves burning in a gutter." Undaunted, the priest goes on to show Tom how to read the smoke as a sign of danger and take action with others to respond to the threat (*TS*, 119), obviously hoping that Tom will understand the metaphorical implications of his instructions.

Smith is using the azimuth (in Arabic, "the way") to show Tom a less abstract way of seeing than the scientistic way he has chosen.[15] Smith wants

Tom to see that the living creation that stretches out beneath them is a place filled with signs where he can discover with others the sacramental "Life" (*TS*, 126) all share beneath the "bright afternoon sun" and amid the "crowns of the longleafs." But Tom sees only a claustrophobic and menacing place where the pines "glitter in the sunlight like steel knitting needles" (compare Percy's identical image in *LR*, 4) and pierce the air that is as "dense and yellow as butter" with pollen (*TS*, 114). About the only significance he can find in this mildly threatening environment is that the uncomfortably bright sun requires him to shade his eyes and the claustrophobic "butter" skies make his nose run (*TS*, 114, 118).

Father Smith continues his sign-reading lesson and begins to talk about all language signs in this century being "evacuated of meaning" (*TS*, 121) because they signify only abstractions, and he explains how the Jews are an exception to this general "evacuation." They are, he declares, a "sign of God's presence" (*TS*, 123). He is trying to teach Tom that there are signs other than the ones immediately before them—signs in the history of the Jews, in the history of the Germans and Russians, and in his own history that might reveal to him some important information about who he is and where he is. He wants Tom to identify himself not as an isolated observer of life separate from these histories, but as a participant in a scientistic, gnostic age in which the pervading scientistic mind-set has resulted in "millions dead for the good of mankind" (*TS*, 129). Finally, when he points his azimuth at Tom and tells him he is "going to end up killing Jews" (*TS*, 128), Tom indifferently says, "Right," and thinks, "I really have to get out of here" (*TS*, 130). Tom is not at this moment considering who he is in the context of real time and real human events, but has psychically withdrawn into his thoughts about his upcoming visit to Pantherburn and into his theories about Smith's mental illness. Because he is convinced that the priest is too seriously "disturbed" to carry out his duties in the parish, Tom plans to help Bob Comeaux close down Smith's hospice (*TS*, 127).

At Pantherburn[16] (*TS*, 133-86), Tom continues to retreat from time-space experience with others and, therefore, from the signs Father Smith advises him to read. Abstracted in his problem-solution mind-set, Tom is still pursuing data that will help him understand the syndrome that his scientific curiosity has prompted him to investigate, and he believes that his "Vassar smart and Southern shrewd" cousin Lucy can assist him in his search. Lucy is an epidemiologist who works with Comeaux and Van Dorn at Fedville, and Tom's trust in her abilities as a truth-seeker implies that at this moment he still has absolute faith in the way of seeing Lucy and her colleagues represent. While Tom believes Father Smith's seeing is the perception of an insane man, he is confident that Lucy is "a sane person, . . . the only one around" (*TS*, 90).

Unlike Father Smith, Lucy encourages Tom to turn away from the here-and-now realities of present time and a consciousness of who he is in it. She lures him into his memories of their genteel Southern family and cultural history and the narratives that have accumulated about it. Tom says at one point that she "reminds . . . [him] of Southern women in old novels" (*TS*, 104), and he, in his memories of their heritage, is tempted to join her in that fictional world. At the ancestral Pantherburn plantation, Tom spends much of his time lost in his personal memories of his family's past and absorbed in his reflections on the family legends he has heard since childhood. Caught up in family stories and the mythological time of Old South history,[17] Tom removes himself from present experience and the possibility of action in it.

This withdrawal from time at Pantherburn provides him with the same kind of psychic freedom from choice that he says he enjoyed in prison (*TS*, 262), a freedom that is actually an ontological imprisonment. While drinking alone in the "dim dark of the dining room" at Pantherburn, he thinks, "drinking . . . frees one from the necessities of time" and therefore frees one from having to make choices. He muses, "one would as soon do one thing as another" (*TS*, 158–59). Tom's removal of himself from time does not create for him a freedom of choice, however, but makes all choice impossible. As Kierkegaard explains, the psychic self-enclosure and detachment from time Tom exemplifies here is based on the tacit assumption that a segment of time from which one is excluded has already ended or has not yet come into existence.[18] Since there is, therefore, no moment of time into which the individual can insert himself, there is no possibility to choose or to act.

Tom, in electing to leave Father Smith's tower and descend to Lucy Lipscomb's Pantherburn plantation, makes a symbolic existential journey away from the open seeing the priest tries to teach him to the psychic imprisonment, blindness, and death symbolized by the plantation and its residents. Although Tom sees the plantation as a "fecund," "green" refuge amid the ruin and "crankcase" smell of the modern wasteland that surrounds it (*TS*, 134), the imagery that Percy uses to describe Pantherburn suggests that it offers Tom only an absence of the "Life" (*TS*, 126) that Smith tries to show him. The small, "dim" "box" of a house, filled with huge "dark paintings" leaning against the walls of the "dark," "not large" rooms (*TS*, 134–35, 158) symbolically encloses Tom in the past it represents. When Tom arrives, waiting for him on the porch of this foreboding "perfect cube" are relatives who are part of that small, enclosed world of memory into which he is about to descend. Both are associated with the past and with death. Uncle Hugh Bob, an eccentric, if not insane, representative of Old South gentility, greets Tom dressed in the "blood-stained camouflage army jacket" he wears for the continuous duck hunting that has become his life. Lucy, the mistress of the plantation, hugs and kisses him, "the smell of her cotton" giving him a "*déjà vu* ." Like any déjà vu, this one causes its victim to lose consciousness of the present moment and to imagine that the current events being experienced have already occurred in some past moment that is forever lost. She then immediately escorts her guest to the family "graveyard," the "tiny enclosure" behind the house where she shows him "the grave of their common ancestor" (*TS*, 135-36). She is inviting Tom to imagine a self that has already been created in a dead past they share and tempting him to ignore his actual self that Father Smith knows is mysteriously and continuously coming into being in an open, living present.

Lucy, when she first meets with Tom in her pickup in the parking lot of the Fedville hospital to talk with him about the syndrome, shows the power she has to cause the deadly déjà vu (*TS*, 102, 103, 106, 156) that he later experiences on the front porch of her plantation home. Inside the pickup, the "smell of hot Chevy metal" (*TS*, 102, 103) transports Tom into the interior world of his memories—his "youth, the past, the old U.S.A.," a time when he was "free to go anywhere." This déjà vu takes Tom into "a forgotten world, [where] bits and pieces of cortical memory like old snapshots [are] scattered through an abandoned house" (*TS*, 106). This inner world is very much like the dark interior of Pantherburn, another house filled with smells of "wet dogs, Octagon soap, [and] scoured wood" that are to Tom "as wrenching as memory" (*TS*, 141). The déjà vu in Lucy's pickup ushers Tom into the forgotten emptiness of his memory and takes him into a lonely, lifeless, fragmented psychic house. As he sits beside Lucy and tries to discuss their problems with their patients and fellow scientists, he is so removed from a consciousness of who he is and where he is at this moment, so imprisoned in his recollections of a lost youth and lost freedom, that he appears to her paralyzed, if not dead. Lucy notices that he is "absolutely motionless" (*TS*, 104), and she is concerned enough to insist on immediately examining him in her office at the hospital.

Tom's dislocation from immediate experience and his psychic paralysis are again demonstrated that evening before he and Lucy go in for dinner at Pantherburn. While they sit on the gallery drinking toddies like a couple of eighteenth-century Southern aristocrats, the sun is "making winks and gleams and casting long shafts of foggy yellow light" (*TS*, 137), illuminating the small figures on the porch and the ancient house at their backs. The light of the personified sun in this image envelops Tom and Lucy in a beautiful and wondrous cosmic immensity that they fail to recognize. Tom turns his back on this light and the sacramental cosmos that invites his attention in order to enter the dim rooms of the past and his roles in it. Inside the darkness of the house, he is conscious only of the "bird-dog reek of memories" of his childhood at the plantation, the lavish Christmas parties and the famous dove hunts that were such important family traditions (*TS*, 160).

At the end of the evening, Tom literally loses consciousness while he is being sexually seduced by Lucy and while he is being figuratively seduced into the past they share. Drunk on Uncle Rylan's bourbon that Lucy has saved for twenty years (*TS*, 158–59), Tom allows Lucy to help him to his bedroom. Collapsing there in a half-conscious stupor, he floats in and out of consciousness and has a series of strange dreams mingled with his memories and fantasies. Within this surreal collage of past and imaginary events, he envisions himself playing a variety of roles in a variety of settings. He sees himself as a carefree child visiting Pantherburn; in another episode, he is a nineteenth-century Southern gentleman waking in the plantation mansion to the sounds of a faithful slave starting the morning fire; in another, he becomes Hemingway's heroic Robert Jordan in war-torn Germany enjoying an innocent love affair with Alice Pratt;[19] abruptly, he returns to more recent memories of his life in prison and prisoner Harry Epps's less innocent "dial-a-girl" phone sex.

In this semiconscious, hallucinatory state, Tom has sexual intercourse with Lucy in a dark upstairs bedroom (*TS*, 161–66). In his dazed condition, he is occasionally aware that he is lying in a feather bed at Pantherburn with the androgynous Lucy, "the sweet heavy incubus" (*TS*, 163, 348), on top of him, but the psychic confusion of dream, memory, and fantasy events that her uncle's bourbon have induced interfere with his efforts at sustained consciousness of the present moment. Lucy is the agent of this confused and helpless state, just as she is earlier the cause of Tom's paralytic déjà vu that transports him into his past. As a result of her literal and figurative seduction, Tom is this night even more detached from this incubus that is sexually assaulting him than he was from Ellen the night he returned from Fort Pelham. The psychic unconsciousness and lifelessness she has induced are revealed when Tom thinks to himself that night, "I don't feel anything" (*TS*, 158, 160).

Tom's journey to Pantherburn and seduction by Lucy have resulted at this point in his being reduced to feeling nothing and becoming a sort of ontological tabula rasa on which Lucy proposes that he write some new identities. After dinner that night she orders him out of his Bruno

Hauptmann suit, what she calls his smelly jailbird clothes, and insists that he dress in the L. L. Bean shirt and jeans she purchased for her Uncle Hugh Bob. Dressed as Lucy's eccentric uncle, Tom is being offered by Lucy the opportunity to shed his current prisoner self and imprison himself in another role; he can become the stereotypical Southern male her uncle represents and grow old with her at Pantherburn. Uncle Hugh Bob is an anachronistic representative of a decayed Southern gentry who does nothing but hunt, fish, and glorify the manly pursuits of soldiers and fornicators. He believes that the cliché "war is hell" is "horseshit," his own experience in World War II proving to him that there is no "better time" to be had (*TS*, 142–43) than in combat. Another of his profound convictions after a lifetime of nothing is that "a little pussy never hurt anybody" (*TS*, 165). Lucy also offers Tom her former husband's bedroom, of course symbolically inviting him to assume yet another identity. She says she has "cleaned all his [her ex-husband's] stuff out" (*TS*, 141), so she is apparently ready for Tom to become the next Buddy Dupre. Tom remembers Buddy as an alcoholic "Southern charmer," a stereotypical Louisiana good old boy who lived a casual, easy life at Pantherburn and "drifted" into state politics before leaving Lucy (*TS*, 104). Lucy tells Tom directly the next day that she wants him and his children to live with her at Pantherburn (*TS*, 230), wants him to consider assuming, then, the identity and lifestyle Buddy exemplifies.

Most of all, in her assisting Tom at Pantherburn with his analysis of the syndrome, Lucy is reinforcing his inclination to reject Father Smith's way of seeing (she considers the priest as "crazy as a jaybird" [*TS*, 212]) and tempting him to see scientifically, as she does. Lucy is the consummate Fedville scientist at Pantherburn as she and Tom search for the truth in her second-floor laboratory that looks like "an office in Fedville" (*TS*, 144). In her computerized lab, Lucy shows Tom a way to look at the syndrome that he is investigating in an even more abstract way than his Freudian and Jungian psychiatric theories provide. Her computer utterly ignores the signs "out there" that Father Smith locates with his azimuth and reduces the individuals in Tom's case studies and the other victims of the Blue Boy project to statistical numbers and symbolic dots on a screen. She does not talk to other human beings as she searches for the source of the Na-24 that has somehow entered the local water supply, but communicates only with data banks (*TS*, 146). She does not see the dehumanization that her data signifies, but instead she is "big-eyed ... like a ten-year-old" in her excitement about her triumphant discovery of the truth that her dots and numbers have revealed to her (*TS*, 155). Gary Ciuba argues that Lucy's way of seeing is a "deadly aestheticism" that allows her to actually enjoy herself and her intellectual calculations while ignoring the deadly effects of the

Fedville projects in which Comeaux, Van Dorn, and she are involved.[20]

Lucy's enthusiasm about her discoveries as she and Tom sit together at the computer terminal makes Tom also turn his gaze to the graphic on the screen and murmur, "that's beautiful . . . . You're beautiful" (*TS*, 155). Tom is being attracted by Lucy to an aesthetic posture toward the phenomenal world beyond his thinking, lured into seeing abstractions where Father Smith sees both life and death. Later, when Lucy advises Tom to "take the job with Comeaux" (*TS*, 212, 229), she is directly insisting that he adopt the aesthetic, scientific way of seeing she and the other Fedville scientists represent. She wants to convince Tom that he has "no choice" (*TS*, 212) but to join them. Ironically, the absence of choice that she is encouraging him to assume is what made Tom feel so good in prison, but it is also what reduced his life to disengaged watching and thinking. Lucy is now urging him to continue to believe that he has no choices in his life and therefore suggesting that he continue to develop the disengagement that has imprisoned him in his small life.

Tom's decision to leave Pantherburn and Lucy and to turn his attention to the actual dangers in his community that Father Smith warned him about indicates that Tom may be in the process of learning that he needs to awaken from the unconsciousness of his small life. He resists the temptations of Lucy's science and the past she represents, finally realizing near the end of the novel what his destiny probably would have been had he accepted her invitation to become the husband and Fedville scientist she wanted him to be. He believes that a life with her at Pantherburn would have lured him into a repetition of their famous ancestor's (*TS*, 136) life, a life that ended with his tying "a sugar kettle on his head and jump[ing] into the river" (*TS*, 348). John Desmond says that by rejecting Lucy Tom is rejecting "spiritual and literal suicide."[21]

Tom's encounters with Lucy and the other residents of the plantation also make him think more precisely about who they are, and, as a result, he is provoked into some new questions about who he is in the world outside the dark house and Lucy's laboratory. An example of this self-inquiry occurs in the final scene of the Pantherburn section of the novel when Tom, Vergil Bon, and Uncle Hugh Bob are arrested for trespassing in Tunica Swamp while searching for the pipeline that carries the Na-24 from the Grand Mer facility. The three men paddle their skiff through the "warm sunshine and open water" of Lake Mary, a "peaceable," "clear stretch of water" that Tom feels is a great "beneficence" after the "funky" bayou that they just left (*TS*, 181). As always, Tom is blind to these sacramental signs in nature around him and therefore incapable of identifying who he is as an incarnate spiritual being wayfaring through a holy place. But at least he does demonstrate in this scene a capacity for escaping the mythological past and self-placement in it and an ability to locate himself in the immediacy of time-space reality.

Similar to the way he earlier saw Lucy as like "Southern women in old novels" (*TS*, 104), Tom imagines for a moment as they glide through the swamp that Vergil is a modern-day Hawkeye and Uncle Hugh in the stern of the boat is a contemporary Natty Bumppo. But then he wonders, "Who am I?" (*TS*, 181) if these men here in Tunica Swamp are fictional characters in an imaginary forest in a James Fennimore Cooper saga? His asking himself this question implies that he knows that he is in the same boat with real men in a real world, not a character in a romantic fiction. As if to verify the actuality of himself, this place, and the people in it, Tom turns his attention to the immediate factual realities of the oars in his hands and "the sun on . . . [his] back" (*TS*, 181). He is waking up to the flesh-and-blood reality of his physical self in present time and resisting the temptation to escape into memory, mythologized American history, and fantasy.

After he leaves behind the temptations and dangers posed by Lucy and Pantherburn, Tom learns directly through Bob Comeaux of the dangers (*TS*, 131) of the German science that Father Smith warned him about at the fire tower. Bob bails Tom, Vergil, and Uncle Hugh Bob out of the Clinton jail after their arrest in Tunica Swamp, and he gives Tom a ride back to his car. They drive through the swamp in Bob's Mercedes Duck, a luxurious German sport utility that "smell[s] of leather, oiled wood" (*TS*, 188-89). This comfortable vehicle has its origin in the country that Father Smith associates with the comfortable illusions of modern science and romanticism. During the drive, Bob rhapsodizes about the Romantic "Strauss waltzes" that play continuously on the tape deck—aesthetically lost in "the golden woods of old Vienna" (*TS*, 190, 195)—and he lectures Tom about the humane goals of the Blue Boy project (*TS*, 190–200) he wants Tom to join. He explains that by adding Na-24 to the water supply, his team of scientists has succeeded in radically reducing teen pregnancies, wife battering, and child abuse, while at the same time increasing the I.Q.'s of their subjects. When Tom voices his reservations about the scientists' violating the civil rights of the citizens by "assaulting" their cortexes, Bob argues that his group is only working to "improve . . . the quality of life for all Americans" (*TS*, 200).

Tom, enclosed in Bob's German car and enveloped in his romantic music and gnostic, scientistic philosophizing, is being tempted again to return to that Cartesian self-enclosure that has alienated him from himself, others, and the world. Like Lucy, Bob asks Tom to consider adopting a new identity, this time senior consultant on the Nuclear Regulatory Commission's Advisory Committee for the Medical Uses of Isotopes (*TS*, 189). Bob tells Tom that he has, in fact, already become "one of us [Blue Boy scientists]" because of his early scientific studies of "isotope brain pharmacology" (*TS*, 200). Bob promises Tom financial security, professional recognition, and, ironically, the opportunity, he says, to be free to continue his scientific research (*TS*, 189–90). This freedom, of course, will require that he forget about who he is and where he is and once again lock himself in that detached scientific mind-set that Bob recommends. Bob's temptations—as well as Lucy's—are very much like the aesthetic temptations of Art Immelman in *Love in the Ruins*, another time when Tom was attracted by the freedom from time and space that Cartesian, aesthetic withdrawal into private thoughts, feelings, and sensations grants.

As he listens to Bob, Tom is apparently beginning to understand some of Father Smith's warnings. In Bob Comeaux Tom can see the kind of "lover of Mankind" and "theorist of Mankind" that the priest claims is responsible for the millions dead in this century, sacrificed for "the good of Mankind" (*TS*, 129). And Tom may be on the verge of seeing that he can, in fact, easily become, as Bob tells him, one of the them. Tom's simple, noncommital refrain is "I see" (*TS*, 194, 196, 199, 200, 201), as he listens to Bob talk about how his team is controlling the sexual behavior of their subjects, how they are killing the "unwanted," and how Van Dorn plans "the sexual liberation of Western civilization." Acknowledging his involvement with the scientists who are promoting this social engineering, Tom murmurs, "So it seems," when Bob identifies him as part of the Blue Boy team. The tone of his responses here suggests that Tom is beginning to scrutinize and reject Bob's gnosticism and science. Tom's deciding immediately after this conversation with Comeaux to investigate Belle Ame and free the children who are being exploited there, indicates that he has seen in Bob some of the moral inadequacies of a self that merely watches life from the narrow perspective he developed in prison.

Tom's responses during their drive through the natural beauty in Tunica Swamp imply that he may even be on the verge of opening his eyes to the sacramental mystery of creation beyond Bob's Mercedes and the aesthetic self-absorption it represents. Symbolically enclosed in the aesthetic pleasures of Bob's music and science as they cruise through the swamp, Tom looks out the window and sees "the Feliciana woods ... bathed ... in the gold autumn sunlight." Tom thinks the Strauss is "very lovely," but prefers the actual woods outside the car, woods that he considers "surely as lovely as the Vienna woods" (*TS*, 194). Again, when Bob is tempting him to accept a position at Fedville and "the Mercedes is filled with Strauss waltzes," Tom notices a "broken V of ibis lowering on Tunica Island," a sight that he obviously finds more interesting and more significant than Bob's music and his scientistic theorizing about his "basic assumptions and goals" in life. As Bob rattles on, the music "coming from all directions," Tom observes that "the wings of the ibis flash like shook foil and drop into the willows" (*TS*, 189–90). Tom uses in his description of the ibis the famous "shook foil" image from Gerard Manley Hopkins's "God's Grandeur,"[22] indicating, of course, that he has read the poem and chooses, consciously or unconsciously, to use Hopkins's words to name the reality before him. The fact that Tom is speaking with Hopkins's words implies that he may also be seeing, at least at this brief moment, with the Catholic poet's sacramental eyes; the world Hopkins sees is a mysterious sacramental world filled with signs of God's grace.

THE PREDICAMENT: WHAT TO DO?

By the time Tom makes his second visit to Father Smith's fire tower and listens to his "Confession" and "Footnote"(*TS*, 239–57), he has learned first-hand from Van Dorn, Comeaux, and Lucy about the dangers that lurk in his Louisiana home like Azazel in the godless, barren desert. Also, as his responses to Tunica Swamp and Bob suggest, he may be developing the skill to read some other signs out there, the sacramental signs Father Smith tried to explain to him (*TS*, 125). Since his release from Fort Pelham, Tom has learned about Bob's Blue Boy project and discovered the connections between it and Van Dorn's perverse Southern version of a German Gymnasium-Hochschule (*TS*, 219). In addition, he has become increasingly aware of the deadly effects of the Fedville scientists who place themselves in relation to the world as detached, beneficent saviors of a benighted and helpless citizenry. He has seen as well the danger they pose for him personally, begun to understand the attractions of the aesthetic, scientistic way of seeing that may have already seduced him and made him one of them. Especially with Lucy, Tom has been tempted to become the romantic Kierkegaardian aesthete withdrawn into a self-constructed interior world of role-playing and intellectual and sexual stimulations, tempted to locate himself in the role of Southern gentleman/physician puttering around in the dark rooms of Pantherburn and watching the sunset from its front porch.

When Tom arrives for his second visit with Father Smith at the fire tower, he has decided to combat the dangers he has discovered at Belle Ame, in Bob's Mercedes Duck, and at Pantherburn, and, near the end of his visit, he shows signs of acquiring a sacramental way of seeing quite different from his earlier watching and theorizing. Mary Howland believes that with Father Smith in the tower Tom begins to look beyond the immediate problems he has discovered in Feliciana Parish and to show more interest in the transcendent dimensions of his experience.[23] Smith tells Tom about his own attraction to the romance of German aestheticism, science, and social idealism, tells of his discovery of the horror (*TS*, 254) in the immaculate room at Eglfing-Harr where Dr. Jäger performed his experiments on the Jewish children, and explains his reasons for choosing priesthood over Nazi gnosticism. Father Smith, in short, diagnoses the ills of the age of death and prescribes what can redeem it. It is this Catholic Christian vision that leads Tom toward hope at the end of the novel, and the vision that forms the central theme of *The Thanatos Syndrome*.[24]

Although Tom admits he doesn't understand (*TS*, 252) Smith's story in the tower, it does seem to encourage him to look more closely at the sacramental signs in the incarnate world and see with an acuity that he has not up to this point demonstrated. Near the end of the priest's tale, Tom sits in silence with him and looks at the woods that stretch out below them. "We sit," Tom thinks, obviously feeling an intersubjective union with the old man beside him and escaping the detached way of seeing of the Cartesian "I." [25] Something he has heard Father Smith tell—and he can't explain what it is—not only makes him conscious of his existence with another, but also causes him to direct his eyes out into the Louisiana night and search the darkness "out there" where they both live. Beneath the radiant moonlight, Tom sees "the sea of pines, without shadows, . . . calm and silvery as water" (*TS*, 255), a tranquil creation filled with stunningly beautiful light and life-giving water. On his first visit to the tower he saw the same pines as lifeless "steel knitting needles" in the glare of a blinding sun (*TS*, 114). Now he sees only a welcoming abundance of space and life that makes him want to look even more intensely and see beyond the pines. In the distance, he spots another sea of light and splendor and is speechless before the "sliver of light in the south where the moonlight reflects from Lake Pontchartrain" (*TS*, 255). While Tom cannot here make the anagogical analogies he articulates at the end of *Love in the Ruins* when he talks about the "great unclassified beast of a fish" he caught being a sign of the Second Coming (*LR*, 387), he can at least sense that he is alive with others in a place awe-inspiring in its peace, grandeur, and beauty.

Ironically, it is Father Smith's horror story that causes this eye-opening experience for Tom, that enables him, at least for a moment, to locate himself in a vast, mysterious, and wondrous world with another. Smith's narrative echoes Tom's recent experience with the "body snatchers" in Feliciana Parish. The priest tells of his visit to 1930s Germany, another society in which the populace was victimized by its scientists and their romantic aestheticism.[26] There the teenage Smith stayed with his cousin, Dr. Hans Jäger, who, (like Tom's cousin Lucy), was a physician and (like Tom's colleague, Bob Comeaux) was a lover of romantic music and grand political ideals. As the teenage Smith was attracted to the German science of the "charming and cultivated" physicians (*TS*, 245, 247) that he met there, so Tom is attracted to the truths of his colleagues' medical science. And just as the youthful Smith was tempted to join the Nazis and locate himself in the future utopia their ideology constructed, so Tom has been tempted to join his cousin and colleagues in their deadly aesthetic plans for an anxiety-free America ruled by beneficent scientists.

"What do you think?" Father Smith asks Tom when he finishes his tale, apparently assuming that Tom will see the similarities between this story and his own recent experiences. He wants to show Tom who and where he is by pointing out the similarities between the German "psychiatrists and eugenecists" (*TS*, 245) of the 1930s and the "Louisiana Weimar psychiatrists" who are currently at work in their Feliciana community. The priest is trying to show Tom who he is—that is, a member of this group—and, to emphasize his point, he calls them "*your* colleagues" [emphasis added]. He wants him to see that just as these scientists sixty years ago in Europe were so abstracted from creation and their existence in it that they were oblivious to the horror they caused in their society, so Tom may be in danger of becoming similarly abstracted. Tom is, in fact, at this very moment when the priest asks him what he sees in the story he has just heard, lost in his scientific thinking about Father Smith's medical condition. Tom thinks, "I was more interested in his story as a symptom of a possible brain disorder than in the *actual events* which he related" (*TS*, 252; emphasis added). Tom remains "up in his head," does not know where he is, and the priest knows it.

Father Smith's "Footnote" (*TS*, 252–54) about Dr. Jäger's laboratory in the children's division of Munich's Eglfing-Harr hospital is an attempt to make his horror story actual for Tom and to show him the brutality and inhumanity that can result from the aesthetic way of seeing of German, as well as Louisiana, scientists. Jäger's special department was a "pleasant sunny room," empty "except for a small white-tiled table" (*TS*, 253). It was an "innocuous" looking place that "conceal[ed] a horror."[27] This is the room where Jäger and his colleagues executed their young "patients" while performing their experiments with deadly drugs and gasses. What Smith found "notable" about this pleasant execution chamber was the "large geranium plant in a pot on the windowsill . . ., a beautiful plant, . . . obviously very carefully tended" by the scientists who worked there. Enclosed in this "small room" (*TS*, 252), the German physicians were able to detach themselves from the world beyond the windowsill and enjoy their scientific data-gathering, intellectual calculations, and the beautiful life they cultivated within the room's sterile emptiness (TS, 253). Their aesthetic self-enclosure blinded them to who they were and what they were doing and to the actual world beyond the intellectual and aesthetic stimulations that they carefully tended.

These scientists were not horrified by the monstrous selves they had created or the macabre little world they inhabited. Nor is Van Dorn horrified in his office at Belle Ame, Lucy in her Pantherburn laboratory, Bob Comeaux in his Strauss-filled Mercedes Duck, or Tom in the fire tower listening to this story. Father Smith admits that he was not horrified either when he saw what Jäger and his colleagues had done, but only interested in the experience in the same way Tom has been merely curious about things since his Fort Pelham imprisonment. At this very moment, Tom looks at the priest "curiously." Trying to encourage Tom to move beyond such curiosity and discover both the dangers and the beauty of the actual world where the self makes its pilgrimage with all others, Smith tells him that recognizing the horror "takes some effort" (*TS*, 254). Father Smith implies that it was his Catholic faith that revealed to him that the essence of that effort lies in the challenges inherent in the existential fact that finally "one must choose—given the chance," between "life or death. What else?" (*TS*, 257).[28] The children at Eglfing-Harr did not have such a chance—and the Na-24 victims and the children at Belle Ame may also be denied a choice—but, the priest is reminding Tom, the rest of mankind, for the rest of time, does.

Tom can choose the deadly abstract truths of the Nazi doctors at Munich and the Fedville scientists of Louisiana, or the life that waits for him when he descends from the fire tower. The scientists construct a self and a tidy interior life abstracted from the moral and spiritual complexities inherent in the choices all must make when they interact with others, abstracted both from the horror of who they are and from the life-giving Christian love that will redeem them from that ontological blindness. "Life," Father Smith tells Tom, is populated "with few exceptions" by either "victims or assholes," and he does not "exclude himself." Even the disciples, he says, were a "sorry crew" that God in his love managed to "put up with" (*TS*, 243). The priest argues that to choose life is to exert the effort to choose this kind of love with this kind of humanity; life is not the scientist's egoistic escape into a self that is abstracted from the world in detached curiosity. Life is instead the "offensive burden" of love,[29] what Father Smith has chosen at the hospice, where he ministers to the sick and dying geriatric patients, AIDS victims, and afflicted children. The world is not a perfectible place where social, political, medical, and moral problems are to be discovered and remedied but a sacramental reality that is, paradoxically, a place of suffering and death that man, like God, must "put up with." The self, the priest concludes, can choose this life and love or death.

Tom does not on the spot, nor does he ever in the novel, become a firm believer in the Catholic faith that has led Father Smith to understand the death he saw in Germany and to choose the life that exists in the face of that horror. But Tom, by accurately identifying his predicament, does in this scene in the fire tower place himself in the position to receive, and benefit from, the news Father Smith delivers. In a 1981 interview, Percy explained that a knowledge of one's existential predicament in the modern world provides the freedom necessary to open the self to an "extraordinary capacity to know things" (*Con*, 205). In a more imaginative and extended explanation of this point, Percy in "The Message in the Bottle" (*MB*, 119–49) describes the problems of the metaphorical amnesiac castaway stranded on the island of twentieth-century culture. The castaway, first of all, needs to understand that he is not at home, but an exile among other anxious exiles. Only after identifying this as his predicament can he take seriously any "news from across the seas" (*MB*, 140) that might offer him some information that he can use in ameliorating his condition—that is, information about who he is, where he is, and what he should do.

It is Tom's confession when he first arrives at the fire tower that he's "in a fix" and does "not know what to do" in response to the discoveries he just made about Van Dorn's school and Comeaux's Blue Boy project (*TS*, 234–35) that prompts Smith to begin his own "Confession." Tom's discoveries about his Feliciana home have made him conscious of his predicament, his exiled, castaway status and his alienation from his fellow islanders. Circumstances have placed him in a position to hear the priest's news. And Tom's instinctive turning to the life that the sea of pines outside the tower represents and his immediate decision to combat the death represented by Belle Ame and Blue Boy suggest that he may have benefited from the news about Dr. Jäger in ways that he cannot yet make conscious.

"What else" (*TS*, 257), Tom thinks, before he descends the fire tower steps; he changes Father Smith's final question to a declaration, as if reviewing the choices he has made in the past and can make in the future. He has used his Jäger-like data-gathering skills and scientific problem-solving powers to identify the Azazel in the desert that he vowed earlier he would "do something about" (*TS*, 64). He has also discovered that the demons in the Feliciana Parish desert have a face very much like his own. Now what to do in this predicament he has identified? He can choose to join the team of scientists at Fedville and spend his life perpetuating the death Comeaux and Van Dorn represent, oppose Comeaux and Van Dorn and risk being sent back to Fort Pelham (they threaten him repeatedly [*TS*, 265, 302, 330]), join Lucy at Pantherburn and become the Southern gentleman/physician she wants him to be, return to his family in the Slave Quarters where he is treated like "a hole in the floor" (*TS*, 38), or just while away his days on the front porch of his office making paper airplanes and waiting for the arrival of a desperate patient he no longer has the power to help.

Tom has spent most of his time since his release from Fort Pelham simply watching others and enjoying the small life (*TS*, 67) of limited choices that the Kierkegaardian aesthetic detachment and self-enclosure that he learned in prison created. Most of the novel after Tom's meeting with Smith (*TS*, 257–334) is about his acting with others to defeat the evil he has uncovered in his society, exemplifying in his actions Kierkegaard's ethical stage. While he has been in the past primarily interested in observation and analyses of his experience in order to discover what is true, now he is determined to choose what he knows is good and to act to make it prevail. Tom's movement from the aesthetic to the ethical stage is illustrated when he is imprisoned at Angola for parole violation after his first failed assault on Belle Ame. Although he in his cell at Angola reflects again on how good he feels having no choice about what to do (*TS*, 261), the next morning he chooses to escape and to solicit the services of Lucy, Vergil Bon, and Uncle Hugh Bob in his second assault against Belle Ame. He is choosing to act in the world with others rather than remain isolated in his good feelings.

Tom's improved consciousness of where he is and who he is is revealed after his escape from Angola as he walks along the levee in the morning sun toward his rendezvous with Vergil and Uncle Hugh Bob. He reflects on where he is and thinks, "walking the levee in flatlands has the pleasant feel of traveling a level track between earth and sky" (*TS*, 272). Unconsciously, he is locating himself in the vastness of creation and seeing himself as a traveler through it, a traveler who is neither entirely a bestial organism of the earth nor a transcendent angelic spirit in the sky, but the self that Percy says locates itself accurately as a "wayfaring creature somewhere between" (*MB*, 113). A few minutes later, when Tom is crossing the river in the pirogue with Vergil and Uncle Hugh Bob, he also demonstrates that he can recognize the actuality of other people and see that he is in the same boat with them. Earlier, in a boat in Lake Mary with these same two men, Tom, wondered, "Who am I?" and, obviously dislocated from phenomenal reality, imagined for a moment that he was sharing the boat with James Fenimore Cooper's Natty Bumppo and Hawkeye (*TS*, 181). But now he sees that his fellow boatmen are real people he has to depend on if he wants to get safely down the dangerously swollen river to the landing at Belle Ame and do what he feels he must do. He does not psychically isolate himself from them and analyze who they are and what they do as one might observe and analyze fictional characters. He knows that his destiny, literally his life or death, is inextricably connected with these two men and what they choose to do in the boat with him on the treacherous river.

When Tom returns to Angola that afternoon after his victory over the child molesters at Belle Ame, he shows in his meeting with Max Gottlieb and Bob Comeaux that he has made another firm ethical decision, this time a decision to close down the Blue Boy project. He is, again, also less abstracted and more conscious of his existence in present time-space experience. Bob and Max have come to Tom's Angola cell to try to persuade him to join the Fedville team, but Tom uses the meeting to inform them about the arrest of the pedophiles at Belle Ame and to convince them to discontinue the Blue Boy project. In the meeting, Bob begins to celebrate the "scientific breakthrough[s]" his team has made and talks about how much they have "help[ed] folks" in their community, but Tom guides the conversation to the here-and-now reality of what Bob and his colleagues have done. Tom tells Bob that he is not "speaking of science," but "speaking of you and Dr. Van Dorn," and he spreads out on the floor of the cell the pictures he found at Belle Ame and Lucy's data "from the NIH and Public Health" (TS, 329–32).

Bob, resisting the ugly truth about his project revealed in the lurid photographs of his Blue Boy coconspirator Van Dorn, questions Tom's motives in exposing this information about the pedophilia at Belle Ame and asks him rhetorically, "What are we doing here?" Max, "in his old abstracted way," also wonders, "What are we doing here?" Meanwhile, the Na-24-afflicted black prisoners in the cotton fields outside the cell window are singing, *Nobody knows the trouble I've seen, Nobody knows but Jesus.* Tom, as if to remind these two abstracted scientists where they are and what they are doing, bluntly informs them: "We are listening to the darkies singing" (TS, 331). When Bob, the consummate romantic aesthete (here appropriately dressed in his "white plantation tuxedo" [TS, 326]), comments on the beautiful songs wafting across the cotton fields from the contented mouths of the picturesque "darkies," Tom sarcastically says, "Right, Bob." Tom rejects Bob's invitation to romanticize the world outside the cell window, a place where the black inmates crouch at their backbreaking work in the Louisiana afternoon sun. Instead, Tom insists that they talk about what they "ought to do" (TS, 332) in order to shut down Blue Boy and stop the death documented by the photographs and printouts lying at their feet.

Released from Angola and once more out of prison, Tom returns to his family in the Slave Quarters where he must decide again "what to do" (*TS*, 335) after solving the problems caused by Comeaux and Van Dorn. He has been successful in identifying some features of the death Father Smith warned him about at the fire tower and has been able to do something in response to his discoveries. But Tom has not yet, apparently, been quite as successful in locating himself in the life the priest believes he must choose, and he therefore cannot decide what to do from day to day in order to make a meaningful life. Finding his medical practice "almost nil" and continuing to feel invisible among his wife, children, Chandra, and Hudeen, Tom for a while reverts to his old life of aesthetic self-enclosure and solitary consumption. He spends his days drinking at the Little Napoleon and his nights with Ellen idly "watching . . . Carson without laughing and reruns of *M*A*S*H* and *Lifestyles of the Rich and Famous*" from his cramped little "convent bed" (*TS*, 335). The fact that he is not luxuriating in the spacious Sears Best (*LR*, 371) he and Ellen enjoyed together at the end of *Love in the Ruins* suggests the diminishment of his life since then.

Plagued now in his daily life by the same kind of aesthetic self-imprisonment that made him want to escape "the necessities of time" and choice at Pantherburn (*TS*, 159), Angola, and Fort Pelham, Tom thinks, "Why not?" when Leroy Ledbetter offers him the opportunity to escape to Disney World in his Bluebird RV (*TS*, 335). Tom once again wants "no grand epiphanies" that might force him to confront the life beyond his comfortable interiorized world. In the spaceship-like Bluebird, Tom and his family lose consciousness of themselves and their lives, become as removed from the world and others as "astronauts" in outer space—the children "enchanted" and "paralyzed by delight," Ellen still "stoned on sodium ions," and Tom drunk most of the time. When they descend into Disney World, they set up their new home on Jack Rabbit Run in Fort Wilderness, beside similarly homeless Canadians and Ohioans (*TS*, 335–37). Tom is symbolically in the prison of his small world once more. In his "private little copse" on his "tiny plantation" at Disney World, Tom reads Stedmann's *History of World War I* just as he did while in prison in Alabama and sees his "stunned neighbors" as "like . . . [his] cellmates at Fort Pelham" (*TS*, 338–39).

As enjoyable as it is for Tom to spend his days chatting with his amiable fellow inmates at Disney World, he knows that he has to escape this pleasant prison and get back to his home. It is Smith's news that has been so important in Tom's decision to combat the death represented by Van Dorn and Comeaux, and, once more here, it may be the priest's influence that makes him resist the delights of life among his cellmates. Tom wonders if he is "beginning to think like Father Smith" when he considers how the individual Canadians around him have "not yet been ossified by" the word

Canadian (*TS*, 339–40). He is obviously recalling Smith's argument that language signs in this century have been deprived of meaning in that they have been made to signify categories and abstractions rather than "something real" in phenomenal creation (*TS*, 122). Also like Smith, Tom is beginning to suspect that the problems he has just faced with his colleagues in Feliciana Parish are only incidences imbedded in a larger reality. It seems to Tom that the stunned Ohioans and Canadians around him have "been zapped by something else" other than Na-24, something that has been "zapping" Americans for this entire century and turning them into selves that are as alienated from others, the actual world, and themselves as "dreamwalkers in a moonscape" (*TS*, 339–40). They are examples of the death in life that he could name ten years earlier in Paradise Estates and that Will Barrett can name in Linwood, North Carolina (*SC*, 147). But Tom can't quite name it here in Disney World. Neither can he make the connections between what he observes about his neighbors and his own inclination toward aesthetic detachment from time-space experience. He does, however, recognize that their condition has something to do with their longing to escape time, their preference for "the wonders of Tomorrowland" over the realities of "Todayland" (*TS*, 339–40).

VALUABLE CONNECTIONS

At the end of *Love in the Ruins*, Tom acquires a home where there is hope, as Percy says, for "reconciliation" (*Con*, 51) among the disparate religious groups, races, and political ideologies represented by the fellow exiles who have chosen to live in the new community (*Con*, 74) in the Slave Quarters. Tom leaves behind the language worlds of Fedville and Paradise Estates, and in the final scene of the novel begins to open himself to a sacramental language that can tell him the sacred secrets in the "holy night" (*LR*, 402) that surrounds him. While Tom also begins to improve his capacity for sacramental reading at the end of *The Thanatos Syndrome*, he remains much more estranged from others than he is in *Love in the Ruins*. Tom returns from Disney World to a home where there is not yet much hope for his reconciliation with his professional colleagues, his family, and his Louisiana neighbors.

In the medical profession, Van Dorn and Comeaux continue to prosper—their continued success evidence, of course, that the world outside Feliciana Parish is still a place where their gnostic, scientific mode of perception dominates. In contrast, Tom's "practice . . . is shot" (*TS*, 356), his community apparently finding little need for what he knows and what he can do. Van Dorn speaks a language that most understand and embrace as a source of truth. After his two-month affair with Eve, a gorilla at the Tulane Primate Center, he published his best-seller, *My Life and Love with Eve*. This former child molester's story of bestiality has become so popular in America that he is now a cultural icon, appearing regularly on *Donahue*, "often with Dr. Ruth" (*TS*, 344). The governor of Louisiana admires him so much that he grants him a pardon. The last time Tom talks with Comeaux he is still pontificating about his "ultimate goal[s]" and confidently expressing his Benthamite faith in "the greatest good . . . for the greatest number." He is excitedly on his way into a busy future as director of a Planned Parenthood clinic in New York or "consultant to the minister for family planning" in the People's Republic of China (*TS*, 345–46).

At home, Ellen, has converted to a Pentecostal Christianity while Tom has begun to attend an occasional mass, even taking Meg and Tom, Jr., to Christmas mass. The gulf between Tom's developing Catholic sacramental consciousness and Ellen's concept of who she is and where she is is suggested by the fact that she has literally begun speaking a new language: "She speaks in tongues." The language of her fervent Christianity is a radically nonsacramental language that leads the believer to aspire to an individual, private spiritual happiness in isolation from the Word revealed in an incarniontal creation and God's image in it. Ellen believes that she has "been baptized in the Holy Spirit," but "says little about Jesus," and generally, Tom says, she does not like the "mixing up of body and spirit" (*TS*, 353).

Tom notes that there are few Catholics left in his Louisiana community, most having converted to the kind of Pentecostal Christianity his wife now practices. While he himself has few strong Catholic convictions, he is not very comfortable with this new evangelism either. Ellen and her congregation separate their interior world of personal happiness from the real world, where they spend most of their energies developing a "sober, dependable, industrious, helpful" self whose primary purpose is to pursue financial success. Tom is pleased that Ellen is happy in this new religion she has discovered, and pleased that his children are happy in the Feliciana Christian Academy where Ellen has them enrolled. He admits that Ellen may have in fact "found Jesus Christ and been born again" and can find nothing to condemn about these Christians who "weep and exclaim and speak in tongues." He certainly does not hold up the spiritual authority of his own church as a contrast, declaring to Ellen that he doesn't think he is "Roman." But, unlike these zealous evangelicals—who, for some reason he can't name, give him "the creeps"—Tom does accept the possible efficacy of the Catholic sacraments and therefore accepts the possibility of the incarnational union of spirit and flesh they celebrate. Speaking of his own baptism, he asserts that he believes that he was "born again when . . . [he] was baptized" (*TS*, 354–55).[30]

Percy says that Tom experiences "no big conversion," "no great return to religion" (*MCon*, 195, 202) at the end of *The Thanatos Syndrome*, discouraging those readers who would like to see Tom find a home in a family, community, and world that has little understanding or sympathy for the sacramental way of seeing that he is unconsciously developing. While he does not experience the reconciliation he enjoys at the end of *Love in the Ruins*, Tom's work at the hospice and his assistance to Father Smith at mass and at the fire tower (*TS*, 363, 367) suggest that Tom at the end of the novel is at least beginning to open himself to the possibilities of the life that Father Smith has told him lies "out there" beyond the aesthetic windowsill of minds like Van Dorn's, Comeaux's, Dr. Jäger's, and Ellen's. Tom illustrates this developing sacramental way of seeing when he looks out across Lake Pontchartrain from the balcony of Max's "high-rise condo" while he and Ellen are visiting the Gottliebs. At this moment, Tom's eyes are directed toward the sky, light, and water, and the birds that inhabit these vast spaces. He gazes out at the "bright mazy sun [that] whitens out the sky into a globe of pearly light into which the causeway disappears like a Japanese bridge into a cloud." He also notes the "light, vapory water" where coots and scaups peacefully bob beneath the brilliant "vermilion flycatcher perched on the bridge rail" (*TS*, 352). These Hopkinsian "inscape" images show that Tom is seeing in these moments on the balcony a startlingly beautiful world enclosed in a globe of precious radiance, an actual phenomenal world accessible only through his sensory data but at the same time filled with significances transcendent of them.

Although he confesses to Smith that he is "no longer sure what ..[he] believe[s]" and that he doesn't "think much about religion," he does in the final scenes of *The Thanatos Syndrome* become a follower, albeit a tentative and uncertain one, of the sacramental way the priest represents. He is at least welcoming the spiritual possibilities of the "valuable connection[s]" (*TS*, 370) that he believes Smith can reveal to him. At the end of the novel, Tom may be on the verge of locating within himself, and within others, that mysterious spiritual "instinct" that O. E. Parker "obeys" in Flannery O'Connor's "Parker's Back"— in Parker's case, an instinct that he obeys in a strange existential journey whose end neither he nor his wife and friends can fully understand.[31]

The last three scenes of *The Thanatos Syndrome*—the mass at St. Margaret's in celebration of the reopening of the hospice, Father Smith's recounting to Tom in the hall of the hospice the story of Mary's appearance to the Yugoslavian children, and Tom's meeting with Mickey LaFaye at his office—reveal Tom's spiritual alliance with Smith and his growing sacramentalism. At the mass at St. Margaret's, when Smith falls silent during the ceremony, Tom literally removes himself from a congregation made up of the physicians, businessmen, friends, and neighbors that make up his Feliciana community. And, even though he admits that he "could not make head or tail of what he [Father Smith] was saying," he chooses to obey Father Smith's instructions and to kneel beside him before the altar as they prepare to celebrate the Eucharist. Tom also now works with Smith every morning (*TS*, 363) at the hospice where they tend to the needs of the sick and dying patients who were formerly victims of the Fedville Qualitarian Center. It is in the halls of the hospice as the two make their rounds a few days later that Tom listens to the news the priest says was sent by the "Mother of God" to the six children in Yugoslavia (*TS*, 364). When the novel ends, Tom is following Smith's advice to continue his "analysis and treatment of . . . [his] patients" (*TS*, 366) and waiting for the "valuable connection" that he believes he will discover the next day when he visits the priest.

Father Smith's diatribe during the mass at St. Margaret's is essentially a public and much more dramatic repetition of the news he delivered to Tom at the fire tower about the inhumanity and dangers that threaten the individual who is trying to discover life in this age of death (*TS*, 114–31). He demands that the perplexed, even "offended" (*TS*, 362), doctors in the congregation think about who they are, where they are, and what they are doing in a twentieth-century culture of death where "tender-hearted souls" like them have killed more people than "in all other centuries put together"(*TS*, 361). "I wonder if you know what you are doing here!" he challenges them (*TS*, 358), accusing all of them of "creaming in . . . [their] drawers from [the] tenderness" (*TS*, 361) that enables them to support without a single moral flinch the daily killing of helpless children and old people at the local Qualitarian Center.

Father Smith is assaulting the scientistic, aesthetic mind-set that isolates Van Dorn, Comeaux, Lucy, and Dr. Jäger from the horror of the world they create and from the horror within themselves. Talking about the Holocaust in a 1988 interview, Percy said that the "tenderness" that marks these aesthetes is caused by the value they grant to the "abstract ideals" (*MCon*, 191) that they consider the truth. Flannery O'Connor in her "Introduction" to *A Memoir of Mary Ann* anticipates Percy's reflections on this modern "tenderness [that] leads to the gas chamber " and condemns the inhumanity of what she sees as a sentimental "tenderness," a "popular pity" that allows the best-intentioned people to wish that afflicted children like Mary Ann had never been "born in the first place." O'Connor is indicting in her essay the modern gnostic who cannot abide the unpleasant reality of "human imperfection"—the suffering and death of the innocent being one of the most shocking of imperfections—and therefore seeks to eliminate it, sometimes with "forced-labor camps and in the fumes of the gas chamber." She contrasts this "tenderness" with Christian charity, a life-giving love that recognizes and welcomes the "communion" of all in their "grotesque state." It is in that grotesqueness, and only there, that Christian love is needed and its salvific work can be done. It is only in the face of the grotesquely cancer-disfigured face of Mary Ann, O'Connor says, that we can see good and promise "under construction."[32]

At their first meeting at the fire tower, Tom dismissed Father Smith's strange message about deprived language, tenderness, and this century of death as the confused ravings of a seriously disturbed (*TS*, 127) old man, and he could not wait to escape and make his report to Comeaux about the priest's condition. At the mass at St. Margaret's, however, Tom no longer observes Smith from the objective posture of the clinical physician but instinctively assumes some different roles and becomes a participant in his message. Smith suddenly falls silent after he directly addresses the "dear physicians" in the congregation, entreating them not to kill their "suffering, dying, afflicted, useless, born or unborn" patients. At that point, Tom rises out of the congregation and moves to the side of the priest, thinking that he is behaving like "a deacon or usher who knows what he is doing" (*TS*, 361–62). Dropping his scientific, Freudian "psyche-iatrist" (*TS*, 16) self that he has has been so pleased with,[33] he thinks, "never mind Freud," as he obeys Father Smith's directions and "kneel[s] beside him like an altar boy." Tom—deacon, usher, altar boy—is placing himself in deference to the priest's authority and literally at this moment following the sacramental way with his new guide as he prepares to go up to "the altar of God" (*TS*, 363) with him to celebrate the Eucharistic sacrifice.

Father Smith's commentary on the story of Mary's appearance before the Yugoslavian children "a few years ago" (*TS*, 364–65) is some additional "news from across the seas" (*MB*, 144) that is intended to show Tom the hope and life that the sacrifice he celebrated at mass can provide. Just as the castaway in "The Message in the Bottle" is, logically, more interested in those messages in the bottles that give him helpful information about his predicament than he is about whether the information they contain is true (*MB*, 122–23), so Smith stresses the possible significance of this miraculous message from Mary rather than the objective truth of its occurrence. He admits that no one knows whether or not the Virgin actually appeared, not even the Church. What is more important is her message for the cast-aways in this century who are searching for a knowledge of their home. She identifies for them their predicament, tells them where they are and who they are: exiles on an island where science and reason have triumphed over faith, where death and despair, therefore, have defeated love and hope. And she tells the castaways who can recognize this exiled self and this menacing world what to do:

> if you keep hope and have a loving heart and do not secretly wish for the death of others, the Great Prince Satan will not succeed in destroying the world. In a few years this dread century will be over. Perhaps the world will end in fire and the Lord will come—it is not for us to say. But it is for us to say, . . . whether hope and faith will come back into the world. (*TS*, 365)

Father Smith in his story of the appearance of Mary is challenging Tom to direct his eyes "out there" to the horizon in order to locate a knowledge that will provide hope for the castaway who happens to have washed ashore on the deadly island of twentieth-century science and tenderness. Even in this century, the "worst of times," Percy says, it is still possible for the individual to defeat his despair and acquire the hope and psychic energy necessary to initiate a search for the "infinite potential of himself." But, he goes on to explain, that "search occurs only if there is hope that a search is possible" (*MCon*, 60). Father Smith is offering this same advice, reminding Tom that he must patiently "wait" (*TS*, 239, 363) for hope and assume that with that hope will come an opening to infinite possibilities for self-discovery.[34] The "secret" (*TS*, 366) that Smith wants to tell Tom is that he need not worry about his inability to believe in the truths of his Church, that it is "only necessary to wait and to be of good heart" (*TS*, 363) and to continue his service to his patients. By these actions, the priest promises, he will be able to discover "a thing or two" beyond what his old mentors "Dr. Freud and Dr. Jung" discovered through their science and interior quests (*TS*, 366).

Tom may be a reluctant and hesitant believer, but he does listen attentively to what Father Smith and Mary, the Mother of God, have revealed to him about his predicament and accepts their advice about what to do. "All right," he replies (*TS*, 366) when Smith tells him his secret. With this knowledge, Tom at the end of *The Thanatos Syndrome* literally waits on the front porch of his office for Mickey, a former patient and Na-24 victim who is once more as terrified by life as she was when Tom treated her two years earlier. At the beginning of the novel he was also waiting for patients (*TS*, 13–21), but there are some differences now. As he waited for Donna

S_____ a few months ago, Tom paid little attention to the sacramental natural world beyond his porch, more interested at that time in the dead past and his memories of his father, the coroner who once worked in the "Cajun cottage" that is now his own office. But out in the yard on this day he sees the "best time: the morning sun booming in over the live oak, the air yellow and clear as light"; he locates himself in the living, present moment in an open place of sky, light, air, and life. He does not retreat into his thoughts about his past and into his lifeless scientific abstractions, but thinks about what he ought to do in the future, whether he should assume the directorship of the hospice or go into private practice with Max. While Tom wanted to see Donna primarily because he wanted another case study for his investigation of the syndrome he was then studying, he is now interested in helping Mickey because he identifies himself as being in the same existential boat with her. Tom no longer sees his patients as mere data, as case studies. He is this day waiting at his office to help patients he feels are his "kind of people" suffering from the same kind of "solitary aching consciousnesses" that he knows so well (*TS*, 366–67). Tom's expression here of the identity he feels with the suffering of others echoes Father Smith's similar statement in his "Confession" about his own unsentimental capacity for *caritas*: "They [the suffering and dying] were my kind" (*TS*, 244), he says, while explaining to Tom his reasons for choosing to become a priest and choosing life over death (*TS*, 257).

Tom, in his treatment of Mickey LaFaye in the final scene of the novel, is turning his attention to the self, one of the "only two signs," Percy says, that "cannot be encompassed by theory" in this century's "desert of theory and consumption" ("Why Are You Catholic?" *SP*, 312). This genuine self is the individual life that is ignored by the angelic Cartesian observer absorbed in the reality of his theorizing and by the bestial consumer lost in his pursuit of happiness. Tom, in his treatment of Mickey, begins searching with her for this "very self" that he believes may live lost and like a "stranger" within her (*TS*, 371–72), searching in a region of being beyond her mere thinking and immanent activities. And, since he sees his own existential condition as a possible "mirror" (*TS*, 372) of hers, the implication is that Tom is joining Mickey in a life-giving search for the self hidden in the desert and is being guided by a sign that he has until now not sufficiently read.

When Tom first began treating Mickey, she was a stereotypical upper-middle- class woman living out the American Dream in a plantation-style house "next to number-six fairway" and enjoying the leisure and privilege that Tom's wealthy neighbors in Paradise Estates, the Vaughts in *The Last Gentleman*, and the Linwood retirees in *The Second Coming* exemplify. Unfortunately, she also suffered from a paralyzing "free-floating anxiety" that caused her so much dread that she was unable to leave her idyllic home (*TS*, 5–6), the same kind of anxiety and terror that she is complaining about during this latest visit to Tom's office. She is also again talking about the "recurring dream" she has in which she is waiting in the "cellar of her grandmother's farmhouse" for a "visitor" who is coming to "tell her a secret" (*TS*, 6) that will reveal to her a life that her wealth and privilege will not provide. The visitor or stranger, she now feels, is the "deepest part" of her self trying to bring her a message about the fear and dread (*TS*, 371) that account for her enclosed death in her life beside the golf course. The visitor, she believes, will tell her about a fuller life beyond her current home.

In his essay "The Coming Crisis in Psychiatry," Percy argues that ours is an "age of anxiety because it is the age of the loss of self" (*SP*, 254), and he is talking about the anxiety and self-loss represented by Mickey LaFaye. Ironically, he goes on to explain, this anxiety, when recognized by victims like Mickey and Tom, can lead to a discovery of the life that has been lost. Percy agrees with Heidegger that anxiety is "a kind of beckoning of the self to a self." Characters in his novels with free-floating anxiety, he says, have greater possibilities for self-development than those who are "perfectly adjusted" (*MCon*, 60). Because Freud and Jung advise that the therapist and patient search the recesses of the self for such anxieties, they can be helpful in a modern world like Feliciana Parish where the goal of most scientists is to eliminate all anxiety through drugs. Percy vowed that "Jung was right" about anxiety being a source for knowledge about the self (*MCon*, 202, 187). In a 1987 interview, he stated flatly: "I consider my two main sources Catholic theology and Freudian psychiatry . . . . Both start out with the premise that man is born in trouble" (*MCon*, 180).[35] And because both insist on a recognition and precise definition of the trouble, both encourage the individual to search the self for a redemption from it.

Percy maintains that the only other sign besides the self for wayfarers who are "lost in the desert" of the modern world is "the Jews . . . the worldwide *ecclesia* instituted by one of them, God-become-man, a Jew" ("Why Are You Catholic?" *SP*, 314). This sign directs the pilgrim beyond the individual self to the final source of all life. As Tom waits in his office for Mickey, he also waits for the next day of his life, which happens to be the Feast of the Epiphany. Father Smith sends Tom a message that asks him to assist tomorrow (*TS*, 370) in the mass that celebrates on that feast day the sign that can guide all wayfarers and castaways for all times to the Word made flesh, the eternal Logos. As the Christmas mass at the end of *Love in the Ruins* reminds Tom of this sign, so the upcoming mass for the Feast of the Epiphany in this novel has the potential to remind him of the necessity of choosing to search, like the first Magi, for a mysterious new life that entered the desert and human history two thousand years before the "age of thanatos."[36]

As the Magi chose to leave their familiar home and accept the possibility that in a strange land beyond it they might discover a "king" whose power was worth whatever treasures they could offer him, so Tom at the end of *The Thanatos Syndrome* may be about to launch tomorrow a similar search to discover the mystery in the desert. This is a search that can lead him to the Nativity and to an understanding of some connections between his ego self, his "very self," others, the world, and God that are more valuable than the ones he may discover in his Freudian and Jungian psychoanalysis with Mickey LaFaye. Among the Jews, he may be able to extend his vision in order to see beyond his individual predicament and locate himself accurately in a barren and Fallen world with all others in all of time. This Fallen world, this ominous desert, is also paradoxically a place filled with a divine *caritas* and life, God having entered it through Christ precisely because it is a place where horror and death live. The sign of Christ is the sign of this paradox. He is the unconquerable divine power for love, forgiveness, and redemption that lives forever among mankind—the innocent Jewish infant the Magi paid homage to in Bethlehem, the gentle shepherd, the patient teacher, the healing physician. But Christ is also a person like all others, who lives in a world filled with other people who can be guided by the signs offered by Herod and Pontius Pilate, a world where he inevitably must become the despised criminal enduring the horror, the suffering and death, of the Crucifixion. Again, paradoxically, it is in this horror, and nowhere else, where promise and hope for redemption from death exist. This is a world "created upon human imperfection," O'Connor says, and it is because of that imperfection that all are joined in a redemptive communion for all time and held "fast in Christ."[37]

The Magi discovered at Bethlehem the miraculous life they thought worth all their treasures, but they also discovered the murderous deceit of Herod. In Herod they found the death-dealing demon that ruled the desert land where they made their journey. Similarly, Tom has discovered in the course of *The Thanatos Syndrome* the "death" represented by those with political, social, and economic power in Feliciana Parish, and, as the Magi did, he has resisted it. Tom not only opposes the Blue Boy project and Belle Ame school but he also recognizes, with the assistance of Father Smith, that he is in danger of joining the Herods of Fedville. He knows that he has spent much of his professional life pledged to the scientific work promoted by Van Dorn and Comeaux, working alongside his fellow scientists to try to make his society in his image. He has in his aestheticism dreamed, as they have, of a world zapped into perfection and tranquility by his lapsometer or by some magical pharmacological potion. His gnostic mind-set is exemplified by his plan to drug long-distance truckers in order to transform their grueling work lives into a bearable, if not pleasant, experience. Now, however, Tom is thinking about a professional future as the director of the hospice, a position formerly held by Father Smith (*TS*, 367). He is thinking about choosing a life among the terminally ill and dying, the life Father Smith chose and the life Christ chose—the only life that exists in the otherwise Herod-ruled desert.

After the Magi chose Christ and rejected the temptations of Herod, they returned to "their country by another way" (Matthew 2.12). On a literal level, this means that they chose another route in order to avoid Herod, but it may also suggest that they became pilgrims whose ideas about the best way to get to their home changed after their epiphany. Unlike the Magi, Tom has not yet completed his pilgrimage nor experienced any radical revelation, but he has located the Herods in Feliciana Parish and chosen to believe Father Smith's secret that he is capable of learning a thing or two that his old mentors Jung and Freud cannot teach him. Tomorrow at the mass for the Feast of the Epiphany he will, like the three pilgrims to Bethlehem, approach that "eternal light . . . [that] has continually shone on us all the time we have been in this world."[38] Tom, after assisting Father Smith at the mass, may also witness a miraculous new light on the horizon that will cause him to choose to return to his home "another way."

Epilogue:
The Way Home

I am going to prepare a place for you. . . . I will come back again and take you to myself, so that where I am you also may be. Where I am going you know the way.

—John 14:2–4

So Jesus reminds his disciples at the Last Supper of where they are now and where they may be at the Second Coming. In the next few days after this meal, they will see in Herod, Pontius Pilate, their Jewish neighbors, and in themselves the inhuman moral cowardice and ignorance regnant in the place where they now make their home, a desert land unredeemed by the Good News Jesus has brought to them. In his assuring them that their final place is with him in a life and home beyond the suffering and death they are about to witness at the Crucifixion, he is urging them to reflect on this place they currently inhabit. He knows that they are about to set out on their wayfaring in that barren place and that they will be tempted by the demons who reside there. Only their knowledge of the way will provide them with the hope and energy they will need to pass by the demons and continue their journey to their home with Christ. Jesus wants to assure his followers that this final home exists and that they know the way because it has been shown to them in his life and in the Jewish account of human history recorded in the books of the Old Testament. Now the disciples must face their desert journey with this knowledge and wait for the parousia when Jesus will return to take them to where he is. The alternative to this faith in the way home, as Father Smith proclaims, is death.

Will Barrett and Tom More, as they wander through the desert of twentieth-century America, also need to be reminded of where they are and what they need to do in order to live with hope in a place of death. The four novels that chronicle their wayfaring emphasize their efforts to understand where they are and their attempts to find a way that will take them out of the desert and reveal to them a home that is not available in its lifeless sands. Tom recognizes in *The Thanatos Syndrome* that this sojourn among the demons is continuous "fits and starts" (*TS*, 75). as the wayfarer tries to discover where he is and choose the right way. Sometimes the wayfarer sees clearly the way, sometimes he is lost and blind. Tom has realized after a lifetime search for a home in Paradise Estates and in the Slave Quarters that the pilgrim's daily travels are a constant—and only occasionally successful—struggle to remember the way his Catholic faith teaches. His wayfaring has shown him that no steady, uninterrupted progress toward God and salvation can be sustained by the wounded, Fallen pilgrim.

Fortunately, Tom is assisted in his fits and starts by Father Smith, who can speak with the authority of the Catholic Church and remind Tom of the way that will lead to the home Jesus promises at the Last Supper. Will Barrett, however, has no authority to guide him through the desert since he has long ago abandoned his Episcopal faith. Father Smith can show Tom the sacramental signs that will direct him past the Paradise Estates golf course, the Fedville mental ward, the ruins of Howard Johnson's, the Qualitarian Life Center, Belle Ame school, Pantherburn, and Tomorrow land. But Will is on his own as he tries to discover another way besides his father's deadly route and the paths he chooses in the sign-filled landscapes of New York, Alabama, Mississippi, New Mexico, and in Linwood, North Carolina. Will has no one who can speak with authority and tell him how to read the signs he encounters on his journey, no one to tell him about the death that waits for him at the Vaughts' castle by the golf course, in his father's attic, at the Linwood country club, and in the Georgia swamp.

At the end of *The Second Coming*, Will knows that he is a "placeless person in a placeless place" (*SC*, 385) but, finally, as Father Weatherbee backs away from him in Jack Curl's office at St. Mark's, he can only desperately wonder about the place Jesus says he is going to prepare. And he can only question himself about what he wants at his current home in the North Carolina mountains and what he wants from God (*SC*, 411) in a possibly apocalyptic future. In contrast, Tom's contemplative "Well well well" (*TS*, 372) as he tries to ease the fears of Mickey LaFaye at the end of *The Thanatos Syndrome* suggests that he has, at least for the moment, acquired a way to live with hope and patience amid the horrors of his home in Feliciana Parish. His anticipation of his visit "tomorrow" with Father Smith and his reflections on the Feast of the Epiphany suggest that he has also discovered the way to his final home—the way marked by the sacramental signs Father Smith has shown him, the way that leads to the home that will be revealed to all humankind when Christ comes again to make the desert bloom.

Notes

CHAPTER 1: INTRODUCTION

1. Percy's first published essay is a 1954 review of Susanne Langer's *Feeling and Form* (1953) in *Thought*. Throughout his career, Percy published many essays on language, philosophy, religion, and culture in scholarly journals and in popular magazines. *The Message in the Bottle* (1975) and *Signposts in a Strange Land* (1991) are collections that include the most important of these essays. Percy's interviews have been collected and edited by Lewis Lawson and Victor Kramer in *Conversations with Walker Percy* (1988) and *More Conversations with Walker Percy* (1993).

2. Mills, "An Essential Walker Percy Bibliography," 129–39.

3. My sources for biographical information about Percy are Jay Tolson's *Pilgrim in the Ruins: A Life of Walker Percy* (1992) and Patrick Samway's *Walker Percy: A Life* (1997). See Bertram Wyatt-Brown's *The House of Percy: Honor, Melancholy, and Imagination in a Southern Family* (1994) for a thorough discussion of the history of depression and suicide in the Percy family.

4. Samway, *Walker Percy*, 56.

5. Allen, *Walker Percy*, 14.

6. Crowley and Crowley, eds., *Critical Essays on Walker Percy*, 1–34.

7. Luschei's *The Sovereign Wayfarer* (1972) is a seminal study of Percy. Lawson's *Following Percy*, a collection of his essays, was published in 1988.

8. Jac Tharpe, *Walker Percy*, (1983); Robert Brinkmeyer, *Three Catholic Writers* (1985); Harold Bloom, ed., *Walker Percy*, (1986).

9. Hardy, *The Fiction of Walker Percy*, 1.

10. Wyatt-Brown, *The House of Percy*, 289–90, 312.

11. Lawson, *Still Following Percy*, xi, xv.

12. Gretlund and Westarp, eds., *Walker Percy* (1991). This collection includes the papers presented at the international conference on Percy at the University of Aarhus in 1989.

13. In Samway, ed., *A Thief of Peirce*, 1995.

14. *Futrell, The Signs of Christianity in the Work of Walker Percy*, 1994.

15. Lawson and Oleksy, eds., *Walker Percy's Feminine Characters*, 1995.

16. Quinlan, *Walker Percy: The Last Catholic Novelist*, 9, 91.

17. Ibid., 13.

18. See the following critics for commentary on Percy's sacramentalism. Some important page numbers are noted, but these critics also refer to Percy's sacramental vision throughout their works. Gary Ciuba, *Walker Percy: Books of Revelation*; John F. Desmond's essays in *At the Crossroads*, and especially his 1986 article in *The Southern Review*, "Walker Percy and

T. S. Eliot" (475–77); Edward J. Dupuy, *Autobiography in Walker Percy* (especially 33-36); Paul Giles, *American Catholic Art and Fictions* (196–202); John Edward Hardy, *The Fiction of Walker Percy*; Lewis Lawson's *Following Percy* and *Still Following Percy*, especially his "The Cross and the Delta" (4–5); Sally McFague, "The Parabolic in Faulkner, O'Connor, and Percy" (122–29); Patricia Lewis Poteat, *Walker Percy and the Old Modern Age*; Jay Tolson, *Pilgrim in the Ruins*.

CHAPTER 2: THE PREDICAMENT: WHERE ARE YOU?

1. Ciuba, *Walker Percy*, 21.
2. In a meeting of the "Jung discussion group" Percy belonged to in Covington, he stated, " I do not think the notion of 'growth' is steady or inexorable" (Samway, *Walker Percy*, 337). From Percy's Catholic Christian perspective, the wayfaring toward a consciousness of the self as a participant in a God-created incarnate creation inevitably involves failures and defeats.
3. Teilhard de Chardin, *The Divine Milieu*, 73.
4. Percy's thinking about the "closure" of the self was probably stimulated by Gabriel Marcel, perhaps his favorite modern Catholic philosopher. Marcel maintains in *The Mystery of Being* that "authentic sin" is "the act of shutting oneself in on oneself or taking one's own self as the centre." The Christian "wayfarer" seeks an escape from this "shut-in" condition (181–82). Philosopher Eric Voegelin's interpretation of history as a product of "closed" gnostic epistemologies is another likely source for Percy's ideas about the subjectification of experience in this century and the social, political, and personal consequences of such a solipsistic, romantic mind-set (*Con*, 13). See Lewis Simpson's *The Brazen Face of History* for a discussion of the modern "closure of history into the finitude of human consciousness" (270–72) and Voegelin's theories about gnosticism. See also Cleanth Brooks's classic essay, "Walker Percy and Modern Gnosticism." Robert Brinkmeyer in "Walker Percy's *Lancelot*" sees the connection between Percy's concept of the closed self and Bakhtin's "enclosure within the self" (31).
5. Lawson, *Still Following Percy*, 11.
6. Samway, "A Rahnerian Backdrop to Percy's *The Second Coming*," 133, 138.
7. Frye, *The Great Code*, xviii.
8. Samway, ed., *A Thief of Peirce*, xv.
9. Lawson, "The Cross and the Delta," 4–5.
10. Samway, ed., *A Thief of Peirce*, 130.
11. Futrell, *The Signs of Christianity*, 89.
12. Robertson, *The Literature of Medieval England*, 29.
13. Josipovici, *The World and the Book*, 29.
14. Maritain, *Ransoming the Times*, 220.
15. Lawson, "The Cross and the Delta," 5.
16. Scullin, "*Lancelot* and Walker Percy's Dispute," 110-11.
17. Gunn, *The Interpretation of Otherness*, 114.
18. Luschei, *The Sovereign Wayfarer*, 39.
19. "Angelism-bestialism" is a key concept in Percy's "anthropology" and important throughout his work, especially in *Lost in the Cosmos*. Paul Giles in *American Catholic Art and Fictions* locates the source for Percy's understanding of this idea in the literary criticism of Allen Tate and in the philosophy of Jacques Maritain. Maritain, in his *The Dream of Descartes* (1944), examines the illusions about reality characteristic of the post-Romantic, "Angelic" sensibility, a kind of consciousness that assumes an autonomy for its knowing and being. Tate says that for one who is afflicted with such a sense of "romantic individualism," "every son-of-a-bitch is Christ" (Giles, 196–202).

20. Foucault, *The Order of Things*, 125 ff.

21. In *Either/Or*, Kierkegaard describes the aesthete's detachment from reality by comparing him to an "eagle" who swoops "down into reality" to capture his "prey." Similarly, the aesthete descends into the world, captures "picture[s]" of phenomena through his observations, and carries them back to the "palace" of his interior life where he "weaves" them into "tapestries." Among those tapestries he lives "as one dead." He creates his own private world made up of his pictures and subsequently "erase[s]" from his consciousness "everything finite and accidental" (*Kierkegaard Anthology*, 35).

22. O'Connor, *Mystery and Manners*, 150.

23. Mrs. Mary Bernice (Bunt) Percy, Walker's widow, told me in a 1994 conversation that Percy always felt greatly indebted to Caroline Gordon for her assistance in the early years of his literary career. See Jay Tolson's *Pilgrim in the Ruins* (197–98, 300–302) on the influences of Gordon. Gordon's letters to Percy (1951–52) in the Walker Percy Papers (Series 3, Box 39, Folders 34, 35) show more specifically how influential Gordon and her husband Allen Tate were in Percy's development as a Catholic novelist and thinker. Besides offering him detailed technical literary advice, they directed him to modern Catholic theologians and philosophers like Mauriac, Bernanos, and Jacques Maritain.

24. Crowley, "*The Thanatos Syndrome*," 235.

25. Frye, *Anatomy*, 141.

26. Frye, *The Great Code*, 142.

27. O'Connor, *Mystery and Manners*, 226.

CHAPTER 3: *The Last Gentleman*: WAITING IN THE DESERT

1. Pindell, "Toward Home," 75, 82.

2. Dupuy, *Autobiography in Walker Percy*, 28.

3. Pindell, "Toward Home," 71.

4. *A Kierkegaard Anthology*, 123.

5. Dupuy, *Autobiography in Walker Percy*, 31.

6. Ciuba, *Walker Percy*, 98.

7. Karl, *American Fiction, 1940–80*, 317.

8. Patrick Samway (*Walker Percy*, 217) explains that Will's journey "from New York to Birmingham and Greenville (Ithaca) . . . [and] Santa Fe" is a "mythic voyage homeward . . . to the City of Holy Faith" very similar to Walker Percy's own "voyage." As Will's scientific worldview is challenged in the Santa Fe hospital by the Catholic sacramentalism of Father Boomer, so Percy's own scientist faith was challenged by the Catholic faith he adopted.

The Last Gentleman is the most autobiographical of all of Percy's novels, and anyone interested in the many parallels between Will Barrett's story and Percy's life can easily find them in Samway's biography and Jay Tolson's earlier biography, *Pilgrim in the Ruins*. Because of the thorough biographical work of Tolson and Samway, it would be redundant in this study of the novel to specify all these parallels, but it does seem useful to note briefly some of the major ways Will Barrett's story echoes Percy's.

In 1924, Percy's father moved his family into a country club home on a suburban Birmingham golf course; the Vaughts in the novel also have a "castle" on a golf course. When Percy was thirteen, his father, like Will's, shot himself in the attic of the family's home. Percy spent his adolescent years at his Uncle Will's in Greenville, Mississippi, the model for Will Barrett's fictional hometown of Ithaca. Also like Will, Percy lived in New York (while in medical school at Columbia) and underwent psychoanalysis there. In 1946, Percy returned to Greenville, then left to vacation in Santa Fe with his friend Shelby Foote. When he returned from New Mexico, Percy decided to marry Mary Bernice Townsend, pursue a writing career, and become a Catholic. As Will Barrett learns to see anew in Santa Fe, Percy apparently also had his revelation in that Catholic "city of faith," one that made him question the objective "truths" that his education in the sciences at Chapel Hill and Columbia had provided him.

9. O'Connor, *Mystery and Manners* ,150.

10. *A Kierkegaard Anthology*, 123.

11. Ibid., 28, 415.

12. Percy said that Will is a troubled searcher "looking for a father-figure" (*Con*, 13). William Rodney Allen in his *Walker Percy* (20, 36, 56) discusses the search for a father as a major theme in all of Percy's novels. Gary Ciuba argues that the first half of *The Last Gentleman* is "dominated by . . . [Will's] memory of" his father (*Walker Percy*, 123). More recently, Bertram Wyatt-Brown (*The Literary Percys*, 62) has declared that all of Percy's novels develop this search-for-a-father theme, and Patrick Samway (*Walker Percy*, 107) has found the "psychic source" of *The Last Gentleman* in Walker Percy's own painful "quest for the missing father."

13. Jac Tharpe (*Walker Percy*, 37,130) notes Gerard Manley Hopkins's influences on Percy's nature imagery and Percy's use of Hopkinsian diction like "dappled" and "pied." Most major critics have recognized Percy's debts to Hopkins, Percy himself in one of his earliest interviews listing Hopkins among the writers that "meant most" to him (*Con*, 5).

14. In his essay, "Uncle Will," Percy remembers William Alexander Percy, the consummate Old South aristocrat, excoriating the modern "new morality" as merely the license to "fornicate . . . like white trash" (*SP*, 58). Ed Barrett's stoicism, romantic sense of honor, duty to community, and sentimental noblesse oblige may be modeled after the similar moral and personal qualities of William Alexander Percy (Tolson, "The Education of Walker Percy," 160).

15. Prochaska, *The Myth of the Fall*, 3.

16. Prochaska, *The Myth of the Fall*, 16-17. John Edward Hardy (*The Fiction of Walker Percy*, 60) sees the falcon as an allusion to both "The Windhover" and William Butler Yeats's "The Second Coming." The bird symbolically suggests to Hardy both Will's spiritual quest and his desire to become an aggressive and predatory male like the falcon.

17. Lawson, *Still Following Percy*, 123–24.

18. Barrett, *Irrational Man*,163–64.

19. In his collection of essays, *Still Following Percy* (17, 49–52,166–69, 189, 193), Lewis Lawson argues that Will's pursuit of "love" with Kitty is an example of the search-for-a-mother theme that can be found in all of Percy's fiction. Lawson sees landscapes such as Central Park, the Vaughts' garden, and the golf course beside their home as symbols of the Edenic maternal womb that Will wants to re-enter. Will wants to return to Eden and to Eve, the mother of all. These places and the women in them, of course, fail to offer Will an escape from his Fallen condition.

20. *A Kierkegaard Anthology*, 26.

21. Barrett, *Irrational Man*, 163–64.

22. Howland, *The Gift of the Other*, 35.

23. In Percy's handwritten notes for *The Last Gentleman*, he has jotted, "theme = solipsism," and close by on the same page is "key to Sutter = love and longing for God" (WPP, Series 1, B.1).

24. *A Kierkegaard Anthology*, 347.

25. Terrye Newkirk ("*Via Negativa* and the Little Way," 197) explains in his discussion of Lonnie's role in *The Moviegoer* that there is in the Catholic faith an ancient belief that it is possible for individuals to "do penance" for others through their suffering and therefore assist in the continuing process of the redemption of the world.

26. "Wait" is a refrain throughout *The Last Gentleman* (5, 168, 224, 226, 241, 277, 331, 354), particularly important because it is Will's last word in the novel (409). The idea that the Christian wayfarer should always be waiting in hope for a life that lies "across the seas" (*MB*, 144) is a recurring motif throughout Percy's fiction and essays. Percy had hanging over his desk at his home in Covington Kafka's motto, "Warte!" ("Wait!") (Tolson, *Pilgrim*, 316). Compare Tom More's thoughts on "waiting and watching" at the end of *Love in the Ruins* (*LR*, 383, 387) and Father Smith's advice on "waiting" at the end of *The Thanatos Syndrome* (*TS*, 363).

27. Referring to the "Oxford riot" of 1962 on the campus of the University of Mississippi, Percy in an essay in *Harper's* (1965) condemned the racial violence in the state and blamed it on the contemporary "Snopeses" who had acquired political power in the state ("Mississippi: The Fallen Paradise," 168–70).

28. Allen, *Walker Percy*, 46.

29. Pindell, "Toward Home," 75.

30. Schwartz, "Life and Death," 124.

31. Ciuba, "The Fierce Nun," 62.

32. Prochaska, *The Myth of the Fall*, 71.

33. Ciuba, *Walker Percy*, 111.

34. Labrie, *The Catholic Imagination*, 143.

35. Stokes, *Stokes Field Guide*, 288.

36. Baker, *The Dynamics of the Absurd*, 113.

37. Rubin, *A Gallery*, 212.

38. Allen, *Walker Percy*, 70.

39. Walker Percy also chose not to practice medicine after his "war" with tuberculosis and also spent his life as "a philosopher of sorts." Jay Tolson's and Patrick Samway's biographies explain in detail the circumstances involved in his choice and the "philosophy" he pursued.

40. *Mystery and Manners*, 226, 228.

41. See my 1996 article in *Renascence*, "The Brownian Leaves."

42. *The Habit of Being*, 128. Patrick Samway says in his preface to *A Thief of Pierce: The Letters of Kenneth Laine Ketner and Walker Percy* that Percy believed that the writer's primary task was to name experience with such precision that the words "go beyond evoking a dramatic sense of probability to representing the real" (xiv). See also John Desmond's excellent article on Percy's naming, "Walker Percy's Triad: Science, Literature, and Religion" (*Renascence*, 1994).

43. *A Kierkegaard Anthology*, 123, 142.

44. Oleksy, *Plight in Common*, 88–89.

45. Bigger, "Logos and Epiphany," 52–53.

46. Lauder, *Walker Percy*, 77.

47. Richard Baker (*The Dynamics of the Absurd*, 118–20), Mary Howland (*The Gift of the Other*, 62), and Bernadette Prochaska (*The Myth of the Fall*, 60–61) comment on Will's opening to intersubjective experience at the end of the novel.

48. In *The Second Coming*, twenty years after the events described in *The Last Gentleman*, Sutter is still alive and working in a "V.A. hospital for paraplegics" (*SC*, 195) in Santa Fe. Apparently, Sutter "waited."

CHAPTER 4: *The Second Coming*: SIGNS OF A GIVER?

1. Tolson, *The Correspondence*, 258. Percy explained to Shelby Foote in a 1979 letter that he wrote about half of the novel and then decided that the hero was Will Barrett. He says he tried to make the events in *The Second Coming* fit chronologically with the events in *The Last Gentleman*, but admitted that he was not as "systematic" as Foote about such mat-

ters (Tolson, *Correspondence*, 260). Again, in a 1980 interview with Edmund Fuller, Percy said that he was "a good way into writing *The Second Coming*" when he realized that he was writing a novel about a middle-aged Will (*Con*, 188).

2. Will, Percy says, is an example of the traditional American "success" whose life has "fallen apart" (*Con*, 236) — at one level, a symbolic character who, with his Harvard education and New York sophistication, is a sociological type who embodies "the best of American life even by the standards of the Northeast" (*MCon*, 46).

In another interview, Percy explains that his story of a "successful" but failed middle-aged Will is based on the life of a "bum" who showed up one day at the front door of his home in Covington. Percy discovered that the man at his door was an old friend from his college days who had gone north to become a successful businessman, retired and built his dream house in the North Carolina mountains, and then "one Sunday after church" just "caught a bus . . . out — anywhere" (*MCon*, 44–45). In his notes for *The Second Coming*, Percy identifies the man who arrived at his home that day as Ansley Cope, one of his fraternity brothers when he was at Chapel Hill (WPP, series 1.E, 1a.i; Tolson, *Pilgrim*, 415).

3. Zamora, *Writing the Apocalypse*, 146.

4. In *Pilgrim in the Ruins* (42–43), Jay Tolson tells of Roy Percy's (Walker's younger brother) memories of a similar hunting trip near Thomasville, Georgia, when he was about ten and Walker about eleven. Although their father did not try to kill either of his sons, he was depressed and drinking heavily, Roy recalls, and his "weird," "out of control" behavior created an emotional atmosphere of "confusion and menace."

5. *A Kierkegaard Anthology*, 255.

6. Pridgen, "Nature as Sacrament," 3–13.

7. Percy was a participant in a Carl Jung discussion group in Covington from 1976 to 1979 (Samway, *Walker Percy*, 331). In a 1979 interview, Percy told Ted Spivey that *The Second Coming* deals "explicitly with Jungian individuation" (Spivey, *Revival: Southern Writers in the Modern City*, 193). Spivey briefly discusses in his *The Journey Beyond Tragedy* some of Percy's uses of Jungian archetypes in the novels (148–64). Jay Tolson also notes some of the Jungian influences in *The Second Coming* (*Pilgrim*, 423).

8. Gary Ciuba calls Ewell McBee the "true son of Lawyer B___." Ewell, Ciuba explains, is another angry unbeliever who shoots at Will (*Walker Percy*, 214).

9. Fowler, "The Cave—the Fence," 80.

10. The following are some of the critical comments on the cave episode that are particularly relevant to this study: Bernadette Prochaska sees the cave descent as Will's search for a redemptive "treasure" that lies hidden beneath the "post-lapsarian Eden" where he lives (*The Myth of the Fall*, 85). The cave is a symbol of "chthonic" energy, according to W. L. Godshalk in his article on Will's redemptive journey in the novel ("The Engineer, Then and Now," 39). Lewis Lawson argues in a number of articles that Percy's heroes seek symbolic womblike places in their quests for a mother who will give them a new "birth," a new self (*Still Following*, 188). In her "Answers and Ambiguity" (115–23), Doreen Fowler discusses Will's failure to learn the limitations of his knowledge in the cave and the novel's confused statement about engagement with and transcendence of the finite world.

11. Dupuy, *Autobiography in Walker Percy*, 99–100.

12. Ciuba, *Walker Percy*, 217.

13. Prochaska, *The Myth of the Fall*, 103–4.

14. Fowler, "Answers and Ambiguity," 121.

15. Jung, *Man and His Symbols*, 171. Speaking of Jung's idea that an exploration of one's anxieties, dreams, depressions can reveal information about the self, Percy said that he agreed with Jung's assertion that "there's gold down there in the darkness" (*MCon*, 187; *TS*, 67).

16. Samway, *Walker Percy*, 349.

17. Gary Ciuba sees Allie and her stove as symbolic of the "newly sovereign life" (*Walker*

Percy, 223) now available to Will. Colleen Tremonte ("The Poet-Prophet," 176) believes Allie has discovered "the divine within the concrete and natural world." Bernadette Prochaska asserts in *The Myth of the Fall* (106) that there is no miraculous rebirth for Will after his emergence from the cave into Allie's "home," but instead a "fall" into a postlapsarian world where healing is necessary. Frederick Karl says that Will's fall is out of the "masturbat[ory]" self-love exemplified by his father and into "mutuality" (Percy's intersubjectivity) with Allie (*American Fiction, 1940–80*, 534).

18.   Advising a similar kind of "opening out" in *The Divine Milieu*, Teilhard de Chardin says that relationships with others should be a "ventur[ing] forth, . . . into the uncharted ocean of charity" (146). In his psychoanalytic analysis of *The Second Coming*, Lewis Lawson says that Allie is yearning to return to the womb, yearning for the Freudian "oceanic experience" ("Will Barrett and the Myth of Marsyas," 17).

19.   Prochaska, *The Myth of the Fall*, 112.

20.   *A Kierkegaard Anthology*, 412.

21.   Kennedy, "The Semiotics," 220.

22.   Ciuba, *Walker Percy*, 243–44.

23.   Ted Spivey (*Revival*, 194), Bernadette Prochaska (*The Myth of the Fall*, 122), Gary Ciuba (*Walker Percy*, 240), and Elzbieta Oleksy ("From Silence and Madness," 129) are among the many to comment on the obvious intersubjective love experience of Allie and Will at the end of the novel. Oleksy maintains that there is no true intersubjectivity between a man and woman in Percy's fiction until *The Second Coming*.

Ann Croce in a 1988 article ("The Making of Post-Modern Man," 218–19) and Susan Donaldson ("Keeping Quentin Compson Alive," 74) argue that there is no intersubjective experience. They both see Will as a patriarchal Southern gentleman lawyer rescuing a helpless Allie. Susan Derwin agrees that the future for Allie looks bleak, both she and Will proceeding toward the same kind of "self-enclosure" that marked the marriage between Will and Marion ("Orality, Aggression, Epistemology," 83–84).

Percy himself suggests a number of times in his interviews that he is interested primarily in the "possibilities" for happiness and self-discovery that exists in the love between Will and Allie (*Con*, 190, 308). He says that Will's solution to his difficulties amounts to a "business proposition," his "figur[ing] out a way to live, to love, and to work" (*Con*, 234). This is similar to Tom's ethical solution at the end of *Love in the Ruins*. There is for Will, however, "a victory . . . of eros over thanatos" in the novel. At least, Percy points out, Will's victory distinguishes him from the desperate Lancelot Lamar, who chooses in a "similar predicament" "the way" of death (*Con*, 184,189).

24.   In *The Last Gentleman*, Will arrives in his hometown of Ithaca, Mississippi, and recognizes suddenly that he has "no address" (*LG*, 313). In a 1980 interview with John Atlas, Percy said that after his bout with tuberculosis in 1946, he left the sanatorium in New York and realized he "had no address . . . no place to live." It occurred to him at the time, he goes on to explain, that the sense of "dislocation" he was experiencing was "the state of man in the twentieth century" (*Con*, 185).

25.   Ciuba, *Walker Percy*, 275.

26.   Tolson, *Pilgrim*, 425–26.

27.   In a 1986 interview in which Percy discusses this key idea in his philosophy and theology, he refers to the Tasaday tribe of Mindanao as an example of how the scientistic secular humanists of the day can be deceived by their belief in the perfectability of man (*SP*, 395). The Tasaday, a small Indonesian tribe "discovered" by anthropologists in 1971, were believed at the time to be examples of modern-day prelapsarian man. The tribe was a popular culture phenomenon, becoming the subject of *National Geographic* articles by Kenneth MacLeish ("Help for Philippine Tribes," "The Tasadays"), stars of a 1972 television documentary, and the topic for a bestseller by John Nance, *The Gentle Tasaday* (1975). By 1986,

anthropologists had proved conclusively that the tribe was a hoax (Headland, *The Tasaday Controversy*, 3).

28. *The Second Coming* has frequently been criticized for its "happy" ending (Hardy, *The Fiction*, 292; Oleksy, *Plight*, 221; Brinkmeyer, *Three Catholic Writers*, 168; Allen, *Walker Percy*, 131). Kieran Quinlan even discovers somewhere in the novel's "forced resolution" that Will converts to the Episcopal faith (*Walker Percy*, 152, 163,172).

Percy also calls his ending "happy" (*Con*, 235; *MCon*, 62), but he also stresses that the happiness Allie and Will achieve is achieved in a "world [that] is dead" (*MCon*, 58). They make their happiness in a "modern world" that Romano Guardini describes in the epigraph to *The Last Gentleman* as a spiritually barren and lonely place where the best that can occur is the rare intersubjective union of two people in love (*Con*, 308). If Will's search for love and God is a happy story, it is happy only in "the old Dantean sense" (*MCon*, 61; Spivey, *Journey*, 64). Whatever "secret joy" (*SC*, 411) Will experiences comes only after his suffering and suicidal despair and occurs in the context of a conspicuously Fallen Linwood world that at the end of the novel remains in its unredeemed condition.

29. Lois Zamora (*Writing the Apocalypse*,146-47) and Gary Ciuba (*Walker Percy*, 234) explain that in traditional Catholic theology the parousia is not a future event but continuously present and continuously happening. Kierkegaard emphasizes that for the clear-eyed Christian God is always here in "present" time (*A Kierkegaard Anthology*, 409).

CHAPTER 5: *Love in the Ruins*: SIGNS OF THE END?

1. Many critics have recognized the obvious importance of the angelism-bestialism theme in *Love in the Ruins*. For particularly interesting discussions, see Ciuba, *Walker Percy*, 142; Kennedy, "The Sundered Self and the Riven World," 115–36; Kieran Quinlan, *Walker Percy*, 130. A brief but highly infomative essay on the angelism in Percy's fiction is included in Ross Labrie's *The Catholic Imagination in American Literature*, 133–51.

2. There have been a number of critics who have pointed out how the satire in *Love in the Ruins* differentiates the novel from Percy's earlier fiction and how it reflects some of Percy's philosophical, political, and personal concerns in the late 1960s. Patrick Samway (*Walker Percy*, 257), Kieran Quinlan (*Walker Percy*, 118), and Jay Tolson (*Pilgrim*, 338) discuss how genuinely concerned Percy was about the racial unrest and political turmoil in the nation, the South, and in his hometown of Covington, Louisiana. Several of Percy's letters to Shelby Foote in the late 1960s and early 1970s indicate his feelings about American politics and the social problems in his own community. In the letters, Percy speaks of his "melancholy and depression" and his sense of alienation amid the racism and religious hypocrisy of his neighbors in Covington. "Christendom" may well have ended in contemporary America, he says, the tragedy being that its demise might go unnoticed by the insensitive and unthinking American masses (WPP, series 3, folder 1).

Gary Ciuba (*Walker Percy*, 131) asserts that Percy is more interested in this novel in creating a dark satire than he is in chronicling the private consciousness of heroes like his earlier Binx Bolling and Will Barrett. William Rodney Allen (*Walker Percy*, 77) believes that Percy's shift to satire makes the novel artistically inferior to *The Moviegoer* and *The Last Gentleman*. John Edward Hardy (*The Fiction of Walker Percy*, 110) views the novel as a satire on Americans' faith in their country as a potential secular "New Eden."

3. Tolson, *Pilgrim*, 362.

4. Samway, *Walker Percy*, 292.

5. Percy defines language as the "center" of consciousness throughout the body of his work, but he is particularly clear about the idea in "A Theory of Language" (*MB*, 298–327) and "The Fateful Rift" (*SP*, 271–91). Basing his discussion of how language connects per-

ception of phenomena and meaning on Charles Sanders Peirce's language theories, Percy asserts in "A Theory" that human consciousness is made possible by the unique power of humans to somehow "couple" sensory data and words and arrive at meaning and knowledge. This "coupler" stands at the center of human consciousness and "is a complete mystery," Percy says — perhaps some type of an "I," a "self" (*MB*, 327), he ventures. In his later "A Fateful Rift," Percy explains that language is the "intersection" of mind and matter in that language is "both words [material and empirically observable] and meaning [immaterial knowing in the mind]" (*SP*, 279). Peirce calls this "coupler" of phenomena and meaning the "mind" or "soul" (*SP*, 286–87). In his equating the "coupler" with the "soul," Peirce is identifying the human language "center" with the metaphysical center of being posited by Percy's faith.

    6.   Samway, "A Rahnerian Backdrop," 138.

    7.   Godshalk, "*Love in the Ruins*," 143–49.

    8.   Edward J. Dupuy's *Autobiography in Walker Percy* is an informative study of Percy's ideas about the placement of the self in time (especially, 4–37).

    9.   Lawson, *Still Following Percy*, 196–98.

  10.   Kennedy, "The Sundered Self," 128.

  11.   See similar ideas about the mythologizing of the American past in Lewis Simpson's *The Dispossessed Garden*. Percy's friendship with Simpson dates from the early 1960s when Simpson was editor of the newly revived *Southern Review* at L.S.U. (Tolson, *Pilgrim*, 316). The degree of influence Simpson had on Percy is suggested by the fact that Percy quotes from page 71 of *The Dispossessed Garden* in his essay, "Diagnosing the Modern Malaise": "The covenant with memory and history has been abrogated [in this century] in favor of the existential self" (*SP*, 209).

John Hardy (*The Fiction of Walker Percy*, 110) discusses the way *Love in the Ruins* explores the American myth of a "New Eden."

  12.   Camus, *The Fall*, 63. Percy in his interviews repeatedly expresses his admiration and debt to Camus (*Con*, *MCon*). *The Fall* is a model for the narrative technique Percy uses in *Lancelot*. In his correspondence with Shelby Foote in July, 1970, he said he was considering taking Foote's advice to use "The Fall Out" as the title for the novel that later became *Love in the Ruins* (Tolson, *The Correspondence*, 145-46; see also Samway, *Walker Percy*, 283).

  13.   Lawson, *Still Following Percy*, 198.

  14.   *A Kierkegaard Anthology*, 408.

  15.   Art Immelmann can be seen as the temptation of "art" and the abstract, aesthetic happiness it provides (Ciuba, *Walker Percy*, 142). Percy says Art, "the Devil" in the novel, is named after a famous German World War I fighter pilot his father told him about, the pilot credited with inventing a combat maneuver called "the Immelmann turn" (*Con*, 206). Frederick Karl explains that the Immelmann maneuver involves the pilot's gaining altitude while "appearing to fly in the opposite direction." Metaphorically, Karl says, Art in *Love in the Ruins* offers Tom "more altitude"—that is, a Cartesian transcendence through abstraction (*American Fiction, 1940–80*, 321).

Percy was never comfortable with the aestheticism of his friend Shelby Foote (Tolson, *The Correspondence*, 30, 60, 80; Tolson, *Pilgrim*, 226–27), to whom *Love in the Ruins*, ironically, is dedicated. Jay Tolson points out that Percy often expressed "an almost puritanical contempt for the artifice of art" and quotes a 1962 letter to Ashley Brown in which Percy said he considered himself more of a "moralist or propagandist" than a literary artist (*Pilgrim*, 233, 300).

  16.   Ciuba, *Walker Percy*, 149.

  17.   Ibid., 156.

  18.   Cunningham, "'The Thread in the Labyrinth,'" 30–31.

  19.   Labrie, *The Catholic Imagination*, 136.

20.   *A Kierkegaard Anthology*, 27–28.
21.   Ibid., 181.
22.   Teilhard de Chardin, *The Divine Milieu*, 145.
23.   Ciuba, *Walker Percy*, 157.
24.   Crowley, "*The Thanatos Syndrome*," 227–28.
25.   O'Connor, *Mystery and Manners*, 227–28.
26.   Link, "An Impotent Savior," 29.
27.   Allen, *Walker Percy*, 84.
28.   Ciuba, *Walker Percy*, 149–50.
29.   William Rodney Allen discusses the similarities between Tom's situation in this opening scene and Robert Jordan's predicament at the end of *For Whom the Bell Tolls* (*Walker Percy*, 83).
30.   Gary Ciuba (*Walker Percy*, 135) notes that the "marsh hawk" here, unlike the falcon in the opening scene of *The Last Gentleman*, is a sign of the general social, political, religious, moral, and psychic disorder described in *Love in the Ruins*. It "balances on a column of air" above the ruins of Tom's community, but loses its "balance" and "slants off . . . toward the swamp" (*LR*, 4). Metaphorically, the hawk, in its flight toward the swamp, can be identified with the politically disaffected hippies in Honey Island Swamp, whose departures from their families' homes are evidence of the dissolution of unity and harmony in middle-class Paradise Estates.
31.   Kennedy, "The Sundered Self," 125–26.
32.   Sweeny, *Walker Percy*, 77.
33.   Ciuba, *Walker Percy*, 154.
34.   An allusion to Jacques Maritain's *Ransoming the Time*.
35.   O'Connor, *Mystery and Manners*, 227.
36.   Dupuy, *Autobiography in Walker Percy*, 215.
37.   William Rodney Allen (*Walker Percy*, 99) comments on the life and death imagery in this scene and the "world of weight and stability" created by Percy's description. John Edward Hardy recognizes the Hopkinsinian sacramental nature depicted, but argues that the images of the spider and the predatory kingfisher also reveal a Hobbesian nature where death prevails and life is "nasty, brutish, and short" (*The Fiction of Walker Percy*, 128). Gary Ciuba believes the imagery shows how Tom has a "renewed sense of the world" that allows him to see how the "natural kingdom disclose[s] a supernatural landscape" (*Walker Percy*, 165–66).
38.   *A Kierkegaard Anthology*, 411–12, 415.
39.   Ciuba, *Walker Percy*, 169.
40.   Lawson, *Still Following Percy*, 203.
41.   *A Kierkegaard Anthology*, 412.

CHAPTER 6: *The Thanatos Syndrome*: LIFE OR DEATH

1.   West, "Extending Walker Percy's Legacy," 18.
2.   Tolson, *Correspondence*, 223.
3.   Samway, *Walker Percy*, 376.
4.   Many scholars have commented on the connections Percy makes between language and the impoverishment or enrichment of consciousness, but Edward Dupuy's discussion in his *Autobiography in Walker Percy* (124ff.) is particularly clear, accurate, and precise.
5.   Coles, *Walker Percy*, 15, 26–27.
6.   John Edward Hardy (*The Fiction of Walker Percy*, 264–66), Gary Ciuba (*Walker Percy*, 257–58), and, more recently, Richard Martin ("Language Specificity," 210–13) are

especially effective in showing how Tom in *The Thanatos Syndrome* is very different from the introspective, despairing wayfarers in Percy's other novels.

7. *A Kierkegaard Anthology*, 314.

8. O'Connor, *Mystery and Manners*, 150.

9. Montello, "The Diagnostic 'I'," 32.

10. Dupuy, *Autobiography in Walker Percy*, 36.

11. See Patrick Samway's *Walker Percy* (102–6) and Jay Tolson's *Pilgrim in the Ruins* (138–42) for information about Dr. Sullivan's friendship with the Percy family and his role in Walker Percy's psychoanalysis in New York (1937–40).

12. Crowley, "*The Thanatos Syndrome*," 227.

13. John Edward Hardy makes reference to the sunfish and cicadas in this scene, seeing them as evidence of Percy's "sacramental and prophetic consciousness" ("Man and Beast," 144–47).

14. Ciuba, *Walker Percy*, 262.

15. Lawson, "Tom More," 31.

16. See Tolson's *Pilgrim* (449–50) and Samway's *Walker Percy* (372) for possible sources for Lucy and Pantherburn in Percy's family history. Also, see Samway's "Two Conversations" (26) for a discussion of other references in the novel to real places in Mississippi and Louisiana. Samway says that Percy actually drew a map of the fictional landscape in the novel, a fact that obviously indicates the importance he attached to such details of setting.

Mrs. Percy told me in a 1994 conversation that Dr. Percy insisted on seeing the actual places he described in his fiction, and she joked about their many drives into the swamps and backwoods of southeastern Louisiana.

17. Desmond, "Disjunction of Time," 68.

18. Dupuy, *Autobiography in Walker Percy*, 28.

19. William Rodney Allen points out a similar allusion to *For Whom the Bell Tolls* in the opening scene of *Love in the Ruins* (*Walker Percy*, 83). Apparently, Tom is, ten years after that scene, still dislocated from his genuine self and still given to role-playing.

20. Ciuba, *Walker Percy*, 268–69.

21. Desmond, "Disjunction of Time," 70.

22. Sue Crowley calls this image and similar ones in Percy's fiction "Christological hierophanies" ("*The Thanatos Syndrome*," 235).

23. Howland, *The Gift of the Other*, 131.

24. Samway, *Walker Percy*, 384.

25. Lewis Lawson says that this exchange between Tom and Father Smith is "not Freud's 'talk' between observer and object," but intersubjective "talk" ("Tom More and Sigmund Freud," 31).

John Hardy argues that whereas psychiatrists like Tom talk with their patients to help them reach their true selves, Smith uses language in seeking the way to the Incarnate Word (*The Fiction of Walker Percy*, 257).

26. See Samway's *Walker Percy* (74–78) and Tolson's *Pilgrim in the Ruins* (115-19) on Percy's 1934 summer in Germany.

27. Labrie, *The Catholic Imagination*, 138.

28. In a 1990 essay, "Why Are You Catholic?" (*SP*, 304–15), Percy humorously reports that when he is asked why he is Catholic, he "usually" replies, "What else is there?" A major point in his essay is that the contemporary world offers little else that is more meaningful, true, or valuable than Catholic doctrine.

29. Ciuba, *Walker Percy*, 275.

30. Gary Ciuba notes Tom's ability here to see baptism as the "sacramental opposite of the deathly river" of Na-24 created by the Fedville scientists (*Walker Percy*, 290).

31. O'Connor, *The Complete Stories*, 527.

32. *Mystery and Manners*, 226–27. For commentary on Percy's indebtedness to O'Connor in *The Thanatos Sydrome*, see Howland, *Gift of the Other*, 142; Crowley, "*The Thanatos Syndrome*," 225; Desmond, "Walker Percy, Flannery O'Connor and the Holocaust"; Pridgen, "Up in His Head," 36-37.

In a 1989 interview with Scott Walter, Percy denied any conscious use of O'Connor's essay in *Mystery and Manners*. When Walter pointed out the parallels, Percy replied, "I am amazed. I would happily admit that I did that consciously [use O'Connor's "tenderness" passage] because I'd love to give her credit" (*MCon*, 229).

33. Ciuba, *Walker Percy*, 291.

34. Compare Will's decision to "wait" at the end of *The Last Gentleman* (*LG*, 409) and Tom's thoughts about "waiting and watching" (*LR*, 383,387) at the end of *Love in the Ruins*.

35. Percy first read Freud in 1939. About the same time, he became interested in Dr. Harry Stack Sullivan's theories concerning anxiety (Samway, *Walker Percy*, 104–9).

36. Ciuba notes the parallels between the mass at the end of *Love in the Ruins* and the mass at the end of *The Thanatos Syndrome*. He believes that Percy wants to show at the ends of both novels that there are people who are still choosing the sacramental way and the spiritual life it offers, even in the age of death (*Walker Percy*, 290) .

37. O'Connor, *Mystery and Manners*, 228.

38. Marcel, *The Mystery of Being*, 187.

Bibliography

Allen, William Rodney. *Walker Percy, A Southern Wayfarer.* Jackson: University Press of Mississippi, 1986.

Baker, Richard E. *The Dynamics of the Absurd in the Existentialist Novel.* New York: Peter Lang, 1993.

Barrett, William. *Irrational Man: A Study in Existential Philosophy.* New York: Doubleday, 1958.

Bigger, Charles P. "Logos and Epiphany: Walker Percy's Theology of Language." In *Critical Essays on Walker Percy,* edited by Donald Crowley and Sue Mitchell Crowley, 49–57. Boston: G.K. Hall, 1989.

Bloom, Harold, ed. *Walker Percy: Modern Critical Views.* Boston: Chelsea House, 1986.

Brinkmeyer, Robert H., Jr. *Three Catholic Writers: Allen Tate, Caroline Gordon, Walker Percy.* Jackson: University Press of Mississippi, 1985.

———. "Walker Percy's Lancelot: Discovery through Dialogue." *Renascence* 40.1 (Fall 1987): 30–42.

Brooks, Cleanth. "Walker Percy and Modern Gnosticism." In *Walker Percy: Modern Critical Views,* edited by Harold Bloom, 53–62. Boston: Chelsea House, 1986.

Broughton, Panthea Reid, ed. *The Art of Walker Percy: Stratagems for Being.* Baton Rouge: Louisiana State University Press, 1979.

Camus, Albert. *The Fall.* Translated by Justin O'Brien. New York: Vintage, 1956.

Chardin, Teilhard de. *The Divine Milieu.* New York: Harper & Row, 1962.

Ciuba, Gary M. "The Fierce Nun of *The Last Gentleman*: Percy's Vision of Flannery O'Connor." *The Flannery O'Connor Bulletin* 25 (1986): 57–66.

———. *Walker Percy: Books of Revelations.* Athens: University of Georgia Press, 1991.

Coles, Robert. *Walker Percy: An American Search.* Boston: Little, Brown, 1978.

Croce, Ann Jerome. "The Making of Post-Modern Man: Modernism and the Southern Tradition in the Fiction of Walker Percy." *Critique: Studies in Contemporary Fiction* 29.4 (Summer 1988): 213–21.

Crowley, J. Donald and Sue Mitchell Crowley, eds. *Critical Essays on Walker Percy.* Boston: G. K. Hall, 1989.

Crowley, Sue Mitchell. "*The Thanatos Syndrome*: Walker Percy's Tribute to Flannery O'Connor." In *Walker Percy: Novelist and Philosopher,* edited by Jan Nordby Gretlund and Karl-Heinz Westarp, 225–37. Jackson: University Press of Mississippi, 1991.

Cunningham, John. "'The Thread in the Labyrinth': Love in the Ruins and One Tradition of Comedy." *South Carolina Review* 13.2 (Spring 1981): 28–34.

Derwin, Susan. "Orality, Aggression, and Epistemology in Walker Percy's Second Coming." *Arizona Quarterly* 45.2 (Summer 1989): 63–99.

Desmond, John F. *At the Crossroads: Ethical and Religious Themes in the Writings of Walker Percy*. Troy, N.Y.: Whitston, 1997.

———. "Disjunction of Time: Myth and History in *The Thanatos Syndrome*." *New Orleans Review* 16.4 (Winter 1989): 63–71.

———. "Walker Percy and T.S. Eliot: The Lancelot Andrewes Connection." *Southern Review* 22.3 (Summer 1986): 465–77.

———. "Walker Percy, Flannery O'Connor and the Holocaust." *Southern Quarterly* 28 (Winter 1990): 35–42.

———. "Walker Percy's Triad: Science, Literature,and Religion." *Renascence* 47.1 (Fall 1994): 3–9.

Donaldson, Susan V. "Keeping Quentin Compson Alive: *The Last Gentleman, The Second Coming*, and the Problem of Masculinity." In *Walker Percy's Feminine Characters*, edited by Lewis A. Lawson and Elzbieta Oleksy, 62–77. Troy, N.Y.: Whitston, 1995.

Dupuy, Edward J. *Autobiography in Walker Percy: Repetition, Recovery, and Redemption*. Baton Rouge: Louisiana State University Press, 1996.

Foucault, Michel. *The Order of Things: An Archaeology of the Human Sciences*. New York: Vintage, 1994.

Fowler, Doreen. "Answers and Ambiguity in Percy's *The Second Coming*." In *Walker Percy: Modern Critical Views*, edited by Harold Bloom, 115–23. Boston: Chelsea House, 1986.

———. " 'The Cave . . . the Fence': A Lacanian Reading of Walker Percy's *The Second Coming*." In *Walker Percy's Feminine Characters*, edited by Lewis A. Lawson and Elzbieta Oleksy, 78–89. Troy, N.Y.: Whitston, 1995.

Frye, Northrop. *Anatomy of Criticism*. New York: Atheneum, 1966.

———. *The Great Code: The Bible and Literature*. New York: Harcourt Brace Jovanovich, 1982.

Futrell, Ann M. *The Signs of Christianity in the Work of Walker Percy*. San Francisco: Catholic Scholars Press, 1994.

Giles, Paul. *American Catholic Art and Fictions: Culture, Ideology, Aesthetics*. Cambridge: Cambridge University Press, 1992.

Godshalk, W. L. "The Engineer, Then and Now; or, Barrett's Choice." In *Walker Percy: Novelist and Philosopher*, edited by Jan Nordby Gretlund and Karl-Heinz Westarp, 33–42. Jackson: University Press of Mississippi, 1991.

———. "*Love in the Ruins*: Thomas More's Distorted Vision." In *The Art of Walker Percy: Stratagems for Being*, edited by Panthea Reid Broughton, 139–56. Baton Rouge: Louisiana State University Press, 1979.

Gretlund, Jan Nordby and Karl-Heinz Westarp, eds. *Walker Percy: Novelist and Philosopher*. Jackson: University Press of Mississippi, 1991.

Gunn, Giles. *The Interpretation of Otherness: Literature, Religion, and the American Imagination*. New York: Oxford University Press,1979.

Hardy, John Edward. *The Fiction of Walker Percy*. Urbana: University of Illinois Press,1987.

———. "Man, Beast, and Others in Walker Percy." In *Walker Percy: Novelist and Philosopher*, edited by Jan Nordby Gretlund and Karl-Heinz Westarp, 141–54. Jackson: University Press of Mississippi, 1991.

Headland, Thomas N., ed. *The Tasaday Controversy: Assessing the Evidence*. Washington, D. C.: American Anthropological Association, 1992.

Howland, Mary D. *The Gift of the Other: Gabriel Marcel's Concept of Intersubjectivity in Walker Percy's Novels*. Pittsburgh: Duquesne University Press,1990.

Josipovici, Gabriel. *The World and the Book: A Study of Modern Fiction*. Stanford, Calif.: Stanford University Press, 1971.

Jung, Carl G. *Man and His Symbols*. New York: Dell, 1964.

Karl, Frederick. *American Fiction, 1940–80*. New York: Harper & Row, 1983.

Kennedy, J. G. "The Semiotics of Memory: Suicide in *The Second Coming*." In *Critical Essays on Walker Percy*, edited by Donald Crowley and Sue Mitchell Crowley, 208–25. Boston: G.K. Hall, 1989.

———. "The Sundered Self and the Riven World: *Love in the Ruins*." In *The Art of Walker Percy: Stratagems for Being*, edited by Panthea Reid Broughton, 115–36. Baton Rouge: Louisiana State University Press, 1979.

Kierkegaard, Soren. *A Kierkegaard Anthology*. Edited and translated by Robert Bretall. Princeton: Princeton University Press, 1946.

Labrie, Ross. *The Catholic Imagination in American Literature*. Columbia: University of Missouri Press, 1997.

Lauder, Robert E. *Walker Percy: Prophetic, Existentialist, Catholic Storyteller*. New York: Peter Lang, 1996.

Lawson, Lewis A. "The Cross and the Delta: Walker Percy's Anthropology." In *Walker Percy: Novelist and Philosopher*, edited by Jan Nordby Gretlund and Karl-Heinz Westarp, 3–12. Jackson: University Press of Mississippi, 1991.

———. *Following Percy: Essays on Walker Percy's Work*. Troy, N.Y.: Whitston, 1988.

———. *Still Following Percy*. Jackson: University Press of Mississippi, 1996.

———. "Tom More and Sigmund Freud." *New Orleans Review* 16.4 (Winter 1989): 27–31.

———. "Will Barrett and the Myth of Marsyas." *Southern Quarterly* 36.1 (Fall 1997): 5–24.

Lawson, Lewis A. and Elzbieta Oleksy, eds. *Walker Percy's Feminine Characters*. Troy, N.Y.: Whitston, 1995.

Link, Eric Carl. "An Impotent Savior: The Messiah Complex in Walker Percy's *Love in the Ruins*." *Southern Quarterly* 34.1 (Fall 1995): 24–31.

Luschei, Martin. *The Sovereign Wayfarer: Walker Percy's Diagnosis of the Malaise*. Baton Rouge: Louisiana State University Press, 1972.

MacLeish, Kenneth. "Help for Philippine Tribes in Trouble." *National Geographic* 140 (August 1971): 220–55.

———. "The Tasadays: Stone Age Cavemen of Mindanao." *National Geographic* 142 (August 1972): 214–49.

Marcel, Gabriel. *The Mystery of Being*. Translated by Rene Hague. Vol. 1. Lanham, Md.: University Press of America, 1979.

Maritain, Jacques. *Ransoming the Time*. Translated by Harry Lorrin Binsse. New York: Harper & Brothers, 1957.

Martin, Richard T. "Language Specificity as Patterns of Redemption in *The Thanatos Syndrome*." *Renascence* 48.3 (Spring 1996): 209–23.

McFague, Sally. "The Parabolic in Faulkner, O'Connor, and Percy." In *Critical Essays on Walker Percy*, edited by Donald Crowley and Sue Mitchell Crowley, 114–31. Boston: G.K. Hall, 1989.

Mills, Henry. "An Essential Walker Percy Bibliography." *Southern Quarterly* 34 (Winter 1996): 129–39.

Montello, Martha. "The Diagnostic 'I': Presenting the Case in *The Thanatos Syndrome*." *New Orleans Review* 16.4 (Winter 1989): 32–36.

Nance, John. *The Gentle Tasaday: A Stone Age People in the Philippine Rain Forest.* New York: Harcourt Brace Jovanovich, 1975.

Newkirk, Terrye. "*Via Negativa* and the Little Way: The Hidden God of *The Moviegoer*." *Renascence* 44.3 (Spring 1992): 183–202.

O'Connor, Flannery. *The Complete Stories.* New York: Farrar, Straus & Giroux, 1971.

———. *The Habit of Being.* Edited by Sally Fitzgerald. New York: Farrar, Straus & Giroux, 1971.

———. *Mystery and Manners.* Edited by Sally Fitzgerald and Robert Fitzgerald. New York: Farrar, Straus & Giroux, 1961.

Oleksy, Elzbieta H. "From Silence and Madness to the Exchange that Multiplies: Walker Percy and the Woman Question." In *Walker Percy's Feminine Characters*, edited by Lewis A. Lawson and Elzbieta Oleksy, 122–33. Troy, N.Y.: Whitston, 1995.

———. *Plight in Common: Hawthorne and Percy.* New York: Peter Lang, 1993.

Percy, Walker. *Conversations with Walker Percy.* Edited by Lewis Lawson and Victor Kramer. Jackson: University Press of Mississippi, 1985.

———. *Lancelot* . New York: Ivy , 1977.

———. *The Last Gentleman.* New York: Farrar, Straus & Giroux, 1966.

———. *Lost in the Cosmos.* New York: Washington Square, 1983.

———. *Love in the Ruins.* New York: Farrar, Straus and Giroux, 1971.

———. *The Message in the Bottle.* New York: Farrar, Straus & Giroux, 1975.

———. "Mississippi: The Fallen Paradise." *Harper's* 230 (April 1965): 166–72.

———. *More Conversations with Walker Percy.* Edited by Lewis A. Lawson and Victor Kramer. Jackson: University Press of Mississippi, 1993.

———. *The Moviegoer.* New York: Ivy , 1961.

———. *The Second Coming.* New York: Pocket, 1980.

———. *Signposts in a Strange Land.* Edited by Patrick Samway. New York: Farrar, Straus & Giroux, 1991.

———. *The Thanatos Syndrome.* New York: Farrar, Straus & Giroux, 1987.

———. Walker Percy Papers. Southern Historical Collection. Manuscripts Department. Wilson Library. University of North Carolina at Chapel Hill.

Pindell, Richard. "Toward Home: Place, Language, and Death in *The Last Gentleman*." In *Walker Percy: Modern Critical Views*, edited by Harold Bloom, 69–82. Boston: Chelsea House, 1986.

Poteat, Patricia Lewis. *Walker Percy and the Old Modern Age: Reflections on Language, Argument, and the Telling of Stories.* Baton Rouge: Louisiana State University Press, 1985.

Pridgen, Allen. "The Brownian Leaves: Sacramental Presence in Walker Percy's *The Last Gentleman*." *Renascence* 48.4 (Summer 1996): 297–308.

———. "Nature as Sacrament in Walker Percy's *The Second Coming*." *Mississippi Quarterly* 51.1 (Winter 1997–98): 3–13.

———. "Up in His Head: Orbit and Sacrament in Walker Percy's *The Thanatos Syndrome*." *Southern Quarterly* 34.1 (Fall 1995): 32–38.

Prochaska, Bernadette. *The Myth of the Fall and Walker Percy's Last Gentleman.* New York: Peter Lang, 1993.

Quinlan, Kieran. *Walker Percy: The Last Catholic Novelist*. Baton Rouge: Louisiana State University Press, 1996.

Robertson, D. W., Jr. *The Literature of Medieval England*. New York: McGraw-Hill, 1970.

Rubin, Louis D., Jr. *A Gallery of Southerners*. Baton Rouge: Louisiana State University Press, 1982.

Samway, Patrick H., S. J. "A Rahnerian Backdrop to Percy's *The Second Coming*." *Delta* 13 (November 1981): 127–44.

——, ed. *A Thief of Peirce: The Letters of Kenneth Laine Ketner and Walker Percy*. Jackson: University Press of Mississippi, 1995.

——. "Two Conversations in Walker Percy's *The Thanatos Syndrome*." In *Walker Percy: Novelist and Philosopher*, edited by Jan Nordby Gretlund and Karl-Heinz Westarp, 24–32. Jackson: University Press of Mississippi, 1991.

——. *Walker Percy: A Life*. New York: Farrar, Straus & Giroux, 1997.

Schwartz, Joseph. "Life and Death in *The Last Gentleman*." *Renascence* 40.2 (Winter 1987): 112–28.

Scullin, Kathleen. "*Lancelot* and Walker Percy's Dispute with Sartre over Ontology." In *Walker Percy: Novelist and Philosopher*, edited by Jan Nordby Gretlund and Karl-Heinz Westarp, 110–18. Jackson: University Press of Mississippi, 1991.

Simpson, Lewis. *The Brazen Face of History: Studies in the Literary Consciousness in America*. Baton Rouge: Louisiana State University Press, 1980.

——. *The Dispossessed Garden: Pastoral and History in Southern Literature*. Athens: University of Georgia Press, 1975.

Spivey, Ted R. *The Journey Beyond Tragedy: A Study of Myth and Modern Fiction*. Orlando: University Press of Florida, 1980.

——. *Revival: Southern Writers in the Modern City*. Gainesville: University of Florida Press, 1986.

Stokes, Donald and Lillian Stokes. *Stokes Field Guide to Birds*. New York: Little, Brown, 1996.

Sweeny, Mary K. *Walker Percy and the Postmodern World*. Chicago: Loyola University Press, 1987.

Tharpe, Jac. *Walker Percy*. Boston: Twayne, 1983.

Tolson, Jay, ed. *The Correspondence of Walker Percy and Shelby Foote*. New York: Norton, 1997.

——. "The Education of Walker Percy." *Wilson Quarterly* 8.2 (Spring 1984): 156–66.

——. *Pilgrim in the Ruins: A Life of Walker Percy*. New York: Simon & Schuster, 1992.

Tremonte, Colleen M. "The Poet-Prophet and Feminine Capability in Walker Percy's *The Second Coming*." *Mississippi Quarterly* 43 (Spring 1990): 173–81.

West, Walter C. "Extending Walker Percy's Legacy: The Story of His Papers at the University of North Carolina at Chapel Hill." *St. Tammany Parish Library 1992 Symposium*, 14–25.

Wyatt-Brown, Bertram. *The House of Percy: Honor, Melancholy, and Imagination in a Southern Family*. New York: Oxford University Press, 1994.

——. *The Literary Percys: Family, History, Gender, and the Southern Imagination*. Athens: University of Georgia Press, 1994.

Zamora, Lois Parkinson. *Writing the Apocalypse: Historical Vision in Contemporary U.S. and Latin American Fiction*. Cambridge: Cambridge University Press, 1989.

Index